CW00958164

An OPUS book

THINKING ABOUT PEACE AND WAR

Thinking about
Peace and War

MARTIN CEADEL

Oxford New York

OXFORD UNIVERSITY PRESS

1987

Oxford University Press, Walton Street, Oxford OX2 6DP

Oxford New York Toronto
Delhi Bombay Calcutta Madras Karachi
Petaling Jaya Singapore Hong Kong Tokyo
Nairobi Dar es Salaam Cape Town
Melbourne Auckland

and associated companies in
Beirut Berlin Ibadan Nicosia

Oxford is a trade mark of Oxford University Press

British Library Cataloguing in Publication Data

Ceadel, Martin
Thinking about peace and war.—(OPUS).
1. War 2. Peace
I. Title II. Series
327.1 JX1952
ISBN 0-19-219200-0

Library of Congress Cataloging in Publication Data

Ceadel, Martin.
Thinking about peace and war.
Bibliography: p. Includes index.
1. War. 2. Peace. I. Title.
U21.2.C43 1987 327.1'7 87-5619
ISBN 0-19-219200-0

Set by Grove Graphics
Printed in Great Britain by
Biddles Ltd.
Guildford and King's Lynn

For Debby

Preface

It was while doing research on the modern British peace movement that the lack of agreed categories for describing the positions taken in the debate about war prevention comparable to those—conservatism, liberalism, socialism, and so on—which are taken for granted in the analysis of domestic politics became apparent to me. Shortly after publishing *Pacifism In Britain 1914–1945: The Defining Of A Faith*, I interrupted work on a companion volume on the non-pacifist section of the peace movement in order to remedy what I continue to regard as an astonishing deficiency in popular political or international-relations theory.

The Warden and Fellows of New College granted me two sabbatical terms in 1985–6, during which an almost final draft was nearly completed, and have at all times provided a congenial environment in which to think and write. I owe special thanks to Alan Ryan, for being so generous and stimulating a colleague and, in the case of this book, a general editor too. I am also grateful to the late Hedley Bull, who first persuaded me to become involved in teaching Oxford University's M.Phil. course in International Relations—an activity from which I have learned a lot; and to all those who attended the lectures and seminars in Oxford and London in which I first tried out the key ideas of this book. By far my greatest debt, however, is to Deborah Ceadel, who has commented on every stage of this project to its great benefit. She would not have been able to give so much time to this labour had it not been for Sylvia Stockton's ability and willingness, often assisted by her husband David, to keep her grandchildren Jack and Jemima entranced for long periods.

New College, Oxford   M.E.C.

Contents

1

The war-and-peace debate

War prevention is the twentieth century's most urgent issue; and this is a guide to the way it is discussed. This 'war-and-peace debate' has always generated a prolific literature—urging particular policies, analysing current predicaments, and theorizing about the international system—and in the past few years has been surpassing itself in this respect.

This book is not a contribution to the debate; it is an examination of its underlying assumptions. It asks the basic but surprisingly neglected question: why do people disagree about war prevention? Its main answer is: because they have different ideological preconceptions. It argues that the war-and-peace debate needs a general interpretative framework of the sort which has long been employed by students of domestic politics. In the latter sphere disagreements over both policy and analysis are normally taken for granted, being generally understood to reflect differences of an ideological nature.

An ideology is a perspective or world-view which helps its adherent find his way through an otherwise baffling cosmos by highlighting what is important and valuable and filtering out what can be ignored. It enables him to explain how the world currently works and also to prescribe both what an ideal world would look like and how it can be brought into being. Thus a communist and a conservative, for example, will disagree about what the laws of economics are and what economic policy should be. Issues are so numerous and individuals so various that the number of such ideologies could in principle be infinite. In practice, however, it is comparatively small, since views on different issues tend to cluster together in popular doctrinal 'packages', such as conservatism, liberalism, and socialism.

There is, of course, endless debate about the exact content of each package: is conservatism a true ideology? what exactly is socialism? and so on. Not everyone finds one to his taste, moreover. Some have world-views but of an idiosyncratic type, made up of opinions which are either unusual in themselves (such as support for paedophilia) or combined in an unconventional way (such as simultaneous support for the nationalization of industry and the privatization of education). And others (such as self-confessed pragmatists) claim not to need to have reality filtered for them by a world-view. Yet even those with various reservations about the standard doctrines normally accept that at its basic level the political debate can usefully be viewed as a competition between them. Thus domestic politics is generally viewed not as a random interplay of disagreements on a multiplicity of issues but as the interaction of a manageable number of easily identifiable ideologies.

The war-and-peace debate is not viewed in the same way. Its issues are not only numerous and constantly changing—in western democracies the debate has ranged over such topics as the merits of the League of Nations in the 1920s, appeasement in the 1930s, containment during the early cold war, *détente* in the 1970s, and nuclear strategy in the 1980s—but seemingly discrete and patternless. They are normally presented as policy choices, such as disarmament versus rearmament. But the war-and-peace debate can only superficially be understood at the policy level, since the same policy can be advocated for contradictory reasons. For example, opposition to Britain's Trident programme has been voiced both by Monsignor Bruce Kent, general secretary of the Campaign for Nuclear Disarmament (CND) from 1980 to 1985 and a pacifist in the full sense of the word, and by Field Marshal Lord Carver, former chief of defence staff and an advocate of greater defence spending.[1] Clearly, however, this policy agreement is less significant than their philosophical disagreements.

To identify the underlying dynamics of the war-and-peace debate it is thus necessary to probe deeper, as in domestic politics, to the ideological level. Those in any doubt on this point should consider how often it is that those who belong to western peace movements for moral reasons happen to view the Soviet Union as peaceful or relatively powerless, whereas those who do not share their scruples tend to make the opposite strategic diagnosis. It is their respective ideologies which bring their moral intuitions and factual assessments into line with each other.

Yet, in contrast with domestic politics, there is no consensus about what the analytically useful ideologies are. In part this is because such academic studies as there have been of the war-and-peace debate have failed to treat it as a whole, in the round, from a perspective which permits comparison, or in such a way as to shed light on the political assumptions of ordinary people. Instead they have been narrowly focused: on one aspect only (in particular nuclear weapons), rather than on war prevention in general; on only one side of the argument (either the peace movement or defence-policy makers), rather than on the dialogue between the two; on one state (most notably the United States, on which the literature is excellent but stresses the ideological peculiarities of its war-and-peace debate without specifying what a normal one would look like), rather than on a representative sample; or on philosophical aspects and the ideas of great thinkers, rather than on the categories used in everyday discussion.[2]

As a result our understanding of the war-and-peace debate is conceptually stunted. Certainly, one structural feature is too obvious to be ignored: the fundamental cleavage between on the one side most governments and their defence establishments and on the other all peace movements and their supporters in opposition parties. But there is no agreed way of describing the respective outlooks of the two groups.

Admittedly, the former's outlook is sometimes referred to as 'militarism'. But it will be argued here that this term should be restricted to the most extreme pro-war viewpoint of all, which has been overlooked as a theory of international relations. It will further be argued that this militarist position must itself be distinguished from 'crusading', another intermittently used label which has yet to receive adequate recognition as a theory in its own right.

Both must be distinguished from 'orthodox' defence thinking. It is the most striking illustration of how little the basic categories of war-and-peace debate are understood that there is no agreed label for this, its most influential ideology by far. Those few—for the most part academics specializing in international relations—who have recognized it as such have somewhat unhelpfully called it 'realism': a term of considerable ambiguity, as I shall frequently show. Instead, the labels 'defencism' and 'defencist' have been coined here as more accurate guides to the distinctive assumptions of the theory which, consciously or not, is accepted by virtually every government in the world.[3]

As for the peace movement, understanding of its thinking has been handicapped by the narrowing since the mid-1930s of the world 'pacifism', in the English-speaking world at least, to mean an unconditional refusal to support war (in which absolutist sense it will, indeed, always be used here). In consequence no word exists to describe that *majority* of the peace movement which has always been pacific but not pacifist. The term 'pacific-ist', to which I have resorted on a previous occasion,[4] will again be pressed into service to fill the gap. It may be inelegant and etymologically dubious (as will be shown in chapter 6); but it helps to make clear the profound differences between pacifism and pacific-ism, the latter being a particularly influential ideology (or, more accurately, set of ideologies).

With proper classification the war-and-peace debate can be seen to have an underlying pattern like domestic politics. It is a competition between five 'war-and-peace theories'. Each is now summarized, with particular reference to the wars (if any) which it believes to be justified, the image it has of the international system, and the domestic political position to which it most closely corresponds.

(a) *Militarism*. This is the view that war is necessary to human development and therefore a positive good. All wars are justified, it argues, even aggressive ones. It views the international system as sheer anarchy: each state is engaged in a struggle for survival; and there is no prospect of abolishing war even if it were desirable to do so (which it is not). Militarism's domestic counterpart is fascism (this term being understood throughout this book in a broad generic sense, encompassing not only obvious variants such as national socialism but also crude applications of Darwinian, Hegelian, or Nietzschean thought and the political practice of states such as imperial Japan).

(b) *Crusading*. Most of the time crusading is indistinguishable from either defencism or pacific-ism, taking the same view of the international system and being related to the same domestic ideologies as one of the two. Its distinctive feature is a willingness under favourable circumstances to use aggressive war to promote either order or justice, as it conceives it, and thereby help to prevent or abolish war in the longer term. If militarism is aggression for its own sake, crusading is thus aggression for the sake of peace.

(c) Defencism. This theory accepts that aggression is always wrong, but insists both that defence is always right and that the maintenance of strong defences offers the best chance of preventing war. It sees the international system not as a complete anarchy but as an 'anarchical society' (to use a term made famous by Hedley Bull) which allows sufficient trust between states for balance and stability often to be achieved, although not sufficient to make the abolition (as distinct from the prevention) of war a reasonable possibility. Defencism represents the application to international relations of conservatism (including what will here be called 'authoritarian' conservatism) and social democracy.

(d) Pacific-ism. This holds that defencism is too pessimistic: war can be not only prevented but in time also abolished by reforms which will bring justice in domestic politics too. It can thus be derived from any 'reforming' political philosophy—from, for example, liberalism, radicalism, socialism, feminism, or the 'green' ideology here known as ecologism. In each case, its image of the international system is of a society, possessing norms and institutions comparable to those of the domestic sphere. Pacific-ism rules out all aggressive wars and even some defensive ones (those which would hinder the political reform for which it is working), but accepts the need for military force to defend its political achievements against aggression.

(e) Pacifism. This is the absolutist theory that participation in and support for war is always impermissible. The ideologies to which it is related are the non-violent versions of anarchism, socialism, certain religions, and humanitarianism. Pacifism comes, however, in three rather different varieties:

(i) An *optimistic* version, which argues that pacifism is even now the most effective defence policy to adopt (since non-violence can deter or repel an invasion). War can thus be abolished without delay. This assumes the international system to be not just a society but a community, possessing even stronger norms and institutions.

(ii) A *mainstream* version, which does not believe that pacifism is yet practical politics although it will fairly soon be so. In the meantime pacifists should, so far as their consciences allow, support pacific-ism as a step in the right direction. This assumes the international system to be already a society and one capable of evolving into a community.

(iii) A *pessimistic* version, which believes that pacifism is a faith rather than a political strategy: it can merely bear witness to those profound values which will be widely adopted only in the very long term when men eventually undergo a change of heart. This views the international system, like domestic politics, as a vale of tears.

The principles on which the typology is based are discussed in chapter 2, after which each theory receives a chapter to itself.

Since this typology is ideological, complete objectivity in its analysis is difficult to achieve. I should at the outset admit, therefore, to being myself a defencist, albeit one who is sceptical about certain policies now being implemented in the name of defence. In the brief epilogue I shall put forward a few personal judgements, for what they are worth; but up to that point every effort will be made to be as impartial as is possible. Each viewpoint will be expounded in the same way, its sincerity and good intentions being taken for granted and its premises and implications examined critically.

Most of this book is thus devoted to arguing that people disagree about war prevention in part because, as in domestic politics, they have different ideological preconceptions. But its final chapter takes the domestic-political analogy further by pointing out that, just as people rarely choose a domestic ideology because of a wholly disinterested belief in its explanatory power, so they often choose a war-and-peace theory partly because it is to their advantage to do so. The role played in domestic politics by the economic interests and class consciousness of different social and occupational groups is played in international politics by the strategic interests and political outlook of different states. For example, the near-invulnerability once enjoyed by the United States became enduringly ingrained in its political culture, so that Robert E. Osgood could acknowledge in 1957: 'Although America's military policies have been revolutionized, her basic propensities, formed during the protracted period of nineteenth-century innocence, remain in effect.'[5] And even today opposition to nuclear weapons is still much weaker in France than in Britain for reasons that cannot fully be explained by looking at what has happened this century, let alone at what has happened since either became a nuclear state. Although its illustrations are drawn from only a limited number of states, this chapter attempts to provide at least the framework for a comparative analysis by arguing that a state's war-and-peace debate is determined by the extent to which its political culture is historically liberal and its strategic situation historically secure.

This book thus emphasizes the continuities in thinking about war and peace rather than the discontinuities. Although it traces the former no further back than the eighteenth century, it is in general agreement with the German historian Klaus Hildebrand, who is struck by the way that

states now in possession of the most terrifying modern weapons continue to think in terms of categories which in principle have been familiar in European politics since the days of Henry II of England (1165–1189), Philippe Auguste II of France (1165–1223) and Charles V of Spain (1500–58).[6]

This is not to deny the importance of the twentieth century's two revolutions in warfare: the 'mechanical revolution',[7] which found full expression in the trench warfare of 1914–18 and the invention of the bomber, and the 'nuclear revolution' of 1945–52 when the atomic and hydrogen bombs were first tested. This book recognizes that the latter in particular, which poses problems for every war-and-peace theory (except the pessimistic version of pacifism), has significantly reduced the importance of ideological and strategic legacies from previous eras. But it nevertheless differs significantly from most recent literature, which assumes that disagreement about war prevention can mainly be explained by the sheer intractability of the moral and strategic dilemmas posed by nuclear weapons.

To provide an introduction to thinking about war and peace in a short book is a hopelessly ambitious task; and a number of short-cuts have been resorted to, in addition to those already acknowledged. The work stands or falls by its analytical categories; and the discussion of the specific events, foreign policies, and states chosen as illustrations amounts usually to a less than rounded treatment. Many terms which have a more precise meaning in the academic study of international relations—'international system', 'isolationism', and so on—have been employed in a looser sense than would have been appropriate had the book's purpose been different. 'Strategic' has been used broadly: to refer to a state's geopolitical interests, as well as to the technical question of how these should best be protected militarily. 'Nuclear' refers to nuclear weapons only (both nuclear and thermonuclear)—a topic which is receiving so much attention from other authors that the special issues it raises are only touched on here. And jargon, references to other works, and running debates with other writers have all been kept to a minimum. In this context it is worth reiterating that the intellectual framework of this study was developed not after reading the work of international theorists, little of which is directly relevant to present concerns anyway, but in the course of research on the modern British peace movement. It is designed to explain the dynamics of actual war-and-peace debates, not to prescribe the content of ideal ones. Thus when it makes distinctions—for example, between crusading and defencism and among the various sub-types of pacifism—it does so not to make implicit value judgements—such as whether intervention is justified or which is the 'best' form of pacifism—but in order to identify fault-lines in the war-and-peace debate. Similarly, when it talks of the strengths and weaknesses of a theory, it is in order to explain its popularity or otherwise. This is, in other words, a work of political analysis, not of political ethics.

2

Principles of classification

Many activists and even some observers have an instinctive hostility towards any attempt to categorize a political movement in which they are involved or interested. For this reason it is essential, before proceeding to the discussion of the five war-and-peace theories—militarism, crusading, defencism, pacific-ism, and pacifism—both to explain the present typology or scheme of classification and to assess its strengths and weaknesses. This chapter will attempt to make two points clear.

The first is that the typology has two dimensions: it classifies theories according to their attitude to force as well as their doctrinal content. It is thus able, for example, to distinguish socialists who are crusaders from those who are pacific-ists or pacifists, as well as to distinguish all socialists from liberals, conservatives, and so on.

The second point is that its categories are 'ideal-types': they do not label viewpoints which necessarily exist in actual war-and-peace debates, but describe those which logically could exist. The purpose of ideal-type analysis is not to replace discussion of what real people in fact think, but to sharpen and focus it. Only by being aware of the full range of intellectual options available is it possible to identify the distinctive features of a particular debate.

1. A two-dimensional typology

As just noted, the typology reflects two dimensions of ideological belief: the different methods by which it is appropriate to advance political values, and the different values themselves.

i. Means

The first axis deals with means rather than ends. The distinctions which it makes are similar to those which can be made between three basic approaches to domestic politics: the 'coercive' approach, which argues that one should if necessary impose one's values by revolutionary or reactionary force; the 'constitutional' approach, which argues that force is illegitimate, and that one should advance one's values by agreed political procedures; and the 'conscientious' approach, which argues that force is wrong and legal procedures insufficient, and that one should advance one's values only by seeking to bring about profound moral or spiritual conversions in one's fellow citizens. In the war-and-peace debate these three approaches argue respectively that military force can be used aggressively, that it can be used only defensively, and that it can never be used at all.

It is crucial to make clear the implications of basing this first axis on attitudes to coercion. It entails, first, that pacifism be defined in an absolutist fashion and that pacific-ism be regarded as an entirely distinct theory. This is no longer very controversial. There is a growing agreement both that 'pacifist' should be reserved for absolutists who reject all wars, and that 'pacific-ist' is a useful generic term for the remainder of the peace movement.[1]

It entails, second, a moral distinction between aggression and defence. This, however, is rather more problematical. It will here be argued that this distinction has become central to common-sense morality and international law: only a defensive cause is now generally accepted as a just one. But it is admitted that this distinction is of surprisingly recent origin, and that some thinkers continue to deny its validity.

The 'shift of norms' which enabled the defence/offence distinction to become generally, though not universally, accepted has been rightly described by the historian F. H. Hinsley as 'a greater displacement of assumptions about relations between states than any that has taken place in history'; and he points out that 'a shift so fundamental . . . will have been a long time in the making'.[2] It is a further illustration of the neglect of war-and-peace thinking that the stages on this long journey are so little known.

That the process began fairly recently can be illustrated by a brief look at the tradition of just-war thinking evolved by Christians, warriors, and international lawyers over at least the last fifteen centuries. Though this is a tradition rather than a precise doctrine, there is general agreement as to its content. It falls into two fairly distinct parts—the *jus ad bellum*, which regulates the ends of war, and the *jus in bello*, which regulates its means—and has been summarized as follows:

The *jus ad bellum* prescribes that war is permissible if and only if:
  (*a*) war is declared by a competent authority;
  (*b*) as a last resort, all available peaceful means of settling the dispute having first been tried and failed;
  (*c*) for the sake of a just cause;
  (*d*) the harm judged likely to result from the war is not disproportionate to the likely good to be achieved.
The *jus in bello* adds two further conditions governing the conduct of war:
  (*e*) the harm judged likely to result from a particular military action should not be disproportionate to the good aimed at;
  (*f*) non-combatants should be immune from direct attack.[3]

Not only is the offence/defence distinction not explicitly mentioned, it was given surprisingly little weight by just-war theorists as a criterion for satisfying condition (*c*). As a result, by the sixteenth century the risk of 'simultaneous ostensible justification'—a situation in which both sides in a war could make an equally good case for having a 'just cause'—had become one of their major preoccupations.

The laxity of early *jus ad bellum* thinking was in accord with the tenacious refusal of either diplomatic practice or international law to restrict the circumstances in which properly constituted governments could resort to force. Until as late as the 1870s, as F. H. Hinsley has pointed out, although states subscribed to the principle of the balance of power 'out of their concern to establish more stable international relations' and in practice enjoyed the benefits of a more or less balanced distribution of power, they 'retained the right to go to war for any reason whatever, indeed for no reason at all'. They did so because they felt too insecure to renounce aggression, believing that while the going was good no state could miss an opportunity to improve its position in case the situation suddenly took a turn for the worse and it needed all the strength it could muster.

This readiness on 'realist' grounds to use aggression was symptomatic of a fatalistic attitude to war. It was generally assumed that, since war was neither an abnormal state of affairs nor one which was sharply differentiated from peace, and since nothing could be done to reduce its incidence, there was no more point in formulating a moral attitude towards it than in doing so towards the weather. This fatalistic view will here be labelled 'bellicism', a term borrowed from the military historian and student of strategy Sir Michael Howard.[4] It is important at once to emphasize the difference between bellicism and the modern theory which it superficially resembles: militarism. Bellicism is morally neutral and applicable only to the period before the offence/defence distinction came to be widely recognized and when defencism had therefore not yet emerged as a distinct position. Militarism can be understood as a deliberate attempt to moralize bellicist assumptions and to keep them alive in a new era: an era in which peace came to be regarded both as the normal state of affairs and as overwhelmingly preferable to war, in which a moral distinction usually tended to be made between the offensive and defensive use of force, and in which it came generally to be believed that security required only the latter.

It was during the period of relative peace in Europe from the 1870s to the First World War that bellicism began to fade out, as public opinion came gradually to regard war as exceptional and peace as both normal and morally superior. At the same time, states began to recognize a restriction on their freedom to declare war, although they could not at first take this too far since, as Hinsley has argued, the previous equilibrium of power was in practice then breaking down: as a result 'the need to preserve or restore it became their main justification of the right to war'.[5] Thus in the late nineteenth century, as Ian Brownlie has put it in his definitive legal study of this question, the right to war 'eroded' for the first time. It seems likely that in most countries public opinion had by then become conscious of an important moral difference between defence and offence: accordingly, it for the most part accepted the defencist or pacific-ist view that, except perhaps in respect of 'primitive' peoples, states should not use aggression to advance their own interests. Between about the 1890s and 1914, in consequence, bellicism began to fragment; and the distinction between militarism and defencism, and between crusading and pacific-ism, began to gain wide acceptance.

Although the First World War marked the completion of this process as far as public opinion was concerned, international law lagged somewhat behind. In 1919 the Covenant of the League of

Nations stopped short of making aggressive war illegal; in Brownlie's words: 'The general presumption was that war was still a right of sovereign states, although signatories to the Covenant were bound by that instrument to submit to certain procedures of pacific settlement.' In 1928, however, the states adhering to the Kellogg–Briand Pact renounced aggressive war, so that by 1939 'a norm of illegality had appeared as a part of the customary law'; although this norm was not formally expressed until the Charter of the United Nations was proclaimed in 1945.[6] This outlawed all non-defensive war other than interventions under the auspices of the United Nations itself. The American military prosecutor at the Nuremberg trials was thus in tune with international law as well as world opinion when he argued in his opening address: 'Our position is that whatever grievances a nation may have, however objectionable it finds that *status quo*, aggressive warfare is an illegal means for settling those grievances or for altering those conditions.'[7]

But, in belatedly catching up with common-sense morality, international law ran into the problem of how aggression was to be defined. Legally it was easiest to define it as the first use of force; but this was soon generally admitted to be too restrictive. As James Turner Johnson, a leading historian of the just-war tradition, put it: whereas *jus ad bellum* thinking had formerly been too permissive, by being 'defined by first use of force vs. second' it was 'sadly truncated'.[8] The way most defencists and pacific-ists solved the problem was by extending the notion of defence to cover selected instances of the first use of force, such as pre-emptive strikes and preventive wars. (These and the other extensions of the meaning of defence will be examined in chapter 5.) The effect of formally outlawing aggression was thus to a certain extent merely semantic: it led some wars to be described as 'defensive' which would not previously have been so labelled.

Nevertheless, since it was impossible plausibly to attach a defensive motive to all wars which would once have been regarded as 'just', the new insistence on defensiveness has reduced the number of legitimate justifications for war. But it has left the just-war tradition in a state of some confusion as regards the *jus ad bellum*. Its modern exponents willingly accept a more restrictive conception than their predecessors, and thus reject most forms of aggression. But for the most part they refuse simply to equate a just war with a defensive one.

This typology follows common-sense morality and international law in accepting this equation. It therefore stipulates that those who fail to do likewise must be either militarists or—as in the case of most of the just-war theorists just mentioned[9]—crusaders. Since they are unlikely so to regard themselves, it must at once be made clear that crusading is not intended to be a pejorative term. Indeed, as chapter 4 will show, it can be a highly scrupulous and honourable position.

Thus it is here acknowledged that this typology is based on a hard-and-fast moral distinction between aggression and defence which has probably been accepted by public opinion only for the past century, which still poses problems of definition for international lawyers, and which is still regarded as problematical by many philosophers, political theorists, and theologians.

Even if this difficulty is overlooked, moreover, categories based solely on attitudes to coercion can distinguish neither between the two types of aggressive theory, militarism and crusading, nor between the two defensive ones, defencism and pacific-ism, nor even between any of the three variants (optimistic, mainstream, and pessimistic) of the no-war theory, pacifism. The typology depends on its second axis to make these distinctions.

ii. Ends

This second axis is concerned with what is being promoted, rather than how: it classifies theories according to their substantive doctrinal content. The simplest and most popular way of doing this for international relations hitherto has been to distinguish simply between 'realism' and 'idealism'.

This is quite useful when combined with the first axis, since the present typology can then be represented as follows:

	coercive/aggressive	*constitutional/defensive*	*conscientious/no war*
realism	MILITARISM	DEFENCISM	'pessimistic' PACIFISM
idealism	CRUSADING	PACIFIC-ISM	'optimistic' and 'mainstream' PACIFISM

But it is evident even from this tabulation that, as a characterization of the doctrinal dimension of the war-and-peace debate, the realist/idealist dichotomy is problematical. For one thing, it produces some strange judgements: all militarists are deemed to be realists, even though some of them assert that every effort should be made to transcend the constraints of 'reality'; all crusaders are branded as idealists, even though some of them are conservatives; and pessimistic pacifists are classified as realists, even though all of them totally reject military force. For another, it has inappropriate philosophical connotations: in particular, although a militarist inspired by a Hegelian conception of the state as a moral being which must expand to fulfil its own destiny is clearly a realist as the term is conventionally used in international relations, he would be classified in orthodox philosophical terminology as an idealist.

Even when combined with the first dimension, realism and idealism are so vague as to conceal important distinctions. It is self-evident that the term 'idealism' cannot do justice to the diversity of ideological approaches adopted by crusaders, pacific-ists, and optimistic and mainstream pacifists, and needs to be broken down into different sub-categories. Less obvious, and therefore more insidious, is the imprecision of the term 'realism'. Its basic meaning is that the nature of 'reality' is such as to render idealistic or utopian reform impossible. But there are two interpretations of 'reality'—the 'moderate' one of normal usage and a more exotic 'extreme' variety—which differ on two closely related issues.

They differ, first, as to whether reality should be regarded neutrally or normatively. The 'moderate' majority of realists accept the need to be realistic about the current distribution of power and the direction in which social rivalries are heading; but they do not necessarily admire this distribution or wish the struggle to reach a final showdown. Indeed, they try to limit the role power plays in human affairs by fostering societal norms at the expense of anarchic tendencies, although they accept that there are limits to what can be achieved in this respect. The 'extremist' minority, however, take a normative view: they regard reality as by definition good, and argue that no attempt should be made to restrain human competition. This distinction has been recognized by Raymond Aron, in the course of comparing the (moderate-realist) outlook of the American school of self-styled Realist scholars in the late 1940s and early 1950s, of whom the most prominent was Hans J. Morgenthau, with the (extreme-realist) approach of the turn-of-the-century German nationalist school, exemplified by Treitschke, with which it shared 'certain similar precepts':

> In crossing the Atlantic, in becoming *power politics*, Treitschke's *Machtpolitik* underwent a chiefly spiritual mutation. It became fact, not value. The American authors who are commonly regarded as belonging to the realist school declare that states, animated by a will to power, are in permanent rivalry, but that they are not self-congratulatory about the situation and do not regard it as part of the divine plan . . . the German nationalists desired power politics for itself. The American realists believe they are obliged to acknowledge its existence and accept its laws.[10]

The other issue is whether reality is wholly or only partially anarchic. Moderates accept that reality is too anarchic for idealistic reforms to be possible, yet not so intractable as to prevent a modicum of order being salvaged in most cases. Extremists believe that it is too turbulent for stability to be achieved for any significant period. Because there are these two distinct variants of realism, the term is a confusing one; and it is here argued that more precise ideological labels are needed.

This point is fully recognized in domestic politics, of course. Although conservatives, in particular, sometimes find it convenient to claim that they are realists and their opponents utopians, they are never tempted either to discard the label 'conservative' or to deny that utopianism comes in significantly different varieties. And, although many on the left admit to being idealists, they do not believe that this obviates the need for additional ideological self-descriptions, such as socialist or liberal.

The best way of introducing more precision into the second dimension of the present typology is thus to introduce as subdivisions the doctrines of domestic politics. To do so is, of course, to assume that every doctrine worthy of the name has a view not only about domestic issues but also about war and peace, even if its view about the latter is often somewhat vague and distant since it cannot be implemented until considerable headway has been made in domestic politics. Thus when socialists, for example, work for social justice they are also working for the world peace which they believe will be achieved only after most states have accepted their views. Likewise, conservatives are sceptical about the possibility of achieving either social justice or world peace, but believe that the states which best conserve their social orders will do most to sustain such international order (and therefore peace) as exists. And, similarly, fascists seek struggle both internally and externally and deny that world peace is a desirable goal.

There have recently been welcome, if tentative, signs that not only academic observers[11] but also activists are starting to recognize the applicability to the war-and-peace debate of domestic-political categories. Socialists, it is true, have always been keen to apply their critique to international relations: for the first half of this century they maintained a running argument with liberals on the issue of whether capitalism or jingoism caused war;[12] and more recently they have challenged the radical mainstream of the nuclear-disarmament movement on the issue of whether class determines the development of weapons or the development of weapons determines the fate of classes.[13]

Moreover, since the Soviet Union came to replace Germany and Japan as the major threat to world order as they conceive it, western defencists have tended to see the peace movement in ideological terms, as an outgrowth of left-wing politics generally. And peace movements in the past two decades have been far more willing than their predecessors to stress their links to ideologies not formerly regarded as directly related to the peace issue. For example, Rebecca Johnson, a leading member of the pioneering women's peace camp at Greenham Common (Britain's first cruise-missile base), has explained the presence there of 'lesbians, punks, blacks and other social embarrassments' in terms of 'the connections between cruise missiles and the systematic rape of the earth, the violent oppression of Third World peoples, racism, and male violence against women. Nuclear weapons cannot be rendered powerless without a clear understanding of the values and practices in society which sustain the arms race.'[14]

The present typology thus claims to strike a better balance between simplicity and comprehensiveness than its few rivals have done (the two most important of which are discussed in an appendix to this book). It achieves this by being two-dimensional and by combining a basically simple structure with the possibility of almost limitless refinement through the introduction as subdivisions of ideologies which are already familiar from domestic politics.

It must be stressed, however, that to understand its theoretical dimension is not to understand the whole war-and-peace debate: there will also be disagreements over policy. Of course, the espousal of a particular theory considerably constrains the policies that can be recommended: a militarist can never recommend disarmament, for example, or a pacifist rearmament. But it is not uncommon to find major disagreements among advocates of the same theory. To give a notorious example: in the later 1930s defencists in Britain and other liberal democracies were bitterly divided over whether to appease or to defy Hitler.

This book has little to say about why believers in the same theory disagree about policy. But reference must briefly be made to one source of disagreement, since it stems from an important cross-cutting cleavage in the war-and-peace debate: that over 'posture'. This is the view taken of a state's proper role in the international system—where its vital interests lie, the directions in which its influence should be extended, and the areas in which commitments should be avoided. For some states the choice of posture is clear-cut: Switzerland, in particular, has never wavered from its policy of self-reliant non-alignment. But for many the issue is complex and controversial. For example, Wilhelmine Germany debated the merits of a naval and colonial *Weltpolitik* as against those of creating *Mitteleuropa*: its downfall in the First World War was in part because it failed to come to a clear decision. Similarly, it was a major political issue in the United States after the First World War whether the country should be isolationist or interventionist; and for a time after the Second, thanks to McCarthy and MacArthur, it was much debated whether Asia should have been recognized as a higher American priority than Europe. For its part, Britain has experienced a long-running three-way debate between 'little England' isolationists, advocates of a world role (who can themselves be subdivided into a traditional school of imperialists and a more modern one of Atlanticists), and Europeanists. Thus to return to the example of disagreements among defencists given in the previous paragraph: one reason why some staunch British defencists such as Leopold Amery favoured appeasement for as long as they did was that they were imperialists who clung to an isolationist posture towards Europe.

Although rarely overlooked, this debate on posture is often

misunderstood. Thus, although the importance of isolationism in particular has been widely acknowledged, it has normally been treated as if it were just another theory—a milder alternative to pacifism—rather than a posture compatible with a wide range of theories. Posture is, in other words, an important intermediate level at which the war-and-peace debate is conducted that helps to shed light on why advocates of different theories can support such very different policies. There is no space here to develop this point further, however, since this book is concerned above all with the theories themselves.

2. Ideal types

Almost every typology suggests that its categories are more rigidly differentiated than they in fact are: in reality they usually blur into each other at the margins, since each axis of the typology is normally a continuum. Thus wherever the dividing lines between categories are drawn some people will straddle them and so be hard to classify.

This is especially true of a typology like the present one, which is made up not of empirical or descriptive categories but of ideal types or paradigms. Its categories, in other words, are not the result of research to discover what the major clusters of opinion actually are, so that the dividing lines on the continuum can be drawn in such a way as to highlight them to the greatest extent possible. They are devised so as to demonstrate the complete range of options available in principle to participants in the war-and-peace debate, even if some of these options attract very little support in most actual such debates, and the dividing lines thus in practice often bisect opinion-clusters rather than keep them separate.

The category of militarism offers a clear illustration of the difference between the ideal-type and the empirical approach. In order to demarcate the opposite pole of the debate to pacifism, this theory has been defined in so 'idealized' a form that exemplars are in practice difficult to find. As a result, many of those conventionally supposed to be 'militarists' are here presented instead as falling on the dividing line between ideal-type militarism and ideal-type defencism. But this is a strength not a weakness of this type of categorization: their thinking, with its equivocations and ambiguities about the precise value of war and aggression, is more clearly understood as an attempt to reconcile two conflicting theories than as a coherent position in its own right. Ideal-type analysis is thus able to accommodate not only 'purists' who fall neatly into a single category but also 'hybrids' who fall somewhere between two or more and who try either to discover a half-way house or to oscillate wildly between them.

Ideal types can also helpfully be applied to those who either reject or do not understand the utility of such an approach. It is highly probable that a number of war-and-peace activists will not like the way they have in effect been classified here. But this is not because the categories are at fault. It is either because they are unaware of the implications of their own beliefs, or because they are too bound up in the debate to take a detached view, or again because they have self-interested reasons—such as the desire to hold a coalition of different viewpoints together—for disputing useful analytical distinctions.

For example, the pacifism/pacific-ism distinction would undoubtedly have been queried by many, if not most, members of the pre-1914 British peace movement, on the grounds that they could reconcile the two categories. Yet it helps to explain which of them opposed the First World War and which did not. Similarly, in 1934 the British novelist Storm Jameson wrote an essay which is hard to label either pacifist or pacific-ist: her memoirs acknowledged that it 'could have been written either by a devout supporter of the League or an out-and-out pacifist'. This was not because the distinction was inappropriate, but because she deliberately tried to evade it. As she later admitted: 'For some years after 1933 I lived in equivocal amity with pacifists and combative supporters of the League of Nations, adjusting my feelings, in good and bad faith, to the person I happened to be with. I swayed between the two like a tightrope walker.'[15] Eventually she plumped for pacifism, joining the Peace Pledge Union; but during the Second World War she recanted.

Activists, in other words, are not necessarily the best analysts of their own ideas and activities. Though a number of them are remarkably shrewd and self-aware, they have as a whole failed to categorize their own thinking adequately, let alone that of their opponents. They have no valid grounds for objecting to a detached attempt to make up for this.

3

Militarism

Extreme positions make the best starting-points; and the first war-and-peace theory to be discussed is the most controversial of all. Not only does it view international relations as wholly anarchical, from which it follows that there is no possibility of any trust or co-operation between states, let alone reform of the international system, and that frequent wars are unavoidable: it welcomes this fact, since it regards war both as a positive good (rather than a lesser evil) and as essential for human development. In the words of one of its most celebrated German exponents, General Friedrich von Bernhardi, writing in 1911: 'The inevitableness, the idealism and the blessing of war, as an indispensable and stimulating law of development, must be repeatedly emphasized.'[1] The theory holds that war is caused not by moral or political mistakes but by man's laudable drive to achieve his full potential. It can be seen as the application to international relations of fascist assumptions, defined broadly.

This viewpoint has never been the subject of a major study. Indeed, it has scarcely been recognized as a war-and-peace theory in its own right. This is partly a symptom of the general neglect of the war-and-peace debate. But it is largely because those who have written seriously about 'militarism'—those, that is, who have not used it simply as a term of abuse—have regarded it not as a view of international relations but as a socio-political phenomenon. They have not been interested, in other words, in what militarists have actually said about the dangers and opportunities of the international struggle for survival. Instead they have assumed that the militarization of society—the prestige attached to soldiering, the maintenance of a powerful army, the insistence on conscription, and the constant harping on threats to national survival—has been motivated by internal rather than external considerations, in particular a desire to preserve social control in an authoritarian state by distracting the workers from their domestic grievances.[2] But, although militarism has indeed often been supported simply as an excuse for militarization, it is nevertheless primarily a theory of war and peace. This chapter will begin by examining it as such, before looking at the conditions in which it can gain some support.

1. The theory

It must be admitted that, even when recognized as a war-and-peace theory, militarism has no neglected intellectual masterpieces to reveal. Its exponents have usually been more interested in practice than in theory, or have moderated their public statements in an attempt to win support. Even Adolf Hitler pulled his punches somewhat when he wrote for publication. Thus, although in *Mein Kampf* he argued that a state had a duty to expand its soil if this was necessary to feed its population, he was quick to deny the necessity for certain wars which 'the foul hurrah-patriotism' of the 'bourgeois nationalists' might precipitate. And in a second book, dictated in 1928 but not published in his lifetime, his hostility to those demanding the return by Italy of the German-speaking South Tyrol led him to argue that, since in war a state experiences 'a preferential destruction of its best elements', any wars 'fought for aims that, because of their whole nature, do not guarantee a compensation for the blood that has been shed, are sacrileges committed against a nation, a sin against a people's future'.[3] The full extent of his belief in the positive value of war must therefore be gleaned from fragmentary private comments, such as that reported by Hermann Rauschning: 'War is life . . . War is the origin of all things.'[4]

For this reason some of the most explicit assertions of militarism have emanated either from men of action in retirement, like Bernhardi, or from those who have never been politically accountable, such as writers and intellectuals. It was, for example, the Futurist Manifesto of 1909 which proclaimed: 'We want to glorify war—the only cure for the world—and militarism, patriotism' (and which went on in the same breath to praise 'the destructive gesture of the anarchists, the beautiful ideas which kill, and contempt for women').[5] And it was the distinguished, if notably eccentric,

German philosopher Max Scheler who in 1915 published probably
the most outspoken book-length statement of militarism, *Der Genius
des Krieges und der Deutsche Krieg* ('The Genius of War and the
German War'). At the time of writing it, according to his
biographer, Scheler

not only accepted the appelation of militarist, he revelled in it, rejecting the
excuses offered by modern liberals who claimed that Germany had
developed a strong army only in order to hold the frontier against the
barbarians of eastern Europe. Scheler admitted that geographical factors
may have played a part, but the decisive factor in the development of
German militarism was *spiritual*. Militarism was simply the natural organic
form in which the Prussian spirit expressed itself.[6]

But Scheler's book was untranslatably incoherent; and by the end
of 1915 he had retreated from militarism into defencism.

Those who have publicly, seriously, and consistently expounded
the theory have thus been so few and idiosyncratic that a purely
historical approach would produce a diffuse catalogue of fragmentary statements by inarticulate, third-rate or eccentric thinkers.
The present attempt to construct an ideal-type militarism involves
considerably more 'idealization', therefore, than is required in any
of the other chapters of this book.

Its basis is nevertheless clear: a belief that the true values are
'martial' in the sense of being created or given their fullest expression by war. In a characteristic passage of *Der Genius des Krieges und
der Deutsche Krieg*, Max Scheler expressed his belief that

mankind would have destroyed itself had not the dignity of war sanctified
force and focused the attention of great peoples on common aims. As Kant
has already pointed out, it is war that populated the earth—particularly in
areas less favoured by nature—and not only made science and culture
possible, but also actively encouraged them. It is war which created existing
societies out of potential ones and led directly to scientific and other
developments being achieved by hard work, the manufacture of tools and
machines, and by setting standards in trade and business. The weapon
preceded the tool, and it is a fact that now all ancient and modern mechanics
stems directly from the science of fortification (Galileo, Ubaldi, Leonardo).
It is war, too, which justifies a noble people in their striving for increasing
expansion and recognition.[7]

By contrast, every other theory of war and peace sees the true
values as 'civilized', in the sense of emanating from civil society in

a condition of peace. This is true even of crusading, despite its belief that in certain circumstances the values of peace can be imposed by aggressive war. Many who at first sight seem militarists in fact fail to meet this 'martial values' test. One example is Anthony Ludovici, a prolific writer on the far-right fringe of British inter-war politics, who accepted that 'a superior race has the incontestable right to spread itself at the cost of inferior races', but who felt nevertheless that 'there can be no ethical justification for imposing an inferior culture by force of arms upon a superior culture'.[8] Thus, although strongly influenced by militarist ideas, Ludovici (here classified as an authoritarian conservative rather than a fascist) was primarily a crusader.

The real militarist believes that, true values being martial ones, the superior culture must by definition be the one that prevails. Admittedly, since militarists are commonly to be found in states which, however powerful, are territorially dissatisfied and thus victims of past setbacks, they are often reluctant to accept the adverse outcome of a single war as a sign of inferiority. Hence the comment by the historian Heinrich von Treitschke, one of Wilhelmine Germany's most famous militarists: 'It is important not to look on war always as a judgement from God. Its consequences are evanescent; but the life of a nation is reckoned by centuries, and the final verdict can only be pronounced after a survey of whole epochs.'[9] But, as he implied, a state's military record over a sufficiently long period must constitute such a judgement. Of this Hitler was certain as early as 1923: 'Always before God and the world, the stronger has the right to carry through what he will. History proves: He who has not the strength—him the "right in itself" profits not a whit.'[10]

Militarism has two complementary explanations for how it is that martial values are generated: through the process of fighting (here called the 'fulfilment' explanation), and through its outcome (the 'hegemony' explanation).

i. Fulfilment

This argues that going to war (and presumably also, if to a lesser extent, undergoing military training) enables man to fulfil his potential more fully than does any other activity. It depends on a romantic or (using the term in a popular sense) Nietzschean view of human nature as engaged in a dynamic struggle for self-realization. 'The duty of self-assertion' was insisted upon by Bernhardi, who also asserted: 'Struggle is . . . a universal law of Nature . . . "Man is a fighter". Self-sacrifice is a renunciation of life.' And in a speech at Chemnitz on 2 April 1938, Hitler made a similar claim: 'Man has become great through struggle . . . Whatever goal man has reached is due to his originality plus his brutality.'[11] Anti-militarists often accept that this side of human nature exists, but insist that progress is achieved by repressing rather than indulging it. Thus a British radical, William Clarke, could insist in 1901:

The first and primary objection to a policy of militarism is that it involves inevitable moral reaction. It plunges man into the very abyss of brute force, from which he struggles to emerge, and from which he must emerge if he is to fulfil the designs of his Creator . . . Our chief business is to eliminate the 'ape and tiger' from our being, and to rise on the stepping stones of our dead selves to higher things. Now, how can war help that onward evolution? It cannot only not help it, but it must hinder it because it calls forth the very qualities that drag us down.[12]

Not all romantics or Nietzscheans are militarists: many believe that struggle can be repressed or sublimated and the need for war thereby avoided. The leader of the British Union of Fascists, Sir Oswald Mosley, was an avowed Nietzschean, capable as late as 1947 of writing: 'Man is neither an animal nor a God; he is a striving being in a world of flux and becoming who will either revert to a final nothing or win heights of achievement and of being whose divine sunlight would dazzle present eyes to blindness.'[13] Yet he believed that peace could be maintained if the human struggle was channelled into the creation of autarchic blocs which pursued their destiny without contact with each other. This will be classified in chapter 5 as a form of defencism, albeit a very extreme one lcoated almost on the borderline with militarism. But true militarists believe that war offers a unique opportunity for human fulfilment. The French writer Pierre Drieu La Rochelle, already an enthusiastic Nietzschean in principle, felt that he had experienced the practical truth of his philosophy in 1914 when he led a charge against a machine-gun post near Charleroi; it was this to which he was referring when he wrote in 1934, the year he became a fascist:

'There are events that suddenly exhaust, by an essential test, all the possibilities of our being.' The same view was taken in 1932 by Benito Mussolini (or his ghost-writer) in his entry on fascism in the *Enciclopedia italiana*:

War alone brings up to its highest tension all human energy and puts the stamp of nobility upon the peoples who have the courage to meet it. All other trials are substitutes, which never really put men into the position in which they have to make the great decision—the alternative of life or death.[14]

But the fulfilment argument is not incompatible with all liberal-democratic values. In particular it does not deny the autonomy of both individual and society, since the benefits of war are directly available to them rather than mediated through the state. Nor does it regard the contribution to human development as being made entirely by the victors, since the losers too have been fulfilled by their martial experience. As Bernhardi acknowledged, with the struggle against overwhelming odds by the Boers in mind: 'Inestimable moral gains, which can never be lost in any later developments, have been won by their struggle'; and on 4 August 1914, the day Britain declared war, Minister for War General von Falkenhayn observed to the German Chancellor that, 'even if we end in ruin, it was beautiful'.[15] In thus rejecting prudence and praising heroic but doomed military activity, the fulfilment argument departs from the 'realist' tradition with which militarism is more conventionally associated. Instead of recognizing the constraints imposed by reality, it urges that they be transcended by a supreme act of will.

Because of its 'idealist' (as distinct from 'realist') connotations, the fulfilment argument for militarism is easy to confuse with what can be called the 'purgative' view: the argument that war to some extent cleanses man and society of their civilian materialism and self-indulgence. The latter is not militarist, however, because it makes no claim that the purgative benefits outweigh the humanitarian costs incurred in the process of fighting, and because it regards war as the source merely of certain beneficial by-products rather than of all values. The argument that war can be a purgative is widely used by non-militarists. Defencists and even pacific-ists have accepted it in order to be able to look on the bright side of a war—such as the First World War[16]—which has been forced upon them. And pacifists have admitted its force whenever they have insisted that society must try to find a substitute for war with the same purgative value—a 'moral equivalent of war', as William James called it.

ii. Hegemony

Because of its relative moderation, the fulfilment explanation has only a weak notion of progress: it sees mankind as developing only in the sense that after each war the quotient of human fulfilment is higher; and it assigns no special value to conquest. This is why militarists normally supplement it with the hegemony explanation, which asserts that human development occurs as weak societies are collectively subordinated to or taken over by strong ones.

They supplement rather than replace it with this argument, since hegemony could in principle be achieved without war—by sheer economic leverage, for example, or by voluntary merger (such as that between Egypt and Syria in 1958). For a militarist, however, hegemony must be achieved by military intimidation at the very least, and preferably by war itself. Hitler implied that he preferred a fight even to a walk-over when he made the famous complaint to his SS entourage after Britain's diplomatic intervention in September and October 1938 had led to the achievement without war of demands against Czechoslovakia: 'That fellow Chamberlain spoiled my entry into Prague.'[17] The militarist, in other words, admires military triumph for its own sake. Thus the main reason why French writer Pierre Drieu La Rochelle collaborated with the Germans after 1940 was admiration for their martial exploits: that it was not ideological sympathy was shown by the fact that, when by 1944 the Red Army had become Europe's most successful military machine, he went through a phase of admiring 'virile communism' instead.[18] The full militarist position thus requires fulfilment and hegemony to be combined.

The hegemony explanation insists that conquest not only ennobles the conqueror but uplifts the vanquished too. Although it most often draws its inspiration from vulgar Darwinism, it has other roots too. It was, for example, stated with particular clarity in the manifesto issued by the newly formed Yuzonsha group of Japanese militarists just after the First World War:

We the Japanese people must be the cyclone centre of a war to liberate mankind. Therefore the Japanese state is the Absolute which will bring

about the establishment of our idea of world revolution. Ideological fulfilment and militant organization of the Japanese state is a sacred
undertaking on behalf of this absolute goal . . . We do not consider it
sufficient to pursue reorganization and revolution for Japan alone, but
because we really believe in the Japanese nation's destiny to be the great
apostle of mankind's war of liberation we want to begin with the liberation
of Japan itself.[19]

But, if 'hegemony militarists' believe that strong states liberate
mankind, how does their hegemony differ from that envisaged by
crusaders, who also believe that their conquest of weak states
represents progress towards a better world? The difference lies
mainly in the nature of the values imposed.

(a) Particularist values. It has already been seen that the values of
crusading—and indeed of all war-and-peace theories other than
militarism—are civilized rather than martial: they are rooted in
peace. It must now be noted that they are also universal rather than
particularist: they belong to mankind as a whole and can in principle
be espoused by all states on a basis of full equality. Particularist
values, in contrast, are those which express the unique qualities of
one state, nation, or race: they can be revealed only in war and
adopted by another only as a form of enslavement. Fascists thus
recognize each other as co-ideologues only to a limited extent. For
example, Ferenc Szálasi, leader of Hungary's fascist movement,
the Arrow Cross, insisted that its movement's ideology was an
indigenous one: 'Hungarism is an ideological system. It is the
Hungarian practice of the national socialistic view of the world and
the spirit of the age. It is neither Hitlerism nor fascism nor anti-
Semitism, but Hungarism.'[20] Similarly, fascist Italy's foreign
minister told the grand council:

Fascism is not—as Mussolini has said and reiterated—an article for export,
neither was it ever meant to be a universal idea or even an ideology; it is
simply a way of life for Italy; it is meant to be the synthesis of our historical
experience and of the aspirations and particular national needs of our people
and our race.[21]

Sometimes, it is true, fascists present their ideology as universalist; but they do so either for opportunist reasons or because
their world-view turns out not to be fully fascist. Pierre Drieu La
Rochelle did so, for example, in 1934 when he portrayed the

fascism to which he had just been converted as socialist rather than nationalist:

> What is important for fascism is social revolution . . . Not only is nationalism but a pretext, it is also but a moment in the socialist evolution of fascism . . . If Europe is not annihilated [by the Communist East], there will be a Geneva [i.e. a League of Nations] of socializing fascisms.[22]

But Drieu was hoping to avoid a conflict between his fascism and his nationalism; and in 1937 he swung decisively towards the latter (although for only three years, as has just been noted).

Sir Oswald Mosley was an even more convinced and consistent universalist. Indeed by the end of the Second World War, after which he renounced fascism and campaigned instead for European union, he had come to the view that fascism had failed because it had not (in Robert Skidelsky's perceptive words)

> been unshakeably rooted in a 'universalist' conception . . . In other words, Hitler's attempt to adapt Europe to the new reality of its 'dwarfing' by the rising superpowers of America and Russia could have succeeded only had it been attempted by political methods and informed by a genuine European idealism rather than by a conception of German imperialism. The heroic and barbaric values embodied in the Nazi enterprise totally overshadowed the rational and humane ends to which, according to Mosley, fascism was basically directed.[23]

Mosley's universalism, like Drieu's, can be interpreted as a desire to avoid seeming unpatriotic. But a more fundamental explanation is that, just as Mosley was not strictly a militarist (as already claimed), so he was never in the full sense of the word a fascist either. (In our terms he was an authoritarian conservative.)

In certain moods, moreover, even Hitler appeared to regard National Socialism as universalist. If Hermann Rauschning is to be believed, he claimed that the Nazi revolution was 'the exact counterpart of the great French revolution', that it would 'run its course in every nation', and that at least in England, France, and America the 'new men' of the national revolutions would 'voluntarily play their part' in the new Nazi order.[24] But Hitler's motives were largely opportunist: he wished to allay the fears of right-wing potential sympathizers in other states. And on closer inspection, in so far as he was rejecting particularism it was only nationalist particularism. Despite his seemingly universalist talk of 'every nation', Hitler was a racial particularist: he privately insisted before the Second World War that there was only 'one good ruling race',[25] and during it that he was 'firmly opposed to any attempt to export National Socialism'.[26] Although he co-operated with Italy and Japan, in particular, in a sort of fascist international, this was a geopolitical expedient and therefore temporary. He gradually lost his respect for the Italians, and always regarded the Japanese as the 'yellow peril', likening his pact with them to 'an alliance with the Devil himself'.[27] To sum up: it is here argued that, although fascists sometimes pretend otherwise, and although they can legitimately differ about whether their particularism is that of the state, nation, or race (as will be discussed shortly), none is ever a true universalist.

(b) Extreme 'realism'. Unlike the fulfilment explanation, the hegemony explanation puts forward what purports to be a prudential case for militarism: in a wholly anarchic international system a rational state must use any and every means, including aggression, to strengthen its position while the going is good, since otherwise it will be overwhelmed when, as is sure to happen, circumstances suddenly turn against it. As Bernhardi put it:

When a State is confronted by the material impossibilities of supporting any longer the warlike preparations which the power of its enemies has forced upon it, when it is clear that the rival States must gradually acquire from natural reasons a lead that cannot be won back, when there are indications of an offensive alliance of stronger enemies who only await the favourable moment to strike—then the moral duty of the State towards its citizens is to begin the struggle while the prospects of success and the political circumstances are still tolerably favourable.[28]

This amounts to the claim that militarism is really either 'bellicism' or 'realism'. But the former term has already been deemed applicable only to the period before a moral distinction between defence and offence came generally to be accepted. And the latter term has been shown to be ambiguous, since it comes in two very different versions, only one of which is 'realistic' in the normal sense. Although militarists wish to imply that they understand realism in the 'moderate' sense, they in fact accept both the controversial assumptions which identify the more 'extreme' version.

They accept, first, that reality is so wholly and inexorably anarchic that a state is normally justified in getting its retaliation in first (to borrow the jargon of unscrupulous footballers). This is, however, rarely a persuasive reading of the international situation; and militarists commonly lay themselves open to the accusation of paranoia. This is true even in vulnerable states at times of international crisis: German militarists in the late 1890s and much of the 1900s became obsessed with the unlikely possibility that Britain might 'Copenhagen' the German fleet—that is, destroy it in a preventive strike as it had done the Danish fleet in 1807; and their 'Copenhagen complex' disappeared only because it was replaced after the 1907 Anglo-Russian agreement by a scarcely less exaggerated phobia about 'encirclement'.[29] Similarly, in Austria-Hungary during the years before 1914, the chief of general staff, Conrad von Hötzendorff, kept insisting that various states—including even Italy—were poised to attack. He was taking an extreme view of the international situation because he was convinced that only a preventive war could prevent the Habsburg empire from disintegrating for internal reasons.[30]

Militarists also accept the second assumption of this extreme type of realism, namely that reality is a good thing and the struggle for power should be allowed to proceed unchecked. This argument is particularly useful for major states which want to improve their position by aggressive war but which are too dominant (in the short term at least) plausibly to pretend that they are compelled by insecurity to get their retaliation in first. They can argue that when the 'realities' of international competition alter in their favour they have a duty to expand their territory accordingly. For example, the last passage quoted from Bernhardi continues with the revealing sentence: 'When, on the other hand, the hostile States are weakened or hampered by affairs at home and abroad, but [a State's] own warlike strength shows elements of superiority, it is imperative to use the favourable circumstances to promote its own political aims.' And Treitschke had made the same point in the 1890s when he told his students:

When a State recognizes that existing treaties no longer express the actual political conditions, and when it cannot persuade the other Powers to give way by peaceful negotiations, the moment has come when the nations proceed to the ordeal by battle. A State thus situated is conscious when it declares war that it is performing an inevitable duty . . . The righteousness of war depends simply and solely upon the consciousness of a moral necessity.[31]

It should be noted, however, that militarists do not in practice push this second extreme-realist argument to what might be thought to be its logical conclusion. They cannot accept that, if what Treitschke called 'the actual political conditions' were to turn so sharply *against* their own state as to make victory impossible, the same argument for 'moral necessity' that justifies its aggression in favourable circumstances would now require its submission. Thus not merely is the hegemony case for militarism 'realistic' only in a highly contentious sense of the term, it is unconvincing even according to extreme-realist assumptions. When faced with a 'reality' which renders aggression on their part futile, militarists have somewhat inconsistently to switch to the anti-realist arguments, already noted, of the fulfilment case.

(c) State, nation, race. Whereas it will be seen that defencists see the political community to which they belong as merely an agency or framework, militarists (like fascists) view it in mystical terms—as a moral being which gives meaning to human existence. In Bernhardi's words: 'Man can only develop his highest capacities when he takes his part in a community, in a social organization, for which he lives and works.' Thus, whereas the fulfilment argument sees development as occurring through individual struggle, the hegemony argument sees it as occurring through the struggle between collectivities.

For some militarists the true collectivity is the nation or the race. But for most—either because they are Hegelians or because they simply recognize it to be the conventional unit of political life—it is the state. To quote Bernhardi again: 'The State alone . . . gives the individual the highest degree of life . . . It is only the State which strives after an enlarged sphere of influence that creates the conditions under which mankind develops into the most splendid perfection.'[32] If a state cannot or will not strive after an enlarged sphere of influence, it is not recognized by militarists as a true state—hence Hitler's remark in 1942: 'A State like Switzerland, which is nothing but a pimple on the face of Europe, cannot be allowed to continue.'[33] From an ideal-type militarist perspective, moreover, the state has two advantages: unlike nationalism, it has no pre-ordained limits on its territorial scope; and, unlike racism, it minimizes the problem of conflicting political loyalties.

The danger of basing militarist loyalty on the nation is the latter's limited perspective. This is most obvious in the case of secessionist micro-nationalisms, such as those of the Basques and Catalans: these provoked José Antonio Primo de Rivera, the Spanish Falangist, to fulminate against 'romantic' and 'local' nationalism and to urge that 'nation' be defined instead as 'the political society capable of finding its machinery of operation in the State'.[34]

But even where a major nation has managed to create a sizeable nation-state there is a danger that it may not aspire to expand beyond its natural (that is, national) limits. The Italian patriot Giuseppe Mazzini provides a good illustration of a nationalist who regarded belligerence only as a means to a pacific end. In the short term, his enthusiasm for the forcible liberation of Italy from the domination of the papacy and the Habsburg Empire was so fervent that historians have sometimes bracketed him with overt militarists.[35] In 1844, for example, he argued:

We must be great or perish. Rome and Venice are today the emblems of our mission. We cannot have Rome without giving Europe a new faith, and without freeing Humanity from the incubus of the past; we cannot have Venice without destroying the double symbol of despotism in Central and Eastern Europe . . . What for others may be simply a moral duty is a law of life for us . . . The destiny of Italy is that of the world.[36]

And he roundly condemned 'cosmopolitanism' for denying the value of nationality.[37] In the longer term, however, once the Italian state had been created, Mazzini expected it to live in perfect harmony with its neighbours; and his belief in 'the unity of the human race'[38] led President Woodrow Wilson to regard him as enough of an internationalist to make a gesture of homage at his grave.[39] Since he approved of force only to achieve political reform (in his case the creation of the nation-state) which would bring peace, Mazzini can be classified as a (liberal) crusader—albeit one whose enthusiasm to fight the good fight was so extreme as to have militarist overtones.

That nationalism could thus be a brake on militarism was appreciated by Hitler, as already noted. Rauschning quotes him as asserting: 'I have to liberate the world from dependence on its historic past. Nations are the outward and visible forms of our history. So I have to fuse the nations into a higher order if I want to get rid of the chaos of an historic past that has become an absurdity.'[40] As a supplement to nationalism, therefore, Hitler emphasized a higher loyalty to race.

The claim that race is the true political community presents militarism with even more complicated difficulties, however, because of its vagueness. On the one hand, as used by arrogant or opportunistic militarists like Hitler it could be extended until it smacked dangerously of universalism and, therefore, of the implication that national socialism could be spread by internal revolution rather than military conquest. On the other hand, as used by the timorous or deferential a fairly precise notion of racial identity could be turned into an argument for lasting peace between states which shared it. For example, Hitler's most devoted British disciple, Unity Mitford, argued in the *Daily Mirror* on 18 March 1939: 'Germans believe the Nordic race to be the greatest in the world, which indeed it is . . . With Germany, the greatest Continental Power, allied to Britain, the greatest Colonial Power, another world war would become an impossibility.'[41] The behaviour both of Nazi Germany in respect of its fellow Nordics and of Imperial Japan (which had at times claimed a pan-Asian racial solidarity with China and Korea) in respect of its fellow Asians suggests that in practice the full-blooded militarist is unlikely to share power or stay at peace for long even with a partner of the same race. Thus racism as a justification for militarism has in practice tended simply to be a cover for asserting or deferring to the superiority of a particular state.

If the hegemony argument is pushed to its logical extreme the whole world might expect eventually to be subdued by one, ultra-virile, state, nation, or race. In this event there would clearly be a longer than usual period of peace—and possibly a very long one indeed. Should militarism therefore be described, albeit paradoxically, as a war-prevention theory, in the sense of explaining what is necessary for the maximum period of peace ultimately to be achieved? Most militarists who have pondered this question have said no. For example, although Treitschke claimed that 'the progress of culture must make wars both shorter and rarer, for with every step it renders men's lives more harmonious', he backed away from the obvious implication of this argument with an explicit assertion that wars would never cease.[42] And Hitler was recorded as arguing on one occasion: 'As a general principle, I think that a peace which lasts for more than twenty-five years is harmful to a nation. Peoples, like individuals, sometimes need regenerating by a little bloodletting'; and on another: 'In future peace treaties we must be sure to have an opening for a new war.'[43] Militarism seems thus to envisage a cyclical pattern to the development of civilization, in which hegemonic states rise, grow soft, and are overthrown.

2. Preconditions

Militarism attracts support only when a state experiences both external and internal insecurity simultaneously and to an extreme degree. The former is needed to make the war-and-peace theory plausible; and the latter—as those who have stressed the sociopolitical function of that theory in domestic politics have made clear—predisposes the rulers of a state towards any theory which can persuade their citizens not to agitate about their domestic ills. Militarism is thus based on something of a paradox. It was initially stimulated by the pressures of both industrialization and democratization, which between them helped abruptly to alter the distribution of power between states (causing the external insecurity just noted) and to generate social tensions and political pressures (causing the internal insecurity, at least for the élites). But industrialization produced war's 'mechanical revolution', of which the military stalemate of 1914–18 on the Western Front was a tragic result. And democratization enabled potential cannon-fodder increasingly to gain a say in their own government's decisions for war and peace at this very time when war was becoming unprecedentedly horrible. The First World War is thus an important dividing line in the history of militarism. It ended a period of a quarter of a century or more in which militarism played a part in the war-and-peace debates not only of authoritarian states but also, if rather more weakly, of those closer to the liberal-democratic model. Thereafter it was confined to a handful of fascist states in which, nevertheless, it was preached and indeed practised with unprecedented fervour.

i. Authoritarian states

Militarism has been strongest in authoritarian states of two rather different types. The first was a disintegrating dynastic state, such as Austria-Hungary (in which war could be viewed, by the likes of Conrad von Hötzendorff, as a way of rallying support for a state beset by Slav nationalism) and Tsarist Russia (in which war and Pan-Slavism could be used to distract from domestic weakness and pressure for reform). Although the First World War brought these hopes to a climax, it soon dashed them in the cruellest way possible, by destroying the élites in Russia and, in the Austro-Hungarian case, the state itself.

The second type of authoritarian state was a rising power undergoing rapid and successful economic modernization, such as Germany and Japan (and to a lesser extent Italy), in which rapid industrialization generated both the power and the will to challenge the international status quo, as well as the pressures for political and social reforms from which the political élites sought foreign-policy distractions. And in the case of the recently unified German and Italian states, the desire for an assertive foreign policy was boosted by their need to ensure that nationalism triumph over provincialism. It was not surprising that it was in these states that militarism survived the horrors of the First World War to reach a peak in the 1930s and early 1940s, being finally extirpated only by total military defeat—a verdict with which it could scarcely quarrel.

ii. Liberal-democratic states

Yet in the period down to 1914 even the most mature liberal democracies experienced the growth of stronger than usual militarist fringes. The international upheavals caused by Germany's unification, the emergence as a great power of the United States, imperial rivalries, and crises such as the Boer War encouraged the belief that a trial of arms would be needed to determine which state or states would win the struggle for great-power status. And the domestic upheavals caused simultaneously by industrialization and democratization made political élites aware of the value of militarization as a source of social discipline.

Treitschke and Bernhardi thus had their counterparts even in Britain, though these were both obscurer and rarer. In the August 1911 issue of the monthly review *Nineteenth Century and After*, for example, Lieutenant-General Sir Reginald C. Hart published 'A Vindication of War', which argued:

History proves up to the hilt that nations languish and perish under peace conditions, and it has only been by war that a people has continued to thrive and exist. Peace is a disintegrating force, whereas war consolidates a people. War is no doubt a dreadful ordeal but it clears the air, and refines the race as fire purifies gold and silver in the furnace. Nations, like individuals, ultimately benefit by their chastenings—this is one of the mysteries of Nature.

Hart also insisted that 'nations that become unmanly and despise the martial spirit will surely succumb to their more warlike neighbours' and that 'the means of improvement' of civilization would always be 'war, relentless war of extermination of inferior individuals and nations'. It was, in other words, the duty of fitter states to suppress the less fit. Although he was honest enough to admit: 'A war kills off many of the fit and from this it might be argued that the less a nation engages in war the fitter it will be', he nevertheless insisted—somewhat obscurely—that 'even if this is so in theory, it is not so in practice . . . And it is a fact that, notwithstanding casualties in war, a warlike nation does not deteriorate.'

But Hart pulled his punches rather more than his German contemporaries tended to. In the face of a naval challenge from Germany such as would have led an outspoken militarist at least to hint at the need for a second 'Copenhagen', Hart insisted instead: 'But far be it from me to advocate a wanton, bullying and aggressive spirit. We must live and let live.' And rather than elaborate his view of war as a positive good he preferred instead to imply that, war being in practice unavoidable, it was the benefits it had brought to humanity that should be dwelt on, rather than its drawbacks, in order to stiffen the country's morale. In this he was characteristic of liberal-democratic militarists in general and British ones in particular: the militarization they recommended was for purely defensive purposes; and their Darwinian rhetoric amounted to little more than a set of clichés.

iii. Imperialism?

It might be objected to the above discussion of militarism in liberal democracies that it overlooks the possibility that the imperialism in which such states freely indulged was itself militarist, albeit of a selective kind, since in respect of 'primitive' peoples it preached racial supremacy and the right of conquest. It is indeed the case that Europe has had a long tradition of applying less stringent moral standards to relations with 'uncivilized' countries outside its continent, so that in regard to what is now called the Third World an attitude of bellicism lingered longer than it had in regard to the developed world. But, since few imperialists would have argued that the sole evidence for the supremacy of the imperial state was its military ability to seize or hold its colony, their thinking can be said to be militarist only in part. Assuming its motivation was to some extent political (rather than simply commercial), imperialism can more plausibly be explained in either defencist or crusading terms.

It was defencist in so far as the motive for acquiring and retaining colonies was to increase the capacity of the colonizing state to defend itself. (This was indeed normally the motive for imperialism, it seems, although as much from a desire to deny territory to other imperial or would-be imperial states as from a belief that colonies could provide extra resources.) For all its defensive intentions, imperialism of this kind was prone to use militarist-sounding rhetoric. In 1913, for example, Lord Milner 'emphasized the importance of the racial bond. From [his] point of view this is fundamental. It is the British race which built the Empire, and it is the undivided British race which can alone uphold it . . .'. But it usually denied that its intentions were aggressive. As Milner made clear: 'It is a mistake to think that it was principally concerned with expansion of territory, with "painting the map red". There is quite enough painted red already.'[44]

Imperialism was a form of crusading to the extent that the colonizing state was motivated by one of two concerns: to improve the international system rather than its own security within that system (a distinction to which we shall return in the next chapter); or to spread civilized and universal values (religious, humane, or political) in the colony. It is doubtful whether either of these concerns was ever more than a subordinate motive for acquiring colonies; but both were frequently used as rationalizations after the event. Thus in an attempt to justify the British empire to an American audience during the Second World War, the historian W. K. Hancock used both the international-system case and the civilized-values argument:

In the anarchical world of the present, the British Empire represents an indispensable contribution of power to the cause of law and freedom. The contribution will be no less indispensable when the international community of the future is taking shape . . . It is trustee for those peoples who are unable as yet to stand on their own feet under the strenuous conditions of the modern world . . . We should never miss an opportunity of driving forward the great work of self-government by every means which we can command.[45]

Imperialism was, in other words, a hybrid phenomenon, for which defencism provided the main motivation, crusading a common justification, and militarism no more than the occasional flash of rhetoric.

iv. Decline and fall

The existence of imperialism does not diminish the fact that, even at its pre-1914 peak, pure militarism was weak in liberal democracies: much of what passed for militarism was either defencism or crusading with a slight militarist tinge. After 1918 even this tinge disappeared. Warfare had become so destructive—and seemed certain to become more so with the development of air power—that Darwinian and racial considerations seemed now to point to anti-war policies. In the United States in 1921 the American Quaker-convert and chairman of the National Council for the Limitation of Armaments, Frederick Libby, warned that another war would mean 'the end of the white race as a force' and the 'twilight of white civilization'.[46] And in Britain ten years later ridicule rather than approbation greeted the pure-militarist claim made in a Rectorial address at Aberdeen University by Sir Arthur Keith, the noted anthropologist who had 'authenticated' Piltdown man: 'Nature keeps her human orchard healthy by pruning; war is her pruning hook. We cannot dispense with her services.'[47]

With hindsight, the only option for militarists was to have reduced the intensity and horror of war so as to enable military struggle to occur without race suicide. Some attempts to explore this possibility were undertaken in the 1920s: the enthusiasm which

J. F. C. Fuller, the pioneer tank commander, military theorist, and future member of the British Union of Fascists, then showed for the prospect that future wars would be fought by bombers dropping knock-out gases—instead of lethal gases or high explosives—suggests that he was looking for a way in which the necessary struggle for survival between the 'supermen' and 'supermonkeys' could be carried on without catastrophe.[48]

In the event, as the Second World War showed, the bomber was used not to humanize war but instead to mount the indiscriminate 'area bombing' of civilian targets, a policy which was contrary to the self-restraint advocated by some militarists, let alone the just-war tradition. On balance, nevertheless, the fighting from 1939 to 1945 did much to rehabilitate warfare after its discrediting twenty-five years previously. Its cause was just; it achieved a clear-cut result; and for fighter pilots at least the opportunity for individual combat presented itself again.

It is instructive to compare Richard Hillary, the Royal Air Force fighter pilot who was killed in January 1943 soon after the success of his moving autobiographical testament *The Last Enemy*, with the man who was in some respects his First World War counterpart, the poet Rupert Brooke. Brooke, who died in 1915 of disease contracted after embarkation with the Royal Naval Division, never saw action, yet had in 1914 depicted war as a bracing experience for all those taking part ('as swimmers into cleanness leaping'). Hillary, however, wrote after having been horribly burned when shot down as a fighter pilot, and insisted that his sense of fulfilment as a result of his ordeal was an essentially private one:

I could not explain that what I had suffered I in no way regretted; that I had welcomed it; and that now that it was over I was in a sense grateful to it and certain that in time it would help me along the road of my own private development.

And, even though convinced of the justice of the British cause, he distanced himself from conventional patriotism: 'I could not explain that I had not been injured in their war, that no thoughts of "our island fortress" or of "making the world safe for democracy" had bolstered me up when going into combat.'[49] Thus even where, as in Hillary's case, war was in a sense welcomed for itself, as well as for the just cause in which it was being fought, it had ceased to be sentimentalized. Not only were Darwinian benefits no longer claimed for it, any fulfilment value was identified by few—and often highly idiosyncratic—individuals only; and there was little general approbation of its purgative effects.

The Second World War hastened the invention of nuclear weapons, moreover, transforming war even from what Hillary had known only a couple of years previously. For a brief period these increased the appeal of aggressive war: it was argued in some quarters that the United States should use its nuclear monopoly to impose international control of all nuclear weapons, particularly after the Soviet Union rejected the Baruch plan for doing so by international agreement. Sir Oswald Mosley argued this in 1947, for example, although he claimed he was doing so to pre-empt a planned Soviet attack:

The plan of Russia is plain: and the answer is clear. The reply should be an ultimatum to impose the American plan for Atomic inspection before Russia is ready to strike. If the showdown were forced before Russia had an equality of weapons she must either give way or be easily defeated.[50]

But this was not evidence of militarism: it was instead a crusading response, and not an uncommon one, as the next chapter will show. As soon as a state of mutual assured destruction was achieved, moreover, it became clear anyway that even if one state might emerge from a nuclear war less damaged than its adversary (and there continues to be remarkable optimism on this score in certain quarters), it would be difficult to argue that it had thereby 'won' in any traditional sense, and virtually impossible to claim that human development had thereby been promoted. More recently, the increase in number of warheads deployed, and a greater understanding of the possible environmental consequences of nuclear war (such as the nuclear-winter prediction), have further strengthened the already powerful 'unwinnability' thesis.

Although this nuclear revolution caused difficulties for every war-and-peace theory except the pessimistic version of pacifism, it proved uniquely disastrous for militarism, finally destroying it as a theory in its own right. It is now detectable only as a weak tinge to other theories, notably crusading. Thus the 'guerrilla' who became a cult figure among the western left during the 1960s could sound at times like a militarist (just as Mazzini and his fellow European liberals had when engaged on their own national-liberation struggles). In 1969, for example, a message smuggled out of the Bolivian jungle from the revolutionary Inti Peredo proclaimed his conviction 'that the dream of Bolívar and Che—that of uniting Latin America both politically and geographically—will be attained through armed struggle, which is the only dignified, honest, glorious and irreversible method which will motivate our people'.[51] The guerrilla also provoked former pacific-ists into remarkable expressions of enthusiasm for violence. Thus even Jean-Paul Sartre claimed in his preface to Frantz Fanon's *Les Damnés de la terre* that 'the rebel's weapon is the proof of his humanity'.[52] The peace movement regarded such rhetoric as militarist: in its review of Fanon's book *Peace News* criticized both 'the assumption that violence is unqualifiedly "cleansing", and the romantic belief that armed guerilla struggle produces forms of organization that makes the concentration of political power in the hands of elites impossible'.[53] But it is probable that the guerrilla warriors were socialist crusaders first and foremost. Much of their enthusiasm for war was based merely on the 'purgative' view already noted, rather than on militarist ideas as such. And they for the most part believed that their struggle was validated not by its martial means but by its socialist (and therefore universalist) ends.

Crusading proved more durable than militarism because it was often able, as the next chapter will argue, to make do with limited forms of fighting. Militarism failed to follow J. F. C. Fuller's lead: it did not work to humanize war as a way of preserving aggression as a legitimate means of struggle. Had it done so it might, ironically, have pioneered both the nuclear-disarmament and alternative-defence movements, since it took a long time for the peace movement to take up these causes. It is, of course, anyway doubtful whether war could still be regarded as vital to human development if it ceased to be an all-out struggle and were instead to be regulated by a form of Queensberry rules. For, if so, why should it not be regulated even more drastically, so that it became a ritualized contest between small teams of combatants? This question is hypothetical, however: having failed to adapt to his changed environment, the militarist has become extinct.

4

Crusading

Crusaders share with militarists the controversial belief that aggressive war may be justified. But they do not accept that it is always or even usually justified, that warfare is a positive good, or that might is necessarily right: their values, in other words, are civilized and universal. Crusaders of a conservative persuasion have the same ultimate goal as defencists, namely order; and those inspired by 'reforming' ideologies—for example, liberalism, socialism, or radicalism—have the same goals as pacific-ists, namely social justice. As well as having the same ends in view as either defencists or pacific-ists, crusaders most of the time pursue them by identical means: above all by peaceful political persuasion, and by force only as a defensive necessity. It is appropriate, therefore, to defer a discussion of the values crusading has in common with these other theories until the latter are examined in the next two chapters, and to deal in this one only with what is peculiar to it. Its uniqueness becomes apparent only in those exceptional circumstances in which it unilaterally suspends the normal rules of politics and resorts to coercion in the interests, as it sees them, of either order or justice and therefore also of peace.

Crusading has always been a minority viewpoint, most conservatives having stuck to defencism and 'reformers' to pacific-ism; it is, moreover, in decline. But because it is an altruistic theory— a crusade aspires to promote a better world rather than to advance the interests of particular states—it has been more influential historically than militarism, and has adapted more successfully to the limitations of the nuclear era. In particular, it survives better in hybrid form—in wars fought for a mixture of crusading and defensive motives—and partly for that reason still constitutes a conspicuous, though declining, strand in the foreign policy of both superpowers. This chapter will thus in turn examine the different types of crusading, its hybrid manifestations, the conditions which give rise to it, and its evolving role in superpower thinking.

1. Types of crusade

As already made clear, the categories of this book assume the validity of the moral distinction, recognized by both international law and common-sense morality, between defence and offence. In consequence, the first use of force can be interpreted here in one of only three ways: as an act of militarism (discussed in the previous chapter); as an act of 'extended' defence (to be discussed in the next, as already noted); or as a crusade. (If it is to be classified as a hybrid, then more than one of these interpretations must be seen to fit it.) Acts of militarism and extended defence are both primarily selfish: they aspire to promote the interests of particular states only. What distinguishes crusading is its essential altruism: it is undertaken for the general good. (In practice, of course, it is difficult for a crusading state to be wholly disinterested since its actions will usually also advance its own interests. That is why hybridity is common.)

Crusading thus covers any first use of force which, by virtue of its altruism, is neither a militarist nor an extended-defensive act. However, most of those who believe that military interventions of this kind can sometimes be justified, and who are therefore here classified as crusaders, would reject the label. They would argue that it should be reserved for certain, unacceptable, forms of interventionism only. According to Michael Walzer, for example:

A crusade is a war fought for religious or ideological purposes. It aims not at defense or law enforcement, but at the creation of new political orders and at mass conversions. It is the international equivalent of religious persecution and political represssion, and it is obviously ruled out by the argument for justice.[1]

In effect Walzer, who had first written about crusading in the context of seventeenth-century Puritan thought,[2] is trying to keep the term as close as possible to its original religious usage.

The present broader use of crusading has no pejorative intent: indeed the existence of admirably scrupulous crusaders was made clear in chapter 2. Nevertheless another label would have been employed had a suitable one been available. The only serious

contender was 'interventionism'; but this can be applied to a
defensive intervention, such as rallying to the assistance of another
state at its own request, as well as to an interfering one which
promotes the intervening state's conception of order or justice
without reference to the wishes of the target state. It is relevant here
to note that nineteenth-century Britain's most famous opponent of
interventionism, the Manchester businessman-turned Liberal MP
Richard Cobden, was hostile not only to its crusading manifestations but to its defensive ones too. He was thus not only a pacific-ist
(as distinct from a crusader) but an isolationist too—hence his
slogan: 'no foreign politics'. The more precise labels which would
have avoided this objection, 'non-defensive (and non-militarist)
interventionism' or 'disinterested interventionism', are too clumsy.
'Crusading' has the merit of simplicity and—apart from its pejorative connotations—of clarity.

As here defined, crusading becomes a more varied theory than is
commonly recognized. The different forms it takes can be ranged
along two axes, as follows:

On the first axis, a 'domestic' crusade is concerned to rectify the
internal behaviour of a particular state, whereas an 'international'
one is concerned to rectify its external behaviour. Admittedly, this
distinction is easier to make in principle than in practice. All
ideologies hold that a crusade which produces a better domestic
regime will automatically produce one which is less a threat to the
international system, and vice versa. Thus, although the brief
western intervention in the Russian Civil War is here classified as
primarily an international crusade (motivated by the belief that the
Bolsheviks were a threat to the international system), it must be
recognized that it also had a domestic dimension (the liberation of
Russia's non-Bolshevik majority).

On the second axis, a 'positive' crusade is motivated by a desire
to impose new values or create a new system, whereas a 'negative'
one is designed to root out and destroy an existing evil. Once again,
many crusades fall somewhere between these two poles, if not right

in the middle. Positive crusades have to destroy before they can impose or create; and negative crusades are keenly interested in what is to replace the evil they are eradicating. Wars of 'national liberation'—a term used in this book to refer only to struggles which, by spilling over state boundaries, become international as well as civil wars—are thus particularly hard to classify. Because their ultimate goal is to create an independent new state, they are to some extent positive. But because they can achieve this goal only by eradicating alien rulers, they will here be treated as primarily negative.

Thus, if actual crusades and would-be crusades are plotted out along these two axes, there is a considerable cluster towards the centre of the quadrant. A sufficient number are dispersed nearer its extremities, however, for it to be possible to use the four poles as ideal-type categories by means of which the various types of crusade can be elucidated. This method helps to make clear, moreover, that the most criticized types of crusade are polar opposites: those which are both domestic and positive, and those which are international as well as negative.

i. Domestic and positive

Crusades in this category accord closely with most people's idea of what a crusade is—the imposition of one's own values on other people—and are criticized on those grounds. Two clear examples are provided by the early history of the Soviet Union: in 1920 it turned an initially defensive war against Poland into an attempt to impose a communist regime on that country; and the following year it fought a successful ten-day crusade in order to bolshevize the Menshevik republic of Georgia. And to the limited extent that empire-building wars were motivated by a desire to 'civilize' colonial peoples, they too must be regarded as domestic-positive crusades.

ii. Domestic and negative

Most domestic crusaders are careful to deny that they are imposing their own values on other people, however: they claim instead to be liberating them. When, for example, on 19 November 1792 the French revolutionary Convention declared 'that it will accord fraternity and assistance to all people who shall wish to recover their liberty',[3] it claimed to be offering help in the destruction of tyranny rather than attempting to impose a radical system of its own choosing. Similarly, the American radicals who in 1898 successfully urged their country to drive Spain out of Cuba believed that the United States was simply removing a repressive colonial regime and permitting the Cubans to achieve self-determination. In other words, domestic crusaders want their intervention to be regarded as negative, in the terminology used here, because they profess only to remove obstacles to the target state's independence and not otherwise to interfere with its future political life.

Such a claim always has at least an element of truth in it, since there will inevitably be some—and there may even be many—citizens of the target state who will approve of the crusader and welcome his intervention as liberating them. This is why someone can almost always be found to invite a crusader in, as will shortly be seen. But, for a domestic crusade to be truly negative, the proportion of the target population who are indeed liberated must significantly exceed the proportion who are merely coerced. In practice, however, the ratio of liberation to coercion is almost impossible to ascertain, because the target state only rarely enjoys freedom of expression. Nevertheless, it is a striking feature of crusaders that they are self-confident enough to give themselves the benefit of any doubt on this score. This is the case whatever their ideological inspiration.

Conservatives are particularly good at convincing themselves that their domestic crusades are merely destructive of evil regimes and therefore have a liberating rather than coercive effect. This is because they are for the most part sincerely sceptical about the feasibility of transplanting new values and structures into a political system. Their scepticism applies to attempts at peaceful reform (by constitutional means) as well as to positive crusades. They believe a political system to be an organism, in other words, rather than a mechanism which can be tinkered with. (They believe this only of 'advanced' states, of course: they do not doubt that positive crusades can profoundly change 'primitive' countries for the better.)

Conservatives accept that negative crusades are sometimes necessary in the same way that surgical operations are required to excise cancerous growths in otherwise healthy bodies. Such crusades are of two types. The first are wars to extirpate a revolutionary regime: it was a 'crusade'[4] of this kind which Edmund Burke wished Britain to undertake against the infant revolutionary regime in France. The second, at first sight, look to have positive-crusading features: these are state-consolidating wars of the sort undertaken by Bismarck to create the German Empire in 1871, by Nehru to expel the Portuguese from Goa and other enclaves in 1961, and by the Argentine junta to acquire the Falkland Islands—albeit only temporarily—in 1982. To conservatives, however, such wars merely remove obstacles to full statehood and are thus negative.

Some critics might concede that wars of this second kind have a negative rather than positive intent, but insist that they are too selfish to count as crusades. They might even suggest that their acceptance of a state's right to expand smacks of militarism. But, although the premiss on which they rest—that there is such a thing as a state's 'natural' territorial extent—is indeed questionable, it is not militarist, since it has the effect of placing limits on a state's legitimate expansion and would, if implemented, ultimately produce a fixed and final distribution of territory. State-consolidating wars can thus claim to be crusades to the extent that they seek to implement the universalist doctrine that every state has the exclusive right to a 'natural' territory of its own.

The conservative case for state-consolidating wars has marked similarities with the reforming case for national-liberation wars, since the latter can claim to be crusades to the extent that they seek to implement the universalist doctrine that every nation or people has a right to self-determination. In the nineteenth century, when Europe itself had yet to achieve a fixed nation-state structure, liberals—such as Mazzini, as already noted—enthusiastically advocated such wars. By the twentieth, however, when the focus of the struggle for self-determination moved to Asia and Africa, liberals had for the most part ceased to believe in the domestic crusade. A striking exception, however, was the attempt late in 1950 by the United States, with the approval of the General Assembly of the United Nations, to turn the war which it was initially fighting in defence of South Korea into a crusade against North Korea. Since the Americans and their western supporters assumed (perhaps wrongly) that the North Koreans would have plumped for a liberal-democratic as well as a united country if they had been given the chance, they regarded their crusade as negative (the elimination of a puppet communist regime) rather than positive (the imposition of liberalism).

For the most part the national-liberation struggle has during this century become a socialist preserve. For example, in June 1950 North Korea, armed by the Soviet Union, launched its own crusade to create a united and socialist Korea: it was this which provoked the United States to rally to South Korea's defence in the first place. A similar but more successful socialist crusade—albeit one which, waged by unconventional military means, lasted more than a decade and a half—was North Vietnam's conquest of South Vietnam. Like crusaders of other persuasions, socialists took for granted that they were simply eliminating illegitimate regimes in the target state and allowing the true wishes of its people to prevail.

The non-defensive military interventions which just-war theorists still accept to be legitimate—and which, as already made clear, cause them to be here classified as crusaders—are exclusively negative. Michael Walzer, for example, admits that 'states can be invaded and wars justly begun', but only under three conditions: 'to assist secessionist movements (once they have demonstrated their representative character), to balance the prior interventions of other powers; and to rescue peoples threatened with massacre'.[5] Thus, while not prepared to intervene to eradicate a people's 'own' tyrants, he accepts, first, that there are cases in which an established regime has become foreign in the eyes of a substantial community within the state, and that in such cases the community can legitimately be assisted to secede and to set up a polity of its own. He believes, secondly, that intervention to terminate interference by another foreign power can also be justified since, as John Stuart Mill argued, it can be regarded as itself upholding the principle of non-intervention. And he approves, thirdly, of purely humanitarian interventions to save a population from an exceptionally cruel regime.

In other words, just-war theorists reject not only all domestic-positive crusades but also most domestic-negative ones. Before approving even the latter they now require stringent proof both of the intolerability of the obstacles to be removed and of the free and self-determining potential of the society to be liberated. They do so because they are aware that humanitarian arguments are frequently deployed in an effort to conceal political or self-interested motives. A blatant example, which they would have no hesitation in rejecting today, was Edmund Burke's argument in support of a counter-revolutionary intervention in the affairs of France:

A more mischievous idea cannot exist, than that any degree of wickedness, violence, and oppression may prevail in a country, that the most abominable murders, and exterminating rebellions may rage in it, or the most atrocious and bloody tyranny may domineer, and that no neighbouring power can take cognizance of either, or afford succour to the miserable sufferers.[6]

Even the claims on behalf of the Spanish-American War of 1898 are dismissed by Walzer, who insists that the war the Americans 'actually fought . . . and the intervention urged by populists and radical democrats were two rather different things', and criticizes the former as in fact 'an example of beneficent imperialism'.[7]

iii. International and positive

Crusades which are 'international' rather than domestic are prompted by concern for the international system directly (and not indirectly, through concern for its member states). Those which are also 'positive' aspire to the building of a new international system. In practice, so ambitious a task is rarely attempted except when a major war has already broken out in which a state is already committed to fighting for 'justice' and in which the existing international system is showing signs of collapse. As Hans J. Morgenthau has observed: 'The political crusader has his opportunity when his country is engaged on a world-wide struggle with another great power, which lends itself to a moral interpretation.'[8]

The best illustrations, which indeed Morgenthau had in mind, are the American war aims of 1917–18 and 1941–5. The United States entered the First World War in April 1917 because of a 'geographical interest in maintaining freedom of the seas and preventing Europe's domination by a hostile power', as Henry Kissinger later put it.[9] Yet these defensive arguments had not on the face of it weighed with President Wilson as late as November 1916, when he had been re-elected on an isolationist platform; and, when his conversion to intervention came, it was expressed in mainly crusading language. He told Congress on 2 April 1917 that the United States would be fighting 'for a universal dominion of right by such a concert of free peoples as shall bring peace and safety to all nations and make the world itself at last free'.

'Wilsonianism' was later analysed by the influential journalist Walter Lippmann, a sometime enthusiast who soon abandoned it in favour of defencism:

The Wilsonian ideology is a crusading doctrine, generating great popular fervour from the feeling that war is an intolerable criminal interference with the nature of things . . . Therefore all wars are wars to end wars, all wars are crusades which can be concluded when all the peoples have submitted themselves to the only true political religion. There will be peace only when all the peoples hold and observe the same self-evident principles.[10]

The goals of the crusade were both the liberal one of achieving self-determination and establishing a League of Nations and the radical one of subordinating old élites to democratic control.

Once these high expectations were disappointed at the Congress of Paris, the United States retreated to isolationism, from which it emerged only after a direct attack by Japan and a declaration of war by Germany. Yet, although the Second World War began defensively for Americans, they agreed for the most part that it should be treated as a second opportunity to create a liberal international system. President Franklin Roosevelt's views were an only slightly modified version of Woodrow Wilson's: he hoped to create an open world order, free of exclusive spheres of influence, colonies, and autarkic economic practices. So did his Republican opponent of 1940, Wendell Wilkie, who in 1943 argued in his million-selling book, *One World*, that America must 'plan now for peace on a world basis' and should work for 'the creation of a world in which there shall be an equality of opportunity for every race and every nation'.[11] Since this would involve the abolition of the empires to which its European allies were still deeply attached, America's crusading goals in the Second World War were thus in conflict with its defensive goals. They nevertheless received widespread support: the efforts of defencists such as Walter Lippmann, who from 1943 onwards urged the United States to think less about ideal international systems and more about her own national interests,[12] did little to undermine what was in effect a consensus in support of crusading.

When after 1945 the Soviet Union obstructed the American

conception of 'one world', and in particular when it rejected a scheme for the international control of nuclear weapons, a number of westerners suggested a crusade to force it to submit, as has already been mentioned. In Britain, as also noted, Sir Oswald Mosley was in favour of such a course; but so were two recently lapsed pacifists: the philosopher Bertrand Russell, and the literary critic John Middleton Murry.

Russell, who had publicly recanted his pacifism only five years before, was so alarmed by the atomic bomb that as early as October 1945 he had published an article in which he admitted

one exception to the condemnation of wars in the near future; a powerful group of nations, engaged in establishing an international military government of the world, may be compelled to resort to war if it finds somewhere an opposition which cannot be peacefully overcome, but which can be defeated without a completely exhausting struggle.

He proposed that the United States 'should forthwith invite the formation of a Confederation of nations' which would have a nuclear monopoly and the duty to enforce it. He hoped that the Soviet Union would accept the invitation, but anticipated that it would be unlikely to do so straight away.

He was clear, however, that 'if the USSR did not give way and join the Confederation, after there had been time for mature consideration, the conditions for a justifiable war . . . would all be fulfilled. A *casus belli* would not be difficult to find.'[13] Although he was later to deny—then admit, re-deny, and finally re-admit—that he had ever talked of war with the Soviet Union at all, he continued to make similar statements, such as (in November 1948): 'Either we must have a war against Russia before she has the atom bomb or we shall have to lie down and let them govern us . . . Anything is better than submission.'[14]

Although he had only just ceased to edit the pacifist weekly *Peace News*, Middleton Murry had come by 1947 to make his crusading intentions even clearer than Russell's. He asserted in 1947 that the world faced a choice between two possibilities:

Either Russia will, however reluctantly, consent to the establishment of a world-authority for the purpose of preventing preparation for war, to whose decisions she will submit; or, if she refuses, then the nations which are willing to submit to such an authority—and they include all the nations of the world outside the Russian bloc—will combine to render Russia harmless. They will, and must, make war on Russia; and they will not be able to wait until Russia has secretly prepared an overwhelming apparatus of destruction.

The war would, moreover, be fought with the west's nuclear weapons, Murry being explicit 'that a post-atomic war fought by a world authority against a recalcitrant nation would be a rational war, even though it might conceivably destroy the basis of the rational life itself'.[15]

An international-positive crusade of this kind found its advocates in the United States too. 'God Almighty in his infinite wisdom [has] dropped the atomic bomb in our lap,' declared Senator Edwin C. Johnson of Colorado in November 1945; now for the first time the United States, 'with vision and guts and plenty of atomic bombs . . . [could] compel mankind to adopt the policy of lasting peace . . . or be burned to a crisp'.[16] One of America's most persistent, though coy, crusaders at this time was James Burnham—lapsed Trotskyist, theorist of the managerial revolution, and former official of the Office of Strategic Services (who probably still retained a CIA connection).[17] In 1947 he called for a full political union of the United States and British Dominions, linked to a federation of non-Communist Europe: this was reminiscent of the Federal Union proposal which *New York Times* journalist Clarence K. Streit had launched in the late 1930s, except that Burnham argued also that the unstable equilibrium between the Anglo-American and the Soviet shares of the globe should be rendered harmless 'by reducing the Communist percentage safely below the critical point'. As to the means of doing this he gave only teasing hints, such as that 'peace cannot be the supreme practical objective of policy' although nevertheless 'it is preferable and we ought to prefer that the smashing of Communism should be accomplished from within, rather than by a war from the outside'. By the eve of the Korean War he had become a little more explicit, however, condemning containment and insisting that preventive war was morally justified, the only issue to be decided being whether sub-military measures might not be more efficacious: 'Whether or not to begin a full military war is a problem of expediency.' But he was still careful to insist that the west would not thereby be starting such a war, but merely recognizing that the communists had been waging it since 1944.[18]

Although the reminder of the methods contemplated for such crusades will bring a shudder of revulsion to most sections of western opinion today, it is noteworthy how much more favourably positive crusades have generally been viewed if they are international than if they are domestic. The construction of a new international system seems a nobler and more ambitious undertaking than the imposition of one's ideology on a single state.

iv. International and negative

Many international crusades aspire not to build a new international system, however, but merely to eradicate those regimes which by their external behaviour threaten its existing norms. It is possible, as already noted, to reckon as a crusade of this type the deliberate continuation of western intervention in the Russian Civil War after the end of the First World War. This intervention had begun as an attempt to protect the western position after the Bolshevik regime made peace with the Germans, and was abandoned as too costly an enterprise before it could become a major undertaking.[19] Nevertheless, the motive for continuing with it after the armistice in even a half-hearted way was unmistakable—the conviction, expressed by Lord Robert Cecil in a Foreign Office memorandum of October 1918, that it was impossible for Britain to reach an agreement with the Bolsheviks 'now or in the future' because 'they are fanatics who are not bound by any ordinary rules'.[20] This belief that the Soviet regime posed a threat to civilization was even more forthrightly expressed by Winston Churchill: 'The Bolsheviks are fanatics . . . Their view is that their system has not been successful because it has not yet been tried on a large enough scale, and that in order to secure success they must make it world wide.'[21]

It is noteworthy, too, how much worse a reputation negative crusades have if they are international than if they are domestic. This is largely because a crusade which destroys a regime because of its foreign policy cannot so plausibly claim to have the humanitarian interests of its inhabitants at heart as one which intervenes explicitly to put an end to domestic oppression. But it is also because a crusade which picks on a single regime is even more vulnerable to the charge of serving the foreign-policy interests of the crusading power than one which purports to be constructing a whole new world order. International crusades of both kinds are frequently only hybrids, as will very shortly be noted; but this is particularly true of the negative variety. For example, many of the best recent examples of international-negative crusades—such as the Anglo-French invasion of Suez in 1956, or the military interventions by the United States in the Dominican Republic in 1965 and in Grenada in 1983—were to a considerable extent also acts of extended defence.

Thus, of the four ideal-type crusades set out here, the two most controversial are diametrically opposed; and they are controversial for paradoxically different reasons. Domestic-positive crusades are unpopular precisely because they conform to everyone's idea of a crusade: they seem acts of moral arrogance. International-negative crusades are unpopular because they do not seem to be true crusades at all: they seem acts of great-power selfishness.

2. The hybrid crusade

As just implied, many wars can be given both a crusading and an extended-defensive interpretation. Hybrid crusades fall logically into two types: wars in which the crusading element is uppermost, and those in which it merely bolsters or provides a rhetorical justification for defensive considerations. The former occur because ideal-type crusades are virtually impossible in the real world: the self-interest of a crusading state is likely to be promoted by its actions, however altruistic its motives. It is the latter on which attention is focused here, since they are particularly dangerous: some wars for which the purely defensive case is either too weak or insufficiently persuasive are embarked upon because a crusading justification, which would also be insufficient on its own, is introduced to supplement it.

A good illustration is provided by the Anglo-French invasion of Suez in 1956. The primary motives of the British and French governments were clearly those of self-interest: they had become convinced that Nasser was a direct threat to their respective national interests in the Middle East and North Africa. But the security of neither state was menaced by Nasser so obviously as to make a war against him a plausibly defensive one. Since they also believed sincerely, if less strongly, that Nasser, whom they frequently likened to Hitler, was undermining civilized standards of international behaviour, they shored up a weak defensive case with the crusading argument that they were acting to eradicate a threat to the international system itself. The two justifications were characteristically jumbled together in an editorial in *The Times* of London on 2 August 1956:

> If Nasser gets away with it, all the British and all Western interest in the Middle East will crumble [i.e. an argument for preventive defence] . . . There can be no stability and confidence in the world so long as agreements can be scrapped with impunity [i.e. the case for a conservative crusade].[22]

It is thus likely that one of the reasons so misconceived a military operation was begun was because, rather than think through the implications of the defencist approach, the decision-makers lapsed into crusading arguments when it suited them.

Sometimes the slide into crusading arguments happens less because the decision-makers are themselves uncertain than because they wish to curry favour with a moralistic public. A classic instance, even if rarely recognized as such, is Britain's entry into the First World War. Although there was some confusion even within Asquith's Liberal cabinet, the government's key decisions had been based on an unmistakably defensive analysis: that the defeat of France had to be prevented for reasons of British self-interest, since Britain could no longer guarantee the imports of food and raw materials upon which its survival depended if Germany were allowed to dominate western Europe. But many Liberal politicians as well as an articulate section of public opinion were opposed to any such Continental commitment. Some of these were defencists who simply favoured a different posture to the government: they believed that it was in Britain's best strategic interests to ignore Europe and orientate itself towards the Empire. But most were pacific-ists who were unable or unwilling to analyse the problem in strategic terms: failing to see any need for the *entente* with France which had been forged in 1904, and morally outraged by the convention with Russia which had been concluded in 1907, they often assumed these commitments to be merely the dangerous whims of the Foreign Office. As a result they took a strongly isolationist posture.

Faced with such ignorance of the case for forward defence,

Britain's policy-makers chose to represent their decision of August 1914 to stand by France in terms of the honouring of a disinterested pledge of Belgian neutrality, thus implying that they would not have gone to war had Germany used a different invasion route into France. For its entire duration, moreover, the war was justified on similarly moralistic grounds—as an international crusade (or counter-crusade, since the Germans had committed aggression first) to eradicate Prussian militarism. It was also justified in international-positive terms as a war to inaugurate a new type of international relations.

This propaganda was, it should be acknowledged, a notable success. The proper course for consistent pacific-ists to have followed after abandoning their isolationist posture would have been to accept the war on defensive grounds. After all, they accepted the legitimacy of defensive war (subject only, it will be seen, to the requirement that such a war is not politically counter-productive). They could thus have argued that the line had to be held in Europe against German aggression. Instead, however, many preferred to assert that 'Prussianism' had to be eradicated in a war to end war. They either were converted to crusading, in other words, or were already crusaders without realizing the fact.

The propensity of pacific-ism either to overbalance into crusading or to reveal itself to have been latent crusading all along can be observed in other contexts. One such is the support given by socialists to the Spanish government's ill-fated attempt to put down Franco's rebellion of 1936. Whether viewed as a civil war or (in view of Italian and German breaches of the non-intervention agreement) as a covert international one, the war was defensive. But those who went to fight often regarded it in a different light. As Jason Gurney, for one, later noted:

We, of the International Brigades, had wilfully deluded ourselves into the belief that we were fighting a noble Crusade because we needed a crusade— the opportunity to fight against the manifest evils of Fascism . . . which seemed then as if it would overwhelm every value of Western civilization.[23]

The preference which American pacific-ists have shown for crusading rather than defensive rhetoric has led to the observation that members of the peace movement are so upset by war that they can support it only if they can convince themselves that it is not only just but also holy. In Robert E. Osgood's words: 'tender consciences find in broader, more exalted goals a kind of moral compensation for the enormity of war and a rational justification for their contamination with evil. Thus the very ideas which proscribe war become the incentive for fighting war.'[24]

To sum up: governments and publics have both been known to resort to a crusading argument to supplement a defensive one. Where neither would have been persuasive on its own, a 'hybrid' of the two has sometimes resulted in unnecessary wars.

3. Preconditions

Crusading requires both ideological and military confidence to such a degree as to be increasingly a rarity in pure form. Ideological confidence is needed if the crusader is to convince himself that he is justified in intervening unilaterally. With exceptions (notably the Islamic revival), such confidence has become harder to muster in recent decades, as will be noted when pacific-ism is discussed in chapter 6. Military confidence is needed if the crusader is to convince himself both that he can win at acceptable cost and that he can do so without concern for his own national interests (since, as has been emphasized, a true crusade must be disinterested). It is obvious that nuclear weapons have not only made major wars almost certainly counter-productive but have also undermined the strategic security which once permitted some states to be genuinely disinterested. Crusading still survives in its purest form in the national-liberation struggle. Not only does such a war have an unequalled moral intensity (hence its tendency to overbalance into militarist rhetoric), it is often best carried on in a low-technology or otherwise limited form, thereby benefiting from, rather than being handicapped by, the risk that a major war will escalate into a nuclear exchange.

Because of the difficulties involved, crusaders are happiest if their claim to be acting for the general good is endorsed by a representative international body. Thus, when the United States, which had already received United Nations Security Council approval for its defensive intervention to save South Korea in 1950, decided to pursue its own crusade into the North, it secured the approval of the General Assembly of the United Nations, as already noted. Since then, however, the UN General Assembly has changed its political complexion so as to give its blessing instead to crusades of a very different political complexion: those for national liberation. As Hedley Bull has pointed out:

By 1965, it had endorsed the conception of the right of nations to launch wars of national liberation against colonial rule, the right of third parties to intervene on their behalf and the illegitimacy of the use of force to oppose them. Ten years later, it had asserted the right of the United Nations' own organs to involve themselves in just wars of national liberation, as with SWAPO's campaign in Namibia; it had extended this conception to embrace the cases of Israel and South Africa; and in calling for mandatory sanctions against the latter, it was giving effect to Christian Wolff's idea of just intervention endorsed by the *civitas maximas* against a recalcitrant member state.[25]

The United States was able, however, for many years to receive the endorsement of the Organization of American States for anti-communist interventions within its hemisphere. The Soviet Union has lacked a regional body of comparable legitimacy, and so has sought instead to validate its interventions in eastern Europe by the Warsaw Treaty and a general duty towards the 'socialist commonwealth'. This was made clear in the 'doctrine' Brezhnev formulated to explain the invasion of Czechoslovakia, which insisted that 'when internal and external forces, hostile to socialism, seek to reverse the development of any socialist country . . . this already becomes not only a problem of the people of the country concerned, but also a common problem and the concern of all socialist countries'.[26] It has been clearly spelled out in a leading Soviet treatise on international law. This asserts that the relations between socialist (that is, communist) states 'represent a new, higher type of international relations', that these relations are new and higher because 'they are permeated with socialist internationalism', and that the Soviet Union

always precisely fulfills its duties arising from the principle of socialist internationalism. A vivid manifestation of this policy is the assistance of the Soviet Union to the Hungarian people in 1956 and the assistance, together with other socialist countries, to the people of Czechoslovakia in 1968 in protecting socialist gains and, ultimately, in defending their sovereignty and independence from sudden swoops of imperialism, as well as the assistance to the Vietnamese people in their struggle against United States' aggression.[27]

Where international authorization is unavailable, modern crusaders attempt to avoid the accusation of moral arrogance by arguing that it is the other side which first broke the normal rules of domestic or international politics. The left, for example, has made use of the notion of 'structural violence'[28] to argue that capitalism is inherently coercive: this means that those resorting to force against it cannot be said to have initiated the use of violence but are instead merely defending themselves and thus permitted to call in assistance from friendly states. The right's version of this argument is that all domestic unrest must be the result of external intervention. Rationalizing his intervention of April 1965 in the Dominican Republic, for example, President Johnson insisted that 'old concepts and old labels are largely obsolete. In today's world, with enemies of freedom talking about "wars of national liberation", the old distinction between "Civil War" and "International War" has already lost much of its meaning.'[29] President Reagan has made the same point even more starkly: 'Let us not delude ourselves. The Soviet Union underlies all the unrest that's going on. If they weren't engaged in this game of dominoes, there wouldn't be any hot spots in the world.'[30]

Where possible, as already noted, crusaders like to buttress such arguments with the claim they were also invited in: for example, the Soviet Union made this claim when it invaded Hungary in 1956 and Czechoslovakia in 1968;[31] and, although Reid Cabral's government had inconveniently fallen before American troops intervened in the Dominican Republic in 1965, the United States nevertheless thought it worth stating that 'military authorities' had invited them to do so.[32]

This desire to be seen to be acting defensively is evident even in interventions for which the humanitarian case is strongest. In the case of the Indian intervention of 1971 in East Pakistan, for instance, which prevented further massacre of the Bengalis by the Pakistani army and led to the independence of Bangladesh, the Indians chose eventually to re-write the record of their submission to the United Nations Security Council so as to alter their case from justified intervention to self-defence following an attack by Pakistan. In 1979 Tanzania intervened to depose the tyrannical regime of Idi Amin; but it first claimed that it was an uprising of the Ugandan people which deposed Amin, and then, faced with criticism of its intervention at the July 1979 conference of the Organization of African Unity, argued in addition that Uganda had attacked it first.[33]

Although crusaders must be powerful enough to impose their will, the more onerous condition, as already noted, is that they be strategically secure enough to be disinterested. In order to be concerned only with the good of either other states or the international system, in other words, they must have no worries about how the war will affect their own position. When the United States mounted its crusade against Spain in 1898, for example, Americans 'had a sense of security *vis-à-vis* their world environment such as . . . no people had ever had since the days of the Roman Empire', to quote George Kennan. Not only did it thus have 'an overweening confidence in [its] strength and ability to solve problems',[34] it had the detachment to do so with the minimum of attention to its own particular interests. Thereafter, although its military capacity was to increase, its developing sense of vulnerability at home and its extended commitments abroad made it harder for the United States wholly to overlook its own self-interest. Thus crusading today faces a paradox: the states with resources sufficient to undertake a major crusade are also those states with interests so widespread that they cannot, in practice, be disentangled from the interests of a particular value, or conception of the international system, which a state may wish to promote.

4. The superpowers

The superpowers and their agents do not have a monopoly on crusading. Once-for-all wars for either national independence or territorial consolidation still sometimes occur. So, more frequently, do the more limited operations carried out by terrorists, and by the individual guerrilla, who became a quasi-militarist cult figure in the 1960s as (in Che Guevara's phrase) 'a crusader for the people's freedom'.[35] Furthermore, the superpowers' crusading streak has been in decline since the Korean War, as already noted. Yet it is their propensity to crusade which most worries other states and which best explains their own continued mutual incomprehension.

i. The United States

The crusading impulse first manifested in the Spanish-American War of 1898 was to reappear with undiminished vigour in both world wars, although each had a defensive motivation too. At the end of the second, the United States had decided not to retreat into isolation despite another failure to achieve a satisfactory post-war settlement, but instead to take on world-wide military commitments in order to 'contain' the Soviet bloc. Such a policy was easy to misinterpret. Was 'containment' simply a form of forward defence? (If so, it could be either a defencist policy, justified by the need to defend the vital interests of the United States against aggression by the Soviet Union or its allies, or a pacific-ist one, justified by the need to protect democratic values against a communist crusade.) Or was it a step towards the creation of a new international system, a breathing space before a renewed attempt to 'roll back' communism and create 'one world'? (If so, it was a crusading policy.) To most policy-makers it was clearly the former. But to the American public, which found it hard to distinguish their country's newly and extravagantly extended security interests from the interests of the international system itself, it sometimes seemed more like the latter.

In 1950 North Korea launched its crusade against South Korea, which, as already noted, gave the United States, after a period of defensive fighting, an ideal opportunity for a liberal counter-crusade. Although this went disastrously wrong, America's first testing of the hydrogen bomb in November 1952 soon renewed its crusaders' confidence, albeit only temporarily: the next month General MacArthur proposed that President Eisenhower convene a summit with Stalin in which the unification under free governments of Germany and Korea, and their permanent neutralization along with Austria and Japan, would be demanded. If the Soviet Union refused, the United States would threaten to use atomic weapons 'to clear North Korea of enemy forces' and 'to neutralize Red China's capacity to wage modern war'.[36] Although Eisenhower rejected MacArthur's plan, it should be noted that in 1953 a tacit threat of nuclear attack was made which had the effect of terminating China's obstruction of the armistice talks in Korea.

For all his subsequent reputation for caution and conservatism, Eisenhower had himself come into office with a strong line in crusading rhetoric. He had talked of the need for 'a crusade' during the election campaign, and shortly before entering the White House described the cold war as 'a war of light against darkness, freedom against slavery, Godliness against atheism'.[37] And in his first eighteen months in office he covertly deposed the governments of both Mohammed Mosadegh in Iran and Jacobo Arbenz in Guatemala, the former by subversion orchestrated by the CIA, the latter partly by similar means but also by the covert use of American bombers.[38] Both depositions had clear crusading features (purging the international system of those subverting its basic norms—in these cases those which protect the rights of foreign companies), as well as defensive ones (enhancing American security by a preventive intervention).

Also, Eisenhower appointed as his secretary of state John Foster Dulles, who since 1946 had been strongly identified with the Republican Party's aspiration to abandon containment and 'roll back' the frontiers of the communist bloc. Revealingly, Dulles was a former liberal pacific-ist who had been active in the Federal Council of Churches, Federal Union, and numerous other peace groups; and his original attitude to the Second World War had been conditional on the United States' using it to achieve fundamental reform of the international system.[39] His style as Secretary of State was so forbidding as to leave many people in doubt whether 'rollback' would be achieved exclusively by peaceful competition between capitalism and communism (which would cause the latter system to go into a decline), or whether military crusades were also regarded as legitimate.

With hindsight, however, the early 1950s marked the point at which the crusading impulse began to weaken, first as policy and then as rhetoric. In part this was due to the failure of the attempt to conquer North Korea, after which the United States had eventually to settle for what was in effect the status quo ante, prompting a historian of the Korean War to stress its significance as 'the first important war in American history that was not a crusade'.[40] It was due also to the developing nuclear capacity of the Soviet Union, which in August 1953 tested its own hydrogen bomb. For, though the American nuclear monopoly had for a time strengthened the crusading impulse, the onset of mutual deterrence weakened it. In 1956, when the Soviet Union crushed the new

Hungarian regime, the United States did nothing, after which missed opportunity 'rollback' was no longer a credible option.

As crusading faded, the case for containment began to be better explained to the American people. On 7 April 1954 Eisenhower formulated the famous 'domino theory', which clearly presented containment as the forward defence of the United States. Even so, it was containment with pacific-ist rather than defencist overtones: it stressed, in other words, the ideological rather more than the strategic threat posed by the Soviet bloc. Thus the 'Eisenhower doctrine' of January 1957, which marked a new level of American involvement in the Middle East, echoed the moralism of the Truman doctrine ten years before.

It laid down two conditions, however, for American military assistance—specifically promised in the 1957 doctrine, unlike that of 1947—which made clearer its non-crusading nature. No troops would be sent unless a state, first, requested them and, second, was suffering 'overt armed aggression from any nation controlled by International Communism'. Admittedly, these conditions were not always observed. Only the first was fulfilled when the doctrine was invoked and troops were sent briefly to the Lebanon in July 1958.

The same was true—although the Eisenhower doctrine did not formally apply outside the Middle East—when the United States sent military advisers to South Vietnam to help contain the revolt ostensibly mounted by the National Liberation Front. By 1965, however, when the United States committed its own ground troops, North Vietnamese intervention had become sufficiently obvious for the second condition also to be seen to be met. Since it was difficult to feel ideological enthusiasm for the Saigon regime, the case for defending it had to rest more on forward-defensive than on moralistic arguments. Had both the Eisenhower-doctrine conditions for a truly defensive intervention not thus clearly been met, it may be surmised that public support for so remote an intervention could not have been sustained for as long as it was, especially in view of the introduction of conscription.

America's Vietnam involvement was itself evidence of a growing willingness to think in non-crusading terms; and its failure reinforced this trend. Failure prompted Nixon and Kissinger to pursue a policy of *rapprochement* with China and *détente* with the Soviet Union which was based to a remarkable extent on a

geopolitical analysis. And it caused moralists to become isolationists for a time: thus the temptation to mount a counter-crusade in
Angola in 1975 was sternly resisted by Congress.

Where America's crusading impulse has never weakened, however, is in its determination to prevent 'communism' gaining a
further foothold in its own sphere of influence: Central and South
America. This concern can, of course, be explained by fears for its
own security; and indeed wherever possible the United States has
used defensive arguments to support the interventions it has
undertaken within its own hemisphere. For example, despite the
counter-crusading doctrine he soon developed, President Johnson's
initial justification for his intervention in the Dominican Republic
in 1965 was the need to protect American lives.[41] The same
argument was used by President Reagan to justify his intervention
in Grenada in 1983; and he also emphasized the threat to American
security posed by the air base which the Cubans were building
there, insisting in explicitly defencist terms that 'we are not
somewhere else in the world protecting someone else's interests. We
are here protecting our own.'[42] Yet the United States has generally
proved reluctant simply to put forward the geopolitical argument
that great powers have special preventive-defensive rights in their
spheres of influence. Such reluctance is, of course, an American
tradition: when in 1823 the Monroe doctrine had first forbidden
interference by the 'Old' World in the affairs of the 'New', it had
used an ideological argument (hostility to monarchism) rather than
a strategic one (the risk that European states would maintain a
military presence in America). Its interventions have usually had an
explicitly crusading flavour.

This is particularly true of those validated, as already mentioned,
by the Organization of American States. Thus at Caracas in 1954
Secretary of State Dulles secured the passing of a resolution at the
tenth Inter-American Conference which declared:

That the domination or control of the political institutions of any American
state by the international communist movement, extending to this hemisphere the political system of an extra-continental power, would constitute
a threat to the sovereignty and political independence of the American
states, endangering the peace of America . . .

His intention was to provide a justification for an overt intervention by the United States in Guatemala to depose Jacobo Arbenz's regime; but in the event it was toppled mainly by American-backed Guatemalan dissidents, the supporting air raids, carried out by the United States Air Force, being kept a secret for many years.

In 1961 the United States mounted the Bay of Pigs invasion, a disastrous anti-Castro crusade by proxy which used Cuban dissidents but no American forces; and in its embittered aftermath the eighth meeting of consultation of American foreign ministers was persuaded in 1962 to declare Marxism-Leninism 'incompatible with the inter-American system'.[43] This was to come in useful not in relation to Cuba, however, towards which it was originally directed, but in relation to the Dominican Republic in April 1965, since it enabled President Johnson to assert during that crisis: 'The American nations cannot, must not, and will not permit the establishment of another Communist government in the western hemisphere.'[44] It was, however, only after the event that he managed to persuade the Organization of American States to transmute the United States army of occupation into an 'Inter-American Peace Force'.[45] Similarly, when President Reagan invaded Grenada in 1983, he arranged for a request for assistance to come from the Organization of Eastern Caribbean States; his administration allegedly drafted the request itself, although it came a little too late to add to the legitimacy of the intervention.[46]

It may be noted that the United States has, where possible, crusaded either by sub-military means, as in the alleged destabilization of Allende's regime in Chile; or by proxy, as in its use of the Honduras-based Contras in an attempt to depose Nicaragua's Sandinistas (who for a considerable time were careful, as one observer put it, 'not to make any incursions across the border' which could give the Honduran military leader 'the excuse he seems to be seeking for a US-backed holy war').[47]

In reaction against both Nixon's and Kissinger's *realpolitik* (as they saw it) and Carter's human-rights pacific-ism which succeeded it, American crusaders enjoyed something of a recovery of confidence in the late 1970s and early 1980s. President Reagan denounced the Soviet Union as an 'evil empire . . . the focus of evil in the modern world',[48] mounted an invasion of Grenada in 1983, as already noted, and in 1986 allowed the United States' Sixth Fleet to come into a military confrontation in the Gulf of Sirte purely to uphold the claims of international law against Libya's unilateral declaration that it formed part of its own territorial waters. Yet this recovery did not amount to a return to the early 1950s, even in terms of rhetoric. For example, although the keynote of Reagan's strongly anti-communist address to the British Houses of Parliament on 8 June 1982 was: 'For the sake of peace and justice, let us move forward toward a world in which all people are at least free to determine their own destiny', his references to military strength were all explicitly defensive. The moralism of the speech was thus pacific-ist rather than crusading in tone and content: it asserted that 'the ultimate determinant of the struggles now going on will not be bombs and rockets, but a test of wills and ideas, a trial of spiritual resolve . . .'.[49] And he resisted the temptation to talk of rollback during the Polish crisis.

That the long-term trend is still for the crusading impulse to weaken in the United States is confirmed by a recent survey of élite opinion.[50] The reasons include a growing public sensitivity both to the complexity of international problems and to the crudity of war as an instrument for seeking their solution. Crusading can nevertheless be expected to enjoy intermittent and spontaneous upsurges whenever there is either a 'communist' advance within the American hemisphere or a surge in national self-confidence.

ii. The Soviet Union

Although crusading plays a similar role in Soviet thinking its roots are differently located—in official ideology, not in public opinion, which is not only politically insignificant but also scarred by the Second World War.

Marxism-Leninism does not regard 'communism' as having yet been attained in any state, so that the prospect of war's eventual abolition is still a long way off. Since capitalist states, like their feudal predecessors, use war as an instrument of class policy, socialist states like the Soviet Union (which currently regards itself as a developed-socialist society and an all-people's state) must in principle do the same. Thus whether or not a war is just or unjust depends not on whether it is defensive or aggressive, but on whether it hastens or delays the coming of communism. As Lenin put it late in 1918: 'The character of the war . . . depends on what class is waging the war and on what politics this war is a continuation of.'[51] Accordingly, during the period of opportunity which presented itself in the aftermath of the First World War the Soviet Union mounted the two crusades already mentioned: against bourgeois Poland in 1920 and Menshevik Georgia in 1921.

Marxism-Leninism does not sanction crusading unconditionally, however: it disapproves of force if there is a more expedient way of making progress; and, believing as it does in the primacy of the base over the superstructure, it regards force as politically ineffective until the economy is ready for it. Thus only if there is no alternative and the economic situation is auspicious is a crusade justified. Its attitude to war has been summed up by P. H. Vigor:

Fundamentally the concept of war is alien to a Marxist-Leninist. War is the result (almost the automatic result) of the existence of classes in society: war is thus a servile thing, a feudal thing, a capitalist thing; it is not a communist thing. When communism has been established throughout the world, war will inevitably vanish; so, from the point of view of a Soviet statesman, war is 'them' and what 'they' do; it has little to do with us.[52]

Thus, although its official ideology permits crusading, the Soviet Union seems genuinely to regard itself—and certainly tries to project itself—as pacific-ist. But its foreign-policy makers seem in practice to be guided by defencist theory. Because of its greater strategic insecurity, moreover, the Soviet Union was forced to restrict its crusading earlier than the United States was. Faced with mounting evidence that any revolution which was likely to take place in inter-war Europe would be fascist rather than socialist, Stalin limited his ambitions to the defence of the Soviet state.

This is not to imply that he pursued this aim rationally or coherently: his attempt to ensure his own political position by means of the purges had the effect of weakening the state's military position; and it remains unclear whether his favoured policy for avoiding war was deterrence (the construction of a strong anti-fascist bloc that would prevent Hitler from risking war) or appeasement (seeking to embroil the fascist states and capitalist democracies in a debilitating repeat of the First World War minus, however, Russia, which would thus emerge as the real victor). Although as an officially socialist state, the Soviet Union was bound to portray itself in its defensive mode as pacific-ist, its policy—especially its pact with Hitler in August 1939—owed too much to *realpolitik* to be other than defencist. Even Stalin's expansionist moves—such as his seizure of eastern Poland in September 1939, his winter war of 1939–40 against Finland (to improve the defences of Leningrad), and his occupation of the Baltic states in 1940—were acts of preventive defence, although not explained in such terms. And his belated entry into the Second World War took place only because he was attacked.

Once it was forced upon him, of course, he showed a private awareness of its crusading possibilities, telling Tito in 1944: 'This war is not as in the past; whoever occupies a territory also imposes on it his own social system. Everyone imposes his own social system as far as his army has had power to do. It cannot be otherwise.'[53] In public, however, he was careful to play this down, which is why he abolished the Comintern in 1943. Only after the Red Army was in control of eastern Europe did he proclaim, in his notorious speech of 9 February 1946, that the war had 'assumed from the very beginning an anti-Fascist liberating character, having also as one of its aims the establishment of democratic liberties' and that this character had been strengthened by the entry of the Soviet Union.[54] Because it also stressed the incompatibility of capitalism and communism, this speech was interpreted in the west as a declaration that the wartime crusade would continue, particularly when the following year Stalin created the Cominform as a partial replacement for the Comintern.

But, although the Soviet Union seemed for a while to be enjoying a second post-war period of crusading opportunity, America's atomic superiority forced it to be cautious. Stalin bolshevized eastern Europe largely to ensure its reliability and therefore its defensibility, and only partly for ideological reasons. The Chinese communists received less than wholehearted support from Moscow in their civil war; and the North Koreans were given Soviet support only, it seems, because the United States was believed not to regard the peninsula as a vital interest. The latter, moreover, was publicly claimed to be a defensive operation following a South Korean attack. Indeed, despite Lenin's statements to the contrary, the Soviet Union and other Marxist-Leninist states have since Stalin's time bowed to international law and western morality and accepted the defence/aggression distinction, if only for public-relations reasons. They now claim, in other words, that even the revolutionary wars they support are defensive. This has become general Soviet-bloc practice: thus when their army deposed Pol Pot in 1979, the Vietnamese claimed that it was really the Cambodian people who had done so, despite the fact that the destruction of so unspeakable a regime could have been supported on humanitarian grounds.

Since Stalin's death, moreover, the practical constraints on crusading imposed by nuclear weapons have received theoretical recognition, most notably in the doctrine of peaceful co-existence which Nikita Khrushchev expounded in 1956. This argued that the socialist camp had become strong enough to exercise some deterrent effect upon the imperialists and could therefore ensure that war was no longer 'fatalistically inevitable'. To avoid the risks of catastrophic escalation to a nuclear level crusading had thenceforward to be carried out by limited wars only.

This type of crusading—or, as it had now publicly to be portrayed, defensive assistance to peoples under attack from imperialism—was indeed increased. Not only did Khrushchev insist that the struggle between systems would continue and in January 1961 make a combative speech offering to support 'wars of national liberation'; he also worked hard to extend Soviet influence into new areas such as the Middle East. Indeed, as during the period of *détente* during the 1970s, it would have been impossible for the Soviet leadership to do otherwise. Although it can reinterpret Marxism-Leninism to some extent, it cannot do so too blatantly because it needs it to ensure its legitimacy. The more conservative Soviet domestic practice becomes, in other words, and the more cautious its foreign policy, the more the promotion of Marxist-Leninist revolutionism in the Third World is needed to establish the Soviet Union's socialist credibility, both at home and within the world communist movement.

Even so, peaceful coexistence and the Soviet reluctance to pursue crusades which carried a risk of major war were sources of great irritation to the Chinese, who had yet to complete their revolution by taking Taiwan and who during the 1950s were prepared to hint at a belief that socialism could emerge triumphant from a nuclear war. On 5 September 1958, for example, Mao Tse-tung argued that, although between a half and a third of the population would be destroyed if the imperialists started a nuclear war, 'When 900 million are left out of 2.9 billion several Five Year Plans can be developed for the total elimination of capitalism and for permanent peace. It is not a bad thing.'[55] But Mao was whistling to keep China's spirits up; even he never developed a consistent rhetoric of crusading.

In one area, moreover, the Soviet Union showed a greater willingness to 'crusade' than the Chinese liked: within its own sphere of influence. In reality these interventions had largely geopolitical motives, like their American equivalents; but the Soviet Union has been no more willing than the United States to admit this publicly. It has thus justified them, as already noted, largely on ideological grounds—in other words, as the bringing to book of heretics, backsliders, or even infidels.

Just as America's crusading impulse underwent a partial revival after a period of decline, so in the second half of the 1970s the Russian one seemed to intensify: even before it invaded Afghanistan in December 1979, the Soviet Union had emerged as 'the leading imperialist power in a new scramble for Africa', as a western commentator has put it.[56] But to a considerable extent this merely reflected a Soviet desire to establish itself as unmistakably a world power—in other words, a classic defencist aspiration.

Although the superpowers' crusading streaks are thus remarkably similar, they have been a major source of mutual misunderstanding. The most dangerous phase of the early cold war, the period from about 1946 to about 1953, can be attributed to the fact that west and east regarded the other as embarked upon a crusade. Even though the crusading impulse had weakened on both sides by the 1970s, it remained strong enough to contribute to the undermining of *détente*. The American public interpreted the Kremlin's increasing activity in Africa as intensified crusading and its own concern for human rights in the Soviet Union as merely pacific-ist, while for the Kremlin, of course, it was simply the other way round. The need to avoid misunderstandings of this kind is one of the most powerful arguments for the next theory to be considered: defencism.

5

Defencism

Unlike militarists and crusaders, most participants in the war-and-peace debate sincerely reject the aggressive use of force, but fear that others may resort to it unless deterred. Some of them are of the opinion that this risk can eventually be eliminated by domestic or international reforms. These are pacific-ists, and will be discussed in the following chapter. But rather more believe that it will remain, indefinitely if not permanently, and that while it does a state must maintain an adequate military capability in order to ensure the highest possible degree of security for itself and the highest possible degree of international order for all. These are adherents of the war-and-peace debate's most popular theory (motto: 'if you want peace, prepare for war'), and are the subject of this chapter.

They differ from militarists in believing that the international system has some of the characteristics of a society. They believe, in other words, that war can be prevented for indefinite periods, and that diplomacy as well as military force plays a part in achieving this. They differ from pacific-ists (and 'reforming' crusaders) in believing that the international system will never become a full society. They believe, in other words, that war can never be abolished, since states are to some extent always in conflict yet will never consent to any effective curbs on their sovereignty. The best to be hoped for is a diplomatic compromise among states which reflects the prevailing distribution of power—an anarchical society, that is, or an armed truce.

The term most commonly used to describe this position is 'realism'. As already noted, however, this term covers the extreme belief held by militarists that 'reality' is wholly anarchic yet good in itself, as well as the moderate belief in question here that it has only partially anarchic qualities and that these should so far as possible be held in check.

But not only is the term 'realism' thus ambiguous, there are indications that its primary meaning is taken to be the extreme or militarist one. In a recent study of the concept of national security, for example, Barry Buzan has recognized the distinction between the 'view of the international system as a struggle for power' and the 'more moderate view of the international system as a struggle for security'. It is, however, the former which he describes as 'realist' in the sense in which scholars have normally used the term, and the latter as 'idealist'.[1] Similarly, the term *realpolitik*, defined in the *Oxford English Dictionary* as 'The policy of putting the material greatness of one's country before other considerations', is commonly understood as implying Machiavellian or belligerent intentions.

If the established term, realism, smacks too much of militarism, what can be put in its place? One possibility would be a term derived from the phrases 'national security' or 'international order', since these are widely acknowledged as realist goals; but it would not make clear that these goals may be pursued by defensive means only. The same objection would apply to a term based on the word 'geopolitics', since, although often used to convey the idea of thinking realistically about national interest and power without the pejorative implications that *realpolitik* carries, it does not make clear that the policies to be deduced from a geopolitical analysis must be defensive ones. (In addition, though used from time to time in this study to describe a way of analysing the international system, geopolitics has an unhelpful connotation which makes it even more unsuitable for present purposes: it is strongly identified with the particular and idiosyncratic opinions of one influential exponent of this approach, Halford Mackinder.)

The word 'defencism' is coined here on the grounds that the notion of defence is central to the theory. Indeed, it is fundamental to both the propositions to which the theory can in its simplest and most utopian form be reduced. The first, a moral intuition, is that a defensive intent is not only a necessary but also a sufficient condition for a war to be just. And the second, an empirical generalization, is that strong defences are the best way to prevent war. This chapter will look at the criticisms which have been levelled at these two propositions. It will also consider the assumptions defencism makes about the international system and the way these differ from those of the peace movement, before tracing its links to the ideologies in the centre and on the moderate-right wing of domestic politics.

1. The propositions and the challenges to them

The appealing moral simplicity and intellectual plausibility of the two propositions just cited explain why defencism is the world's leading war-and-peace theory. But both have been criticized on at least two grounds; and it is through these challenges that the nature of the defencist case can best be illuminated.

i. 'Defensive intent is necessary and sufficient for a just war'

This moral intuition is unique to defencism. It has already been noted that militarism and crusading regard it as too restrictive, because they deny that a defensive intent is necessary. It will now be seen that members of the peace movement regard it as too permissive, because they deny that a defensive intent is sufficent. And it will also be noted that just-war theorists criticize it as an inaccurate representation of defencist practice.

(a) The peace movement's criticism. Pacific-ists insist that even a defensive cause is just only if it is not also 'reactionary', in the sense of making it harder to achieve those political reforms on which it ultimately pins its hopes of lasting peace. Pacifists, of course, reject all idea of necessity and sufficiency and assert that no cause, not even a defensive one, ever justifies fighting. The peace movement thus argues that it is wrong to defend reactionary regimes or unjust dispositions of territory and economic resources even against un-equivocal aggression. In November 1936, for example, the British Labour Party's leading socialist pacific-ist, Sir Stafford Cripps, asserted: 'I do not think it would be a bad thing for the British working classes if Germany defeated us. It would be a disaster for profit makers and capitalists but not necessarily for the working classes.'[2] Shortly afterwards, the pacifist Laurence Housman was one of many in Britain who argued that the 'haves' should not resist the just demands of the 'have nots':

Not unless we are ready to extend to other nations and races equal access to the means of prosperity which we ourselves enjoy, are they likely to credit us with the love for peace and liberty which we possess . . . We can only have collective security in collective well-being; that is the true way to the preparation of peace.[3]

That the force of this argument was acknowledged even in official circles can be seen from the private admission by the First Sea Lord to the head of the civil service in 1934: 'We are in the remarkable position of not wanting to quarrel with anybody because we have got most of the world already, or the best bits of it, and we only want to keep what we have got and prevent others from taking it away from us.'[4] Such arguments were not confined to the 1930s, of course: the successful and undeniably defensive British campaign to recover the Falklands in 1982 was condemned by some socialists on the grounds that Britain had no right to colonial territory.

But there is, it should be noted in passing, a problem for the pacific-ist who argues that in certain circumstances states should not defend themselves: he appears to be encouraging their adversaries to start a crusade. Although he may himself deplore aggressive war, and argue that states should not seize by force even that to which they are in principle entitled, his arguments will encourage crusading or militarist states to attack regardless. Where his own state is the one to which the right of self-defence is being denied, as in the examples just given, he has at least some chance of persuading it to back down, so as to prevent its adversaries from going to war. But where he is denying it to another state which, in common with its adversaries, is unlikely to be swayed by pacific-ist arguments—such as South Africa under its present regime—he is in effect licensing a crusade. A retort which defencism can thus use against its moralistic critics is that it is the theory which most consistently disapproves of aggression.

(b) The just-war criticism. Whereas the peace movement takes it at its face value, just-war theorists argue that claiming defensive intent to be necessary and sufficient for a just war gives a false impression of defencist practice. Their objection is that, by emphasizing the righteousness of self-defence, defencist theory implies that each state has the duty, and certainly the right, to fight a defensive war. They contrast this with defencist practice, which, they point out, not only allows states in certain circumstances to appease their enemies or even to surrender to them without a fight, but also insists that some states must do so even if they would rather not.

Defencism does so, however, not because of doubts about the justice of the status quo, but because it accepts at least some of the restraints on even defensive wars recommended by the just-war tradition. It should be noted that this tradition emanated to a large extent from the secular notions of chivalry which warriors themselves had devised,[5] so that for many centuries the constraints it imposed were acceptable to warriors, who do not seem to have been thereby deprived of any weapons or strategy they really wished to use. Only with the development of 'area bombing' during the Second World War and the considerable reliance by leading states on nuclear deterrence since 1945 have mainstream defencist practice and just-war thinking come into conflict, with the latter becoming something of an academic and clerical preserve. But although most defencists do not favour too strict an adherence to certain parts of the tradition—particularly the *jus in bello*'s condition (*f*) as set out in chapter 2 (p. 11), which declares that non-combatants should be immune from direct attack—they continue out of common sense and basic decency to endorse most of it.

They observe restrictions on defensive wars emanating from both the *jus ad bellum* and the *jus in bello*. The former's condition (*d*) specifies that the harm judged likely to result from a war is not disproportionate to the likely good to be achieved. And many states have been known to observe this requirement: for example, it was presumably because a war of resistance to annexation by the Soviet Union would in 1940 have had a negligible chance of success that the Baltic states felt it to be unjustified. If such examples of non-resistance to invasion are few, it is because small states avoid provoking powerful neighbours in the first place and accommodate themselves as far as possible to their demands. Finland since the Second World War is a textbook example, even if the degree to which it is constrained is often exaggerated. So are states such as Sweden and Switzerland, which have opted for neutrality on the grounds that it is a less provocative policy than alignment. With about 160 states now belonging to the United Nations, it should be remembered that a considerable majority of the world's states have to exercise prudence in their relations with the greater powers.

Not all states voluntarily accept that the proportionality rule of the *jus ad bellum* requires them at times to back down: some have prudence imposed upon them. The latter are required to abandon their right of self-defence and sometimes also part or all of their independence in the interests of avoiding a disproportionately

serious war. Involuntary sacrifices of this kind were once commonplace, of course. Hedley Bull has, for example, drawn attention to

the great process of partition and absorption of small powers by greater
ones, in the name of principles such as 'compensation' and the 'balance of
power', that produced a steady decline in the number of states in Europe
from the Peace of Westphalia in 1648 until the Congress of Vienna in
1815.[6]

And in more modest form they are a feature of the twentieth
century: the Czechs were induced by Germany, Italy, Britain, and
France to make territorial sacrifices in the 1938 Munich agreement;
and the states of eastern Europe have since 1945 been forced by the
superpowers to accept in practice, though not in theory, a considerable abridgement of their independence.

Defencism is willing to accept this aspect of the just-war tradition
because it agrees that the requirements of international order should
prevail over those of national security for particular states. And,
since it does not believe that the international system is capable of
agreeing any democratic mechanism for deciding what the requirements of international order are, it in effect allows the greater
powers to decide the fate of the lesser ones. Sometimes this is done
co-operatively, by a formal concert of powers, as at Munich. More
often it is done competitively, by such mechanisms as the balance
of power and war, both cold and 'hot'.

Unlike militarism, which explicitly denies that weak states are
proper states, defencism pays lip-service to international law's
doctrine of the sovereign equality of states (including the right to
self-defence); but it behaves as if it believed in special privileges for
great powers. The latter in this context are states with the resources
always to maintain the strong defences which, according to the
simplified version of defencist theory, all states should. Since such
states have not only the greatest capacity but also the greatest
incentive to maintain order, they are licensed to manage the
international system even though the formal rights of small powers
may thereby be infringed. In particular, the great powers are
allowed to maintain spheres of influence within which other states
are in practice not entitled to full sovereignty. In a century like the
present one in which the right of self-determination is so strongly
supported, this doctrine would be intolerable to the generality

of states were it not for the vastly increased awfulness of modern and in particular nuclear warfare, which, as well as exacerbating the differential between strong and weak states, has made the avoidance of all-out war a vital interest for all.

As well as the prudential requirements of the *jus ad bellum*, defencists accept at least some of the humanitarian arguments of the *jus in bello*. The latter has its own proportionality requirement—condition (*e*), which stipulates that the harm judged likely to result from a particular military action should not be disproportionate to the good aimed at—as well as the noncombatant-immunity requirement of condition (*f*). It is generally agreed that, read strictly, both of these conditions, and especially the latter, prohibit a nuclear attack. And many members of the peace movement believe that they also rule out the making of deterrent threats (other than bluffing ones, which are not generally regarded as credible), on the grounds that, if an act is immoral, so is the conditional intention to commit it.[7] As already noted, most mainstream defencists believe that this strict reading of the *jus in bello* nullifies the *jus ad bellum* and produces a just-war doctrine which wills the end (protection against aggression) while denying the means (a nuclear deterrent and other modern weaponry). But they do not completely reject the principles of proportionality and discrimination. It seems likely, for example, that an important reason why after considerable discussion the Eisenhower administration avoided war with China during the crises of 1954–5 was that it believed that this would necessitate a major use of nuclear weapons, about which it had humanitarian scruples.

ii. 'Strong defences are the best way to prevent war'

Defencism's second proposition is that resolute but defensive methods by all states can reliably resist and therefore also deter aggression. This empirical generalization is also attacked on contradictory grounds: by militarists; and, once again, by the peace movement.

(a) The militarist criticism. In addition to denying the moral superiority of defensive methods, militarists insist that they are almost certainly too weak to produce security. Making the extreme-realist assumption that the world is profoundly anarchical, they insist that it will often be suicidal for a state to postpone the use of

force until it is actually attacked. Once again defencists—and in this case many pacific-ists too—in practice accept much of the force of this criticism. They have endeavoured to meet it by allowing themselves a considerably expanded definition of defence.

In its purest and most restricted form, of course, defence is the interception and parrying of a direct attack on the homeland (either by taking a stand at the frontier or by falling back and practising 'territorial' defence). But, as an outspoken British defencist, F. S. Oliver, put it in 1915: 'A war is not less a defensive war if you strike at your enemy in his own territory, or if you come to the aid of your ally, whose territory has been invaded or threatened.'[8] There are, it will here be suggested, at least seven extended forms of defence (some already mentioned): defence of overseas dependencies, forward defence, retaliation, deterrence, pre-emption, prevention, and retrospective defence.

Defence of overseas territories. Defencists have normally regarded an attack on their territory overseas as tantamount to an attack on their homeland. They have often believed such territory to be essential to their state's international position, because of the prestige and influence it brings as well as the additional military and strategic resources. Pacific-ists commonly regard the title to such territory as dubious, and regard it as illegitimate to invoke the concept of 'national' security in support of even a genuinely defensive colonial war. The Falklands War, already noted, is a clear example.

Forward defence. Often a state decides to take a stand not at its own frontier (whether that of the homeland or of an overseas territory) but at the frontiers of another state forward of this. It was in consequence of such decisions that Britain went to war in both 1914 and 1939; and the incomprehension with which its decision to enter the First World War was greeted indicates that forward defence can seem less legitimate even to its own citizens than homeland defence. It was this seeming lack of legitimacy which F. S. Oliver was attempting to remedy in the comment cited above and which led the government to use crusading rhetoric, as noted in the previous chapter.

Forward defence can appear a form of manipulation, moreover, to the state to which assistance is being rendered. When, for example, Britin decided in March 1939 to guarantee Poland it was with its own self-interest in mind: it had decided that if Hitler made further gains in eastern Europe he would become too powerful to be stopped when he attacked western Europe, in which case Britain would be imperilled. One school of thought on the British guarantee interprets it as motivated primarily by fear that the Poles would otherwise accommodate themselves to Hitler and deny Britain the opportunity for the forward-defensive stand it sought. It thus suggests that in this case forward defence was tantamount to preventive war[9]—a far greater extension of the notion of defence, as will very shortly be noted. Even though this accusation was not levelled against the first forward-defensive commitment entered into by the United States in the cold war, that to Greece and Turkey in the 'Truman doctrine' of 12 March 1947, there was criticism of the extent to which these states were being used for American purposes. Even a defencist like Walter Lippmann unfavourably contrasted the Truman doctrine with the greater consideration shown to Europe by the Secretary of State, General Marshall, in his famous Harvard lecture on 5 June 1947, out of which Marshall Aid grew. In Lippmann's own words:

The Truman Doctrine treats those who are supposed to benefit from it as dependencies of the United States, as instruments of American policy for 'containing' Russia. The Marshall speech at Harvard treats the European governments as independent powers, whom we must help but cannot presume to govern, or to use as instruments of an American policy.[10]

As well as sometimes worrying both its own citizens and the states which are supposedly being assisted, forward defence is often provocative to those states which it is intended to deter. This is true whether the forward line which is laid down is flexible or fixed. A flexible line is produced by a balance-of-power policy of practising forward defence only when the 'balance' needs to be restored after a shift in the distribution of power. But this produces arbitrary changes of policy: Britain's sudden support for France after 1904 alarmed the Germans without convincing them that Britain would intervene when war broke out. In other words, British policy was provocative without gaining much deterrent value from it. If the forward line is fixed, however, as in the case of NATO and the Warsaw Pact, it can be too rigid and institutionalize conflicts, at least according to defencism's critics. Forward defence is thus more likely to be controversial than waiting for one's own territory, home or overseas, to be attacked.

Retaliation. Few acts of defence—whether carried out at the frontiers of the homeland or of an overseas territory, or at a point forward of either—are pure interceptions and parryings of an attack, in the way that the trench warfare of the Western Front during the First World War and the aerial dogfights of the Battle of Britain during the Second were. Most are really counter-attacks or retaliations carried out as soon as possible afterwards. For example, the war against Japan which ended victoriously for the United States in 1945 was a long drawn-out act of retaliation for the attack on Pearl Harbor.

Retaliation is more controversial than interception because it can appear to place the punishment of an aggressor before the ostensible first priority of a defensive operation: the restoration of the status quo and the discouragement of future aggression. This is particularly true in the case of nuclear retaliation. It is an axiom of deterrence theory that, in order to avoid preventive attacks on its own missiles, each side must possess an invulnerable 'second-strike' capability. Yet any retaliation using second-strike weapons by a state which has already been the victim of a crushing first strike would in effect be an act of posthumous revenge which would do great harm without making anyone better off.

Despite these objections, however, defencism normally regards retaliation as an acceptable form of defence, provided it is undertaken in the context of a war. Because further attacks are to be expected once a war has started, a counter-attack appears less an act of revenge than a legitimate pre-emptive strike. Would-be retaliators are thus normally expected to declare war before acting; but it is increasingly common for them to argue instead—and more controversially—that a *de facto* state of war already exists. It is significant that, in order to justify military action against states indulging in terrorist actions, the Reagan administration has started to claim that terrorism is itself an act of war, albeit one of low intensity. In April 1984, for example, Secretary of State Shultz argued: 'State-sponsored terrorism is really a form of warfare . . . As the threat mounts . . . it is more and more appropriate that the nations of the West face up to the need for active defense against terrorism.'[11] Two years later the United States demonstrated what

Shultz meant by 'active defense' when it bombed selected targets in Libya as a response to terrorist attacks on its citizens in Europe for which it blamed Colonel Gaddafi, and claimed this retaliation to be an act of self-defence under Article 51 of the United Nations Charter.

Deterrence. The object of defencism is to deter aggression. The ideal way of doing this would be to possess so evidently infallible a capacity to intercept and parry an attack that an enemy would be deterred by an assured inability to deliver a crushing blow—a strategy much hankered after by advocates of alternative defence, who refer to it as 'defensive deterrence' or 'inoffensive deterrence'.[12] But infallible defence has been rendered utopian by the development of the bomber plane and missile, which are harder to intercept and parry even than land armies. Even the success of 'star wars' technology would not alter this since Reagan's scheme could not exclude low-trajectory projectiles, such as cruise missiles. The deterrence of aggression thus rests largely on threatening to retaliate with overwhelming force if, as is probable, an attacker succeeds in landing his initial blow. (All the alternative-defence movement can really hope to achieve is to reduce, rather than abolish, the retaliatory component of modern defence strategies.)

In order to deter effectively, the retaliatory threat must be credible, which means—or so it is usually argued—that an intention must exist to carry it out. It must also be insufferable, which means that it promises to infringe the traditional *jus in bello* requirements of discrimination and proportionality, as already noted. As well as being open to moral objection, deterrence can be criticized on practical grounds. The more a state relies upon the threat of retaliation the more it gives its opponents an incentive, whether through fear or opportunism, to try to eliminate its deterrent in a pre-emptive attack. Its security thus depends entirely on the extent to which its retaliatory capacity is perceived to be both invulnerable and likely to be made use of.

Pre-emption. Pre-emptive defence occurs when a defender surprises with a first strike an aggressor who has already formed an intention to attack but has simply not got round to carrying it out. It is legitimately defensive because, although it involves the first *use* of force, it does not involve the first *intention* to use it. Germany believed that its resort to war in August 1914 merely pre-empted the aggression on the part of the Franco-Russian alliance which would have occurred as soon as Russia's lumbering military machine had completed its slow mobilization. It will, as just hinted, probably also be the justification offered if nuclear weapons are ever used to start a war.

It is, however, very hard to be certain that an adversary has in fact formed an intention to attack: almost all historians would now argue, for example, that Germany was mistaken to believe that Russia and France had done so in 1914. Thus, although a genuinely pre-emptive strike would not be controversial, it is in practice often had to distinguish from a preventive one. Indeed, although the difference is clear enough in principle, there is no agreement about terminology, which means that many writers describe even clearly pre-emptive attacks as preventive.

Preventive defence. Prevention differs from pre-emption in admitting that the enemy state has yet to form even an intention to attack. The claim that a preventive action is defensive is that unless prevented by war the potential adversary will find itself in so preponderant a position that, according to basic defencist assumptions, it will soon be tempted to form an aggressive intention.

There are two types of preventive defence, each of which pushes to the extreme a standard defencist assumption. The first picks a fight with a likely future adversary on the grounds that a small or victorious war now is better than a big or humiliating war later. One clear example, though it did not lead to war, was the 1962 Cuban missile crisis: the United States felt the installation of Soviet missiles to be an unacceptable alteration of the distribution of power, so it took preventive action, blockading the island and threatening an air strike against the missile silos. Another example was Israel's attack on Egypt on 5 June 1967 which precipitated the Six-Day War. Michael Walzer, for example, accepts that the war was preventive rather than pre-emptive (as here defined), arguing that 'it is unlikely that the Egyptians intended to begin the war themselves', but concludes nevertheless that Israel's action was 'legitimate anticipation' because Nasser's actions in expelling the United Nations Emergency Force from the Sinai and Gaza Strip, closing the Straits of Tiran (an international waterway) to Israeli shipping, and mobilizing his troops, had placed Israel in real danger should Egypt ever form an aggressive intention.[13] (Walzer's approval of certain preventive-defensive acts is thus additional to his support for the crusades noted in the previous chapter.) Preventive wars of this first type take to an extreme the doctrine of the balance of power, which is normally taken to justify only forward defence. As already noted, the British guarantee to Poland in 1939 was a possible instance of a forward-defensive application of the balance of power shading into a preventive-defensive one.

A second type of preventive defence is directed at neighbouring states which, being themselves too weak to constitute an effective defensive buffer, hinder the deterrence of an aggressor. The acquisition of colonies in the late nineteenth century was often motivated at least in part by preventive considerations of this kind. So, it may be surmised, were the Soviet Union's partition of Poland with Germany in August and September 1939, its attack on Finland in November of that year which resulted in the extortion of a strip of territory, and its unopposed annexation in 1940 of both the Baltic States and a portion of Romania. In other words, the best justification for Soviet actions was that these states, which were vital for Russia's forward defence, would fail to help it deter Germany from attacking the Soviet Union. The 1970 American incursion into Cambodia had similar motives, being intended to permit action against North Vietnamese infiltrators which the Cambodians themselves were too weak to take, and thereby to contribute to the defence of South Vietnam. Since in practice only the strongest states are able to do this, it is in effect an extreme application of the doctrine of special rights for great powers—a doctrine which is controversial enough, as already noted, without being extended to allow preventive war.

Retrospective defence. It would at first sight appear that defencism rules out the rectification by war of ancient grievances. While it may be reasonable to regard retaliation against a very recent attack as defensive, it seems overtly aggressive to start a war over a long-standing wrong. Thus, while France could have claimed a defensive justification had it started a war to retrieve Alsace-Lorraine shortly after losing it in 1870–1, it could not so plausibly have done so forty years later. Yet defensive rationales have been put forward for actions of this kind. A notable example is the doctrine of 'permanent aggression', according to which a long-standing occupation of territory is morally equivalent to a current attack. This was

developed by Nehru to justify the Indian seizure of Goa in 1961—
an action classified in the previous chapter as a state-consolidating
crusade. The implication of Nehru's argument was that the Indian
action was 'retrospective defence', in the sense that it attempted
to do what a successful defensive war would have achieved at the
time of the original aggression—in this case, Portugal's original
acquisition of its South Asian territories. Of all the ways of
stretching the idea of defence, this is both the rarest and most
extreme.

Although these seven extensions do something to rebut the
extreme-realist charge that strong defences alone are insufficient to
provide security, they considerably undermine defencism's appealing moral simplicity and encourage the idealist argument that strong
defences contribute to insecurity.

(b) The peace movement's criticism. Because it for the most part
views the international system as latently harmonious, the peace
movement is inclined to blame conflicts on defencist policies
themselves. It argues that defencists take far too optimistic a view
of each state's seeking to build up strong defences. It insists, first,
that an arms race will result and, second, that war will thus be made
more rather than less likely. Indeed, the litmus test for membership
of the peace movement is assent to these two assertions.

The first assertion is persuasive. When Michael Heseltine,
then British Secretary of State for Defence, told the 1983 Conservative Party conference: 'We do not expect the Soviets to abandon
their proper defences, to act naïvely, or to surrender their interests . . .',[14] he was admitting that by its own logic defencism must
also accept the right of rival states to be strong. Yet there are two
factors which prevent defencists in competing states agreeing what
each other's 'proper defences' should be. The first is the difficulty
of distinguishing qualitatively between 'proper' and 'improper'
methods of defence: each side feels that the other's supposedly
defensive weapons and strategies are potentially offensive. The
United States Army is sincere in its view that its role in Europe is
defensive; but some of its suggested contingency plans for seizing
the initiative in a war—such as Airland Battle—have recently been
criticized for appearing aggressive. This has led to calls by the
alternative-defence movement for a switch to an unambiguously
non-provocative policy based on anti-tank weapons, fighter aircraft,

and even 'Maginot line' fortifications, which is sometimes also described as 'just defence', or 'transarmament' (as distinct from disarmament).[15] But the disagreement during the World Disarmament Conference of 1932–4 over whether a submarine was aggressive or defensive is indicative of the conceptual problems involved. Likewise, Germany's ability to by-pass France's Maginot line in 1940 is a reminder of the practical dangers of pure defence. And the neutron bomb in the 1970s and the strategic defense initiative in the 1980s are indications that even unmistakably defensive weapons can be controversial and unpopular. If the absence of an agreed qualitative criterion is the first factor explaining why defencists cannot agree on the appropriate level of defences for potential adversaries, the second factor is the failure to establish a quantitative one. Thus, although defencists often talk of a wanting to achieve a 'balance' or 'parity' with their rivals, they not only find it hard to measure relative strengths, but in practice want to build in a margin of superiority for their side too. This automatically ensures a continuous and potentially destabilizing arms race.

Even though the second argument—that arms races cause war—is much more questionable, it too has widespread support. Indeed, as the next chapter will show, it is sometimes assumed that this is all that needs to be said on the subject of war prevention.

2. The armed truce

It will have become apparent that underlying defencism's two main propositions is a distinctive view of international relations which falls between the pessimism of the militarists and the optimism of the peace movement.

Unlike the former, as already noted, defencism believes that a measure of international order exists; indeed the armed truce is a form of order. Even if order depends largely on an appropriate distribution of power, it gives rise to the autonomous norms and values which Hedley Bull has described as the 'institutions' of international society: 'the balance of power, international law, diplomacy, the role of the great powers, and war.' As Bull implies, it is not Thomas Hobbes or Niccolò Machiavelli who should be regarded as defencism's archetypal thinker, as academic 'realists' normally assume, but a theorist who accepts the notion of an international society, however anarchical, such as the Dutch jurist Hugo Grotius (1583–1645).[16]

But, although international society exists, it is an anarchical one and will so remain for the foreseeable future. Defencists do not expect war to be abolished: they believe, in the words of Julian Critchley, a British Conservative MP specializing in defence, that 'the best that can be hoped for is a continuation of the armed truce which (wishful thinking apart) is what has obtained between Russia and the West since 1949'.[17] It is symptomatic of a latent crusading streak when those who otherwise appear to be defencists express unhappiness with the armed truce, as West Germany's former defence minister Franz Joseph Strauss did in 1984, for example, when he wrote: 'World peace for me and my political colleagues is more than a state of no-war, no-fighting. There is no war in Poland and yet the people do not have peace.'[18] To the peace movement defencism seems both unduly complacent and unduly pessimistic.

i. Complacency?

Defencism seems complacent because it is content with the armed truce, on the grounds that it allows the basics of civilized life to continue. In the words of Michael Howard, who has articulated with uncommon clarity the basic premises of defencist theory:

I would not disagree with those who say that 'true peace' is more than the absence of war. I would only claim that the absence of war, and even more the absence of generalized random violence, is a blessing not to be underrated; as those who have experienced war know only too well.[19]

In this way defencists throw anti-war rhetoric back in the faces of the peace movement, accusing it both of ignoring the horror of actual warfare in order to attack the armed truce and of encouraging the belief that crusades to establish true peace might be justified.

Defencists also play down the net cost of the defence effort, either by pointing to its compensating benefits (the stimulus to the economy of defence expenditure, the improvement of social discipline by conscription, and so on), or by likening it to an insurance policy—a small sacrifice which averts the risk of total ruin. The peace movement finds both these arguments complacent, pointing to various drawbacks of the defence effort (the consumption of scarce resources by rearmament, the infringement of civil liberties by conscription, and so on), and likening it not to an insurance policy but to a crude vaccine which, on the grounds of staving off a serious disease of which there is only a slight risk anyway, guarantees debilitating side effects which undermine the very health it professes to preserve.

ii. Pessimism?

If in the eyes of the peace movement defencists appear too complacent on some issues, on others they seem too pessimistic. Although defencism can abstractly conceive of a 'true' or 'positive' peace founded on perfect order, it does not in practice expect to attain this; and it is certain that 'peace as harmony' and 'peace as justice' can never be achieved. Some defencists deny that this shows them to be pessimists; according to the French journalist Jean-François Revel, for example, in his alarmist recent study of the Soviet threat: 'It's the case that is pessimistic, not the person stating it.'[20] But others admit to pessimism, and seek to justify it by the explicit or implicit use of one of two different arguments.

(a) The 'positivist' argument. The first holds that the laws of international relations can be inferred from the discoverable truths of human nature. According to the leading exponent of this view, Hans J. Morgenthau:

Political realism believes that politics, like society in general, is governed by objective laws which have their root in human nature . . . The realist parts company with other schools of thought before the all-important question of how the contemporary world is to be transformed . . . The realist cannot be persuaded that we can bring about that transformation by confronting a political reality that has its own laws with an abstract ideal that refuses to take those laws into account.[21]

The laws of human nature thus rule out the utopian reforms mistakenly pursued by pacific-ists and pacifists but not the stable truce with which defencists rest content. One of Britain's most vocal defencists, Brian Crozier, has explicitly expounded these laws as he sees them in a formal statement of the 'axioms' of his thinking: 'Man is innately envious and aggressive. His nature is not subject to change . . . His behaviour, however, is susceptible to change, either for the better or the worse . . . He has an overwhelming need of order.'[22]

(b) The 'sceptical' argument. The second argument for pessimism asserts that there are no simple laws or truths of human existence; man must above all learn to cope with uncertainty. Thus Michael Howard takes the view, which he attributes also to Raymond Aron and Hedley Bull, that although 'force is an ineluctable element in international relations', this is 'not because of any inherent tendency on the part of man to use it but because the *possibility* of its use exists'. It is purely because of this risk that force has 'to be deterred, controlled and if all else fails, used with discrimination and constraint'.[23] Sceptics also argue that man must accept that his knowledge of how society (international or domestic) coheres even to the extent it does is limited, and that his attempts to improve it are liable to make matters worse. Thus, although Howard does not oppose the attempt to replace nation-states by higher forms of association, he counsels caution:

Clearly it is desirable, so far as possible, to continue this move from lower to higher loyalties, from Britain to Europe or to the Commonwealth or the Atlantic Community; ultimately to the Planet Earth. But this can be done effectively only if the roots of national loyalties are well nourished, and this higher loyalty carries the whole nation with it: not just the highly-educated few. Otherwise national unity is disrupted and nothing gained in its place.[24]

To the sceptical defencist, society is an organism which is too complex to tinker with, changes only slowly, and is unlikely even in the long term to conform to any utopian blueprint.

3. The peace and defence movements

i. The positive-peace movement

The defining characteristic of the peace movement is its belief that, contrary to what defencists say, 'positive' or 'true' peace is in fact within reach. This point is worth stressing since defencists have often complained that the term 'peace movement' is obsolete, dating as it does from a time when militarists and crusaders were in evidence and when even defencists, in their eagerness to mobilize their societies in response to military threats, tended to sound more enthusiastic about war than is now politically acceptable. To talk of a peace movement, they argue, is symptomatic of the view which has been expressed, for example, by the eminent philosopher and member of the Roman Catholic peace group Pax Christi, Michael Dummett, in the context of believers in world government: that 'though generally understood to be cranks . . . they have at least addressed a question to which most people think it not worth attempting to give an answer, namely how can wars be prevented?'[25] Defencists insist that they too have addressed this question and given an answer which most people accept; those who reject this majority view should be described as the protest movement. The view taken here, however, is that, although 'positive-peace movement' would be a better label, the more conventional term is an acceptable shorthand.

ii. Unorthodox, eccentric, and fastidious defencists

It follows from this definition of the peace movement that there is a category of people which falls between it and orthodox defencism. By taking theoretical or principled objection to defencism as its criterion for membership, this book limits the peace movement to pacific-ists and pacifists, and excludes those whose objection is not to the defencist critique of international relations as such but merely to certain policies being carried on in its name. Although such an exclusion can easily be justified in the case of what can be called 'unorthodox' defencists, it will be seen that it is more questionable in the case of 'eccentric' or 'fastidious' ones.

(a) Unorthodox defencists. Two kinds of defencists are here described as unorthodox. The first are those whose disagreement with mainstream defence policy is a matter not of principle but of either 'gaullism', micro-nationalism, localism, neutralism, isolationism, or defeatism. These are defencists whose dissent is a matter either of different political loyalties or of different postures. The second kind are those who do not pretend to be 'peace' campaigners since not only is their disagreement with the government merely over how to achieve more efficacious defence, the reforms they propose are relatively moderate. They include Lord Carver on the Trident issue (as noted in chapter 1) and such influential Americans as McGeorge Bundy, George F. Kennan, Robert S. McNamara, and Gerard Smith, who have together pressed for a no-first-use

nuclear policy for NATO.[26] These are defencists with a dissenting view of certain policy issues; and it is not helpful to include them in the peace movement.

(b) Eccentric defencists. Exclusion from the peace movement is more questionable, however, in the case of those who, though believing themselves to have effective defence as their only consideration, advocate reforms that are so radical—for example, reliance on non-violent defence—as to be dismissed as simply eccentric by the vast majority of defencists. Eccentric defencists can come very close to pacifism, as the case of Commander Sir Stephen King-Hall serves to illustrate. In 1957 he became convinced that Britain and Europe should abandon both nuclear weapons and the 'maintenance of conventional weapons for use in major wars' and develop instead a capacity for non-violent resistance; and for the next five years or so he continued to expound this viewpoint vigorously. His views were thus easy to confuse with what will be identified in chapter 7 as 'nuclear-era pacifism'—the belief that the risk of even conventional wars escalating to the nuclear level is so great as to make pacifism the only rational strategy. But King-Hall was not a pacifist: he made clear that small conventional forces should be retained for limited wars outside Europe, took a distinctly un-pacifist attitude to the Soviet Union (claiming that the purpose of his strategy was 'not only to defend our way of life but to destroy Communism'),[27] and insisted that he had arrived at his new position because it made sense in defence terms and 'not because of a repudiation of my past beliefs'.[28] But he found himself so closely identified with the peace movement that it seems odd not to regard him, and similarly 'eccentric' cases (for example, defencist supporters of such organizations as the Alternative Defence Commission), as having at least associate membership.

(c) Fastidious defencists. It also seems unreasonable to exclude from the peace movement those who take a similarly unorthodox view but do so on grounds not of defencist common sense but of morality: it is because they take so absolute a view of the just-war tradition that they have to rule out the more orthodox means of defence. Admittedly, most such people are pacific-ists, and thus part of the peace movement anyway. Their critique of the international system is thus sufficiently optimistic for their diminished capacity to resist aggression to be offset at least in part by a belief that such an

eventuality will only rarely arise. But some are defencists and therefore experience a major intellectual conflict between the considerable role they expect force and the threat of it to play in international relations and the limited types of counter-force and counter-threat they believe to be morally permissible. They can thus be called 'fastidious defencists' since they retain a defencist scepticism about the reformability of the armed truce, while being highly scrupulous about the methods which may be used to counter aggression. Many fastidious defencists would regard themselves as belonging to the peace movement, though they are sceptical of its political optimism, and are more likely to support limited defensive wars such as that by which the Falklands was recaptured. So, like eccentric defencists, they are here regarded as associate members.

4. The ideological base

Even more obviously than the other theories discussed in this book, defencism is a continuum of positions rather than a single theory: it ranges from those whose pessimism is so great as to take them close to militarism to those whose optimism is not far removed from pacific-ism. This is reflected in its domestic political base, which ranges from 'authoritarian' conservatism through mainstream conservatism to social democracy.

All three positions, it will be noted, give considerable priority to the claims of the sovereign state. Except in an emergency where the needs of international order take precedence, as already noted, the latter is recognized as having not only the right but the duty to promote its own security by any defensive means it can. As Stanley Baldwin put it in 1927 when replying as British prime minister to a pacifist petition:

is it not the privilege as well as the duty of every Englishman to take up arms in defence of his home and his country? A war of aggression is an abomination and a horror; a war of defence is very different. Is it not our inalienable right to govern ourselves, to develop our liberty and our institutions in accordance with our own national ideals, not subject to foreign domination?[29]

Defencists even talk of states having 'honour' and 'prestige' in the same way as individuals do. Indeed defencism is excessively state-centred according to pacific-ists, who, it will be seen, prefer to stress the importance for both domestic and international politics of other, 'transnational actors'.

It must be stressed, however, that none of defencism's domestic counterparts attempts to subordinate society to the state. Notwithstanding their attribution to the state of characteristics normally belonging to individuals, all three believe it to be only an agency or framework for moral action—albeit a unique one—rather than a moral being or source of value itself. They would thus agree with Michael Howard's observation that 'the state is a condition of ethical values: it provides the circumstances in which ethical activity may be carried on at all'.[30] Moreover, all three viewpoints are universalist rather than particularist. Even an 'authoritarian' conservative, while strongly attached to his own society, not only tolerates others but identifies in them many qualities common to his own, such as order, custom, and religion.

i. 'Authoritarian' conservatism

This is the view that society, domestic and international, will overcome its anarchical tendencies only with great effort and difficulty. Internally, it lays great stress on the need to maintain national strength and combat subversion even at the cost, if necessary, of restrictions on civil liberties. Internationally, it doubts whether stability can be achieved without major disruption to normal life. Just as authoritarian conservatives are more likely than mainstream conservatives to believe that domestic society can be made still less anarchical by a spot of reactionary social engineering, so they are more likely to espouse the crusade in an attempt to do the same for international society.

As suggested in chapter 3, Sir Oswald Mosley was an authoritarian conservative rather than a true fascist, despite his explicitly Nietzschean views. His international views, in consequence, always fell short of militarism. But, although he believed in the durability of the armed truce, he had so little belief in the strength of international society as to insist instead on international apartheid: he argued that the anarchical tendencies of the international system could be tamed only if states formed themselves into autarkic and heavily armed blocs which pursued separate development with the minimum of contact with each other. Before and indeed during the Second World War he insisted that Britain must recognize the existence of other 'leader Nations' who, like ourselves, had the natural duty to lead and to organize the more backward countries in their sphere of influence and thereby enrich not only themselves but the world by the production of fresh sources for civilization. If this natural leadership of other great Nations was denied by British interference, in regions where we had no concern, world explosion became inevitable.

After the war, when he abandoned fascism, he advocated a unitary European bloc, to be founded above all on Anglo-German partnership. Although he also preached a crusade against the Soviet Union, he came to accept the possibility of peace with the Russians if they directed their energies away from western interests: by 1950 his advice to NATO was thus to 'hold Europe, leave Asia'.[31]

The weakness from a more orthodoxly defencist perspective of this 'dissociative' approach to war prevention (as the pioneeer of peace studies, Johan Galtung, would classify it)[32] was that small states might not want to join blocs dominated by their powerful neighbours. If so, the creation of hierarchical blocs would itself necessitate aggressive war, for, although Britain had already created its own (imperial) bloc, other major states had yet to do so. Thus Mosley's German counterparts, such as Professor Carl Schmitt who urged that Germany proclaim its own counterpart to the Monroe doctrine, had to advocate aggression: indeed, Schmitt's *Raumtheorie* (theory of space) became an inspiration for Hitler's overtly militarist ideas of *Lebensraum*.[33]

If some authoritarian-conservative defencists thus overbalance into fascist militarism, others are closer to the mainstream. An example of a more moderate authoritarian conservative is Brian Crozier, whose views have already been cited. His defencism is of a fairly alarmist variety none the less: he has called for greater vigilance and a much expanded defence effort, has cited James Burnham with approval, and has even argued (in 1978) that 'the real Third World War has been fought and is being fought under our noses, and few people have noticed what was going on'.[34] Other examples could be found among the membership of the Committee on the Present Danger established in the United States in 1976.

ii. Conservatism

Mainstream defencism is conservative in the Tory sense of respect for the organic quality of society. Michael Howard, for example, has acknowledged that because he 'equate[s] peace with that unfashionable word "Order" ' he brands himself 'as a temperamental Tory rather than a temperamental Whig'.[35] Since society's organic quality is often taken to be an embodiment of religious values, conservatism as here defined is taken to include such variants as Christian democracy. Whereas authoritarian conservatives are more drawn to positivist arguments, mainstream conservatives are characterized by scepticism. Their intellectual affinities with defencism should by now have become sufficiently apparent not to require further elucidation.

iii. Social democracy

At the pacific-ist end of the defencist spectrum is social democracy. This term relates, first and most obviously, to the self-styled social-democratic parties of western Europe which (at least when in office) have been undoubtedly defencist, although for the most part only moderately so. They have thus accepted, if sometimes only grudgingly, that security above all requires military preparedness, while nevertheless allotting a greater role to diplomacy than conservatives do. As Helmut Schmidt put it in 1971, for example, it would be 'foolish to strive for *détente* while neglecting to provide for the military protection of one's own existence—and no less irresponsible to underestimate the risks inherent in a continuous and uncurbed arms race'. His conclusion was 'that peace tomorrow rests on perception of the need for equilibrium and . . . equally on heed for the interests of other countries and on the general will to bring about an equitable compromise'.[36] Moreover, Johan Galtung has recognized the strength of the social-democratic commitment to defencism, claiming even 'that it is easier to find alternative thinking about security matters among conservatives than social democrats'. But he has also acknowledged their pacific intent, writing emphatically that '*no social democratic government in Europe ever went to war as an aggressor*'.[37] (That, incidentally, is why there was no mention of social-democratic crusading in the previous chapter.) It must also be recognized that the Euromissile controversy of the 1980s and the passing into opposition of the West German SPD in 1982 have led most of western Europe's social-democratic parties (though emphatically not the British SDP) to move to the left and thus further towards pacific-ism.

The term social democrat can be applied, secondly, to moderate members of officially socialist parties such as the British Labour Party, and, thirdly, to 'étatists' among the New Liberals of Edwardian Britain and the New-Nationalist, New-Deal, and Great-Society strands of American Progressivism. This means that some of those here classified as social democrats have regarded themselves as socialists, radicals, or liberals. Because of this and the move to the left in western Europe just noted, it might be thought that social democracy is more appropriately linked with pacific-ism than with defencism. After all, not only does it take a relatively optimistic view of man's sociability, it is also interested in supra-nationalism: social democrats have been among the most enthusiastic supporters of the European Communities, for example.

But when social democracy is critical of the nation-state it is more on grounds of its domestic inefficiency than any threat it poses to peace: it is concerned to find the unit that best promotes welfare, and believes in the economies of scale offered by larger state-units. It was the social-democratic element in the thought of J. A. Hobson and H. N. Brailsford which led them to produce proposals for a League of Nations emphasizing the need for a federal body capable of tackling the world's social and economic problems, whereas pacific-ist blueprints for the League tended to envisage a confederal organization concerned first and foremost to curb aggression. And it was the social-democratic strain in the thinking of H. G. Wells, a Fabian as well as an early campaigner for a League of Nations, which accounts for his advocacy of the world state at a time when pacific-ists were as yet interested only in confederations.

What makes the social democrat a defencist is thus his étatism. Even though he is not so strongly committed to the traditional nation-state, and even though he envisages a more interventionist role for the state in domestic politics, he is at one with the conservative on the need to defend the nation-state as (in Michael Howard's words) 'still . . . the only mechanism by which the ordinary man and woman achieve some sense, however limited, of participation in, and responsibility for, the ordering of their own society and the conduct of the affairs of the world as a whole'.[38]

This étatism separates social democrats from pacific-ists. The latter refuse to regard the state as the only significant and constructive unit of international politics, and work instead to emphasize and increase the influence of 'transnational' ones. As the next chapter will show, the liberal, for example, may believe that each nation has a right to a state of its own; but he insists also that such a state should play a limited role in both domestic and international politics, and that it should be prepared if necessary to compromise or even sacrifice its sovereignty in order to permit confederal, federal, or even world-governmental institutions to assume a greater degree of the management of international society. Likewise the radical, to whom the social democrat is often closest on domestic issues, regards the state as inherently dominated by élites and vested interests and hopes that it can to the greatest extent possible be replaced by the rule of 'the people'. And the socialist believes that in the last resort the worker has no country, since the state is a tool of those controlling the economy.

The social democrat, in contrast, has often shown an intensely patriotic commitment to his own state, albeit not of a bellicose variety. This is easy to illustrate from modern British experience. Douglas Jay, for instance, a self-styled social democrat though remaining loyal to the Labour Party, fought doggedly against British membership of the European Communities, and concluded his memoirs by wondering:

What other country after all, has preserved an unbroken record of constitutional government for nearly 300 years, and fought right through two Great Wars, without attacking anyone else or being first attacked themselves, to eventual victory? In a morass of transient controversies let us not forget that. It is one reason why I can conceive of no better fortune, when the time comes to cultivate private rather than public aspirations, than to live, love, garden and die, deep in the English country.[39]

In the Falklands War, moreover, social democrats in both the Labour and Social Democratic parties were among the strongest supporters of Britain's decision to fight. Social democracy is thus a complex mixture of idealism and realism; but the latter has the upper hand. If not—as may be the case with many self-styled social-democratic parties of Europe in the mid-1980s—it is not true social democracy, as here defined, but (moderate) socialism. Even though firmly on its pacific-ist wing, social democracy is thus here regarded as an integral part of the defencist movement.

Defencism flourishes wherever defence is both necessary and likely to be effective. This excludes only the most secure and the most vulnerable or impotent of states, as will be seen in chapter 8. Even the superpowers are becoming more overtly defencist, as the previous chapter noted. Being so ubiquitous a theory, it has been taken for granted, receiving attention only when (as in the case of the challenge nuclear weapons pose to the just-war tradition which it shares with pacific-ism) it has run into intellectual difficulty. Compared with its ideological influence, its theoretical expositions have been few and fragmentary. In the sharp but not wholly unfair words of an advocate of non-violence: 'Human thought on defence is an extraordinary combination of science and mysticism, every question of detail being drawn into the sunlight of scientific investigation while foundation questions are allowed to remain in the shadows of nebulosity.'[40] Even the admirable writings of Michael Howard, cited frequently in this chapter, take the form of disparate essays rather than a unitary work of the kind he has devoted to pacific-ism. There is no shortage of material for such a work: it can be found in the speeches and writings of numerous twentieth-century figures, such as Charles de Gaulle, George Kennan, Henry Kissinger, and Walter Lippmann.

The career of Winston Churchill provides a particularly good example, since it shows that defencists need not be cynical in their approach to international relations. An emotional man for whom resistance to tyranny was a moral duty, Churchill briefly over-balanced into anti-communist crusading as a first response to the Bolshevik revolution; and throughout his career he remained convinced of the righteousness of his country's cause in two world wars and the cold war. Yet this did not prevent him analysing its predicament in geopolitical terms. He was one of the few members of the Asquith cabinet clearly to understand the strategic case for helping France; and two decades later he was the leading campaigner for the view that Britain must rearm so as to be able again to help France resist the threat posed by Hitler to the European order. (Admittedly, in the mid-1920s he had abruptly changed his mind and denied that Britain had vital interests in Europe; but this was a brief aberration at a time when, as chancellor of the exchequer, he was under pressure to restrict public expenditure; and he argued his new case on explicitly strategic grounds.)[41]

Churchill's defencism was most apparent when his moral preferences came into conflict with strategic reality. As prime minister when Germany broke its pact with the Soviet Union, Churchill subordinated his anti-communism to the characteristically geopolitical attitude that an enemy's enemy must be a friend, telling his private secretary: 'If Hitler invaded Hell, I would at least make a favourable reference to the Devil in the House of Commons.'[42] Visiting Moscow in October 1944, moreover, he concluded the famous 'percentages' agreement with Stalin, which conceded to the Soviet Union a sphere of influence covering in particular Romania, Bulgaria, and Hungary, in return for having Greece and Turkey recognized as lying within a British sphere.[43] The United States, it should be noted, was unenthusiastic about the deal. But Churchill was prepared to reconsider an agreement if, unlike the 'percentages' deal, it failed to reflect the realities of power. In the final months of the war he thus urged the United States, in order to improve its bargaining position, to retain or even seize territory already allocated to the Red Army in central and eastern Europe. The United States refused; and the Soviet Union gained a slightly larger occupation zone than, it seems, the military situation dictated. Yet, once it became clear that Stalin was determined to retain a tight hold over this zone, Churchill and his compatriots were in general readier than the United States to acknowledge that on power-political grounds nothing could be done. It was a tribute to their geopolitical understanding that they so calmly accepted that they were right both to have fought for Poland in 1939 and not to do so again in 1945.

As the cold war intensified, Churchill was unusually quick to recognize that the division of Europe would last: his 'iron curtain' speech at Fulton, Missouri on 5 March 1946, which made this point in memorable language, proved controversial in the United States. Despite his belief that the western sphere had to be strengthened militarily, he never lost his faith in diplomacy. In 1953 he was prepared to contemplate an agreement over Germany with Stalin's successors even though West Germany would thereby be lost to NATO. And the following year, while visiting the White House, he uttered what in simplified form was to become a famous phrase: 'Talking jaw to jaw is better than going to war.'[44] Churchill's thinking was thus remarkably consistent (apart from his emotive initial reaction to the Bolshevik revolution): he thought in geopolitical terms, and believed in the need both for strong defences and alliances and for rational bargaining with adversaries.

Defencism is by far the most popular war-and-peace theory because it seems both realistic and humane. It seems realistic because (unlike pacific-ism and pacifism) it recognizes the importance of the state, and takes account of the anarchic and power-political features of the international system. And it seems humane because (unlike militarism and crusading) it rejects aggression, and works for order, stability, and co-existence. It is a broad and apparently simple ideology, which manages to conceal many of its complexities and difficulties, and which offers a choice of perspectives ranging from near-militarist pessimism to near-pacific-ist optimism. Yet defencism tolerates a perpetual and ever more dangerous arms race. And it offers no inspiring vision of the foreseeable future. It has thus appeared sufficiently complacent and sterile to stimulate influential challenges, above all from the numerous varieties of pacific-ism.

6

Pacific-ism

As well as denouncing aggressive war, the peace movement rejects the defencist assumptions that strong defences are the best way to prevent war and that the abolition of war is impossible. A few of its members do so because they are pacifists, who believe that defensive force can immediately and entirely be dispensed with, and that the only way to abolish war is to persuade as many individuals as possible to refuse to take part in it. But most have always been, in the words of a writer on the recent American peace movement, 'peace-oriented non-pacifists [who] have considered warfare a conceivable, if distasteful possibility'.[1]

Like pacifists, the latter criticize defencists for exaggerating the extent to which peace and security are produced by military as distinct from political or diplomatic factors: in Britain, for example, the editors of a symposium on nuclear-free defence asserted in 1983 'that all countries' prospects of security rest ultimately not in military strength but in the justice of their relations with other countries, and of the relations between their own citizens'.[2] But, unlike pacifists, they accept that it will take time to phase the military component out altogether: this will follow, they believe, from the reform of political structures. It will be seen that, although many different reforms are proposed, all would reduce the role which states play in the international system and enhance that played by 'transnational' actors, as they are sometimes called, such as international organizations, ordinary people, the working class, ecological groups, and women.

Ever since the word 'pacificist' and its more common contraction 'pacifist' were almost totally taken over by pacifists in the strict sense understood here, the majority of the peace movement have lacked a generic term with which to describe themselves. 'Anti-militarist' is sometimes used; but in this study it would apply also to crusaders, defencists, and pacifists. 'Pacifier' is an ingenious recent suggestion,[3] but one which does not specify how the theory is to be described ('pacifying', perhaps, or 'pacificationism'?). The terms used here, 'pacific-ist' and 'pacific-ism', were originally suggested in 1957 in a casual footnote by A. J. P. Taylor, but not followed up by him. (When I started borrowing them he observed that they were terms 'which I gladly lend him'.)[4] 'Pacificism' was also briefly used in 1965 by the sociologist David A. Martin to distinguish 'the pacific doctrine', as he called it, from the pacifist one with which he was primarily concerned.[5] I adopted this usage systematically in 1980; and, as noted in chapter 2, it seems recently to have been gaining in acceptability.

It must be admitted, however, that the pacific-ism/pacifism distinction is etymologically artificial: 'pacificism' is really the correct form of the word now almost invariably contracted to 'pacifism'. Yet it is not wholly contrived, since when originally coined (soon after 1900), the word 'pacificism' connoted exactly what pacific-ism is here defined as meaning. As its meaning narrowed to absolute rejection of all war (which it more or less had done by the mid-1930s), so the original and correct form of the word dropped out of common usage. Since the 1930s, in consequence, there has been no word to describe non-pacifist peace sentiment. As early as July 1936, for example, the British prime minister, Stanley Baldwin, experienced this lack when telling a deputation of Conservative backbenchers of the 'very strong , I do not know about pacifist but pacific feeling in the country after the war' (which had, he claimed, hindered rearmament).[6] So, for all its inelegance, pacific-ism is here pressed into service again.

How old a theory is it? Plans for the abolition of war are presumably almost as old as war itself, as F. H. Hinsley has pointed out; and modern plans are often simply re-inventions of the wheel.[7] Yet pacific-ism cannot be said properly to have existed before two related developments took place. The first was a gradual and partial stabilization of the international system so that the bellicist view that war is inevitable did not seem so indisputably true. The second was the emergence of a domestic political process in some states, so that there was some prospect of mobilizing support for peace plans.

The late eighteenth century thus saw the origins of pacific-ism, and the mid-nineteenth its taking root. It was in the period from the 1730s to the 1760s that peace plans—which since medieval times had been backward-looking and had treated Europe as 'a fallen empire or a faded federation in need of reconstruction', in F. H. Hinsley's words, rather than as 'a collection of independent, if interlocked states'—began to take on a more modern form.[8] And, with both French *philosophes* and British political economists stressing the harmony of interests between states during the eighteenth century, it can be said that by its end, to quote Michael Howard, 'a complete liberal theory of international relations, of war and peace, had thus already developed'.[9] The Napoleonic Wars led during 1815–16 in the United States and Britain to the formation of the first peace societies (as distinct from pacifist religious sects) and also brought into being a recognizably modern international system. In these years, moreover, the combined impacts of the American, French and industrial revolutions were inaugurating modern politics within many states.

Pacific-ism thus presupposes a considerable measure of optimism regarding the prospects of domestic and international progress. It will be seen that its utopian fringe—believers in the immediate feasibility of world government, for example—require a very large measure indeed. But its mainstream needs this to be offset with a moderate dose of pessimism, since excessive optimism harms it in two ways. First, if the domestic and international outlook is too rosy then war will not be feared, and the abolition of war will not be a salient issue. Second, if those who even so become interested in this issue are too optimistic about the chances of success, they may opt for more extreme approaches such as pacifism of the optimistic variety or, in powerful states, crusading. On balance, therefore, pacific-ism flourishes where there is the right blend of optimism and pessimism.

It has been convenient so far to talk of pacific-ism as if it were a unitary viewpoint, albeit one with a utopian fringe as well as a mainstream. In fact, however, it is not only highly variegated—a set of theories, like crusading, rather than a single theory—but also at the margins notably inchoate. Thus before examining the five major forms it takes—those based on liberalism, radicalism, socialism, feminism, and ecologism—this chapter will explain why a number of popular positions are best not regarded as pacific-isms in their own right.

1. Marginal pacific-isms

The number of pacific-isms is in principle infinite since there is no limit to the number of reformable ills on which war can be blamed. Factors as diverse as psychological and sexual repression, the calendar, and diet ('The soldiers march/Because of starch') have at various times been singled out.[10] But to form the basis of a pacific-ism a factor must be an independent rather than a dependent variable: it must, that is, be a cause rather than a symptom. That is why three of the commonest 'theories' put forward by the rank and file of the peace movement can only with difficulty be recognized as such. These blame war on the failure to follow religious (and especially Christian) precepts, on the failure to disarm, and on the failure to practise 'conflict resolution'. It will be argued that religion is most commonly an inspiration for adopting one of the major pacific-isms which will shortly be discussed, rather than a pacific-ism in its own right, and that disarmament and conflict resolution are essentially policies rather than theories.

i. Religious pacific-ism?

A true religious pacific-ist, like a religious crusader, would assert that the spreading of his faith alone brings peace. This claim has indeed been made, in particular by followers of Islam, which 'unlike Christianity, sought to establish the Kingdom of Heaven on earth' (in the words of Majid Khadduri) and of which 'the ultimate goal . . . was the subordination of the whole world to one system of law and religion to be enforced by the supreme authority of the imam'. Once this had been achieved, peace would automatically follow: a *jihad*, even if ostensibly aggressive, was thus 'in theory . . . a temporary instrument to establish ultimate peace'.[11]

It is not unknown for Christians to imply, similarly, that their faith alone can bring peace. 'The present evils of the world are due to the failure of nations and peoples to carry out the laws of God', Britain's Christian leaders asserted in a joint letter to *The Times* on 21 December 1940. 'No permanent peace is possible in Europe unless the principles of the Christian religion are made the foundation of national policy and of all social life.' And, when Arab and Israeli representatives met in Washington during the 1948 war in the Middle East, Senator Warren Austin inquired of them: 'Why can't you Jews and Muslims settle this conflict in the true Christian spirit?'[12]

Yet in practice most Christians who have espoused pacific-ism have endorsed political viewpoints which non-believers also support: between the world wars, for example, the British churches supported the liberal pacific-ism of the League of Nations movement; since the late 1950s Christians have provided much of the leadership of a mainly secular anti-nuclear movement; and recently Christians active in the peace movement and other cause groups have been criticized by some of their more conservative co-religionists for 'whoring after strange ideologies'.[13] In other words, Christians who are pacific-ists do not seem to take a distinctively Christian-pacific-ist viewpoint. Indeed, in so far as there is a distinctively Christian (and non-pacifist) position, it is the just-war tradition; and this is not a theory in itself but a set of conditions which other theories—defencism, pacific-ism, and even crusading—must meet.

ii. 'Armaments cause war' pacific-ism?

One of the twentieth-century peace movement's commonest concerns has been 'the danger that the guns may suddenly go off, as it were', as G. H. Perris put it in 1912. Even the long-serving British foreign secretary, Sir Edward Grey, concluded after the First World War that 'great armaments lead inevitably to war'; and so widespread did this argument become in the 1920s and early 1930s that the staunchly defencist MP Leopold Amery was moved to complain at the end of a House of Commons debate in 1933: 'The whole of the discussion has been based on the entirely false premise that armaments are the cause of war . . . Wars are brought about by causes deeper than armaments.'[14]

Once Hitler's intentions became apparent, the armaments-cause-war thesis dropped out of the war-and-peace debate for almost two decades; but it returned with a vengeance when nuclear weapons became an issue in the second half of the 1950s, the emphasis now being on the possibility of an accidental war. In a famous *New Statesman* article on 2 November 1957 which helped to found

CND, the British novelist and playwright J. B. Priestley warned that

> as one ultimate weapon after another is added to the pile, the mental climate deteriorates, the atmosphere thickens, and the feeling is such that something may snap . . . Three glasses too many of vodka or bourbon-on-the-rocks, and the wrong button may be pushed.

Four years later, on 25 September 1961, President Kennedy proposed general and complete disarmament to the United Nations General Assembly on the grounds that everyone now lived 'under a nuclear sword of Damocles, hanging by the slenderest of threads, capable of being cut at any moment by accident or miscalculation or by madness'.

After the Cuba missile crisis and the partial test-ban treaty disarmament again faded from the public agenda—so much so that by the late 1960s it could even be asked: 'What has happened to disarmament?'[15] But it returned in the 1970s, first in response to the SALT process and then, more dramatically, in the wake of NATO's decision of December 1979 to deploy a new generation of Euromissiles (Cruise and Pershing 2) and the Soviet Union's invasion of Afghanistan later the same month. By 1981 even the American author of the containment doctrine, George F. Kennan, was warning that 'this competitive build-up of armaments conceived initially as a means to an end' had become an end in itself, 'taking possession of men's imagination and behaviour . . . and leading both parties invariably and inexorably to the war they no longer know how to avoid'.[16]

To argue that without armaments there would be either no war or merely harmless war is a truism, however. Even those who give disarmament a high priority regard it as complementary to other, more profound, strategies of war prevention: many, for example, would argue that effective disarmament requires so stringent a system of inspection as to presuppose a form of international government. Many active disarmers have become irritated with those who fail to take this point. For example, Salvador de Madariaga, who had been director of the disarmament section of the League of Nations Secretariat in Geneva, complained in 1929 of 'a certain type of fanatical pacifist who, by insisting on armaments as the sole cause of *all* wars, has brought discredit on the view that they can be the cause of some wars, and that they are in any case *one* of the causes of *all* wars'.[17] Thus, although such 'fanatics' believe that they have discovered a new form of pacific-ism, most participants in the war-and-peace debate regard disarmament as a policy—albeit a crucial one—rather than a theory.

It might be objected that those regarding armaments as a cause rather than a symptom of international conflict are for the most part really making a subtler claim: that it is either the arms *race* or *provocative* weapons (those that threaten, and therefore also invite, pre-emptive strike) which cause war. At best, they argue, arms races and provocative weapons generate tensions with which decision-makers may not be able to cope and which can therefore produce unintentional war. At worst, these factors encourage the development of hair-trigger deterrents which can be activated through computer failure and can produce accidental war.[18]

But the objection already made to the cruder version of the theory applies also to the subtler. While not denying the seriousness of these risks, most members of the peace movement regard the theories that 'arms races cause war' and that 'provocative weapons cause war' as confusing symptoms with causes. They point out that even accidents are neither wholly random nor wholly determined by technological factors: the decision to set up a hair-trigger defence system or to create a situation in which an adversary is likely to do the same is a deliberate one. It will thus be seen that radicals regard such decisions as a result of giving excessive power within a closed and largely undemocratic system of decision-making to defence bureaucrats and the armed forces.

iii. 'Conflict resolution prevents war' pacific-ism?

What has just been said applies also to the belief that the resolution of conflict and the creation of mechanisms for peaceful change hold the key to war prevention. Just as armaments are what wars are always fought with, so disagreements about the international system are usually what they are fought over. The peace movement has long been aware of the need, in Jonathan Schell's words, 'to create a political means by which the world can arrive at the decision that sovereign states previously arrived at through war'.[19] Defencists argue that this can be achieved only by a policy of appeasement, according to which the weaker side anticipates the verdict of a military clash and backs down in advance. But enthusiasts for conflict resolution imply that it can be used by statesmen to achieve 'positive' peace rather than the mere absence of war, if only they set their minds to tackling injustices—including the deep-rooted economic sources of conflict—before their judgement is clouded by crisis.

Such enthusiasts were comparatively numerous, of course, in the late 1930s. As the British pacifist and Labour MP Dr Alfred Salter told BBC radio listeners early in 1938: 'Peace will come from justice, from economic appeasement, and a sharing of the illimitable resources of the world.' A few months later, following a personal peace mission to Hitler, Mussolini and other European leaders, his better-known colleague and former party leader George Lansbury asserted:

It is certain that if all the statesmen I have met were to meet in the same friendly manner as I was met they would soon discover that being honest and straightforward with each other is the one and only way of averting war; that they must give up diplomacy and instead think and speak to each other as men.[20]

In Britain at least, 'peaceful change' replaced 'collective security' in 1937 as the peace movement's leading slogan, a number of academic studies appearing under this newly fashionable title.[21]

Growing fears of nuclear escalation have led since the late 1950s to renewed academic interest in this subject, now more normally called 'conflict resolution'.[22] The specialists in this field, like those who work on disarmament, do not believe that it can be a value-free science. Yet a popular belief in the achievability by conflict-resolution of an objectively fair international system is implied by statements such as that made in a letter to *The Times* on 7 April 1980: 'What we want for our children is a peace where all nations live in harmony together and have fair access to the world's raw materials, including energy', or that printed on a lapel-badge for sale at CND's north London bookshop in 1983: 'Peace means sharing.'

Despite such statements, however, it is likely that relatively few members of the peace movement have ever regarded peaceful change or conflict resolution as a theory rather than a policy. Most have subscribed to one of the major war-and-peace theories—such as pacifism in the case of Salter and Lansbury—and have at least implicitly accepted that their conception of justice is an ideological one from which those subscribing to different theories are likely to dissent.

2. The major pacific-isms

Since theories of war and peace are ideological, it is to be expected that the most coherent pacific-isms will be derived from the leading 'reforming' ideologies. Of the five to be discussed here, three—liberalism, radicalism, and socialism—have been influential enough to merit quite detailed discussion. The others—feminism and ecologism—will be treated more briefly, although both have been gaining in popularity of late.

i. Liberal pacific-ism

Liberalism was intellectually the most influential reforming ideology from the emergence of modern politics until well into the twentieth century. This is true both of states such as Britain with important Liberal parties and those like the United States, where there was no 'feudal' enemy to bring a self-styled Liberal movement into existence, but where, as a result, liberalism permeated the outlook of almost all parties. (No simple description of America's heterogeneous and pragmatic major parties can ever be wholly satisfactory; but it seems reasonable to describe the Republicans as liberals of a conservative tendency and the Democrats as liberals tinged with radical—and at times even social-democratic—ideas.) Where independent liberalism has clearly declined during the twentieth century, moreover, it has bequeathed some of its values to the parties taking its place.

Liberalism is here defined as the belief that the basic interests of human beings are in harmony with each other, which is why human individuality can be allowed free expression. Liberals are not anarchists, however: they accept that a state is necessary to enable a society to govern itself. Just as the growing pressures for intervention have caused difficulties for liberalism's traditionally *laissez-faire* approach to domestic politics, so in the war-and-peace debate they have forced it to retreat from a *laissez-faire* belief that states can live in peace if only they emancipate themselves from certain irrational practices and to move towards an acceptance of the permanent intervention by some supranational body—to such an extent, in fact, that liberalism has seemed to part company with its original assumptions. Four distinct phases of liberal pacific-ism can be identified: internationalism (down to 1914), confederalism (from 1914 to the 1940s), federalism (from the late 1930s to the 1950s), and transnationalism (since the 1960s).

(a) Internationalism. In its earliest and most negative form liberalism had much in common, as will shortly be seen, with radicalism: indeed, arguably the most influential pacific-ist of his time, Richard Cobden (1804–65), was influential in the development of both traditions. The liberal belief that feudalism was the major obstacle to political freedom in domestic politics and the source of the irrational jingoism which impeded peace between states was hard in practice to distinguish from the radical belief that aristocratic self-interest was the major obstacle to the pursuit of policies which were in the true interests of the people.

But whereas radicalism focused on the domestic power-structure, liberalism was concerned primarily with international reforms. For Continental liberals in the nineteenth century, the most important of these was to ensure that every nation had its own state (and, as already noted, some of them felt that this justified crusading). For their British and American contemporaries, the most hopeful international reform was the removal of tariffs—'an organized system of pillage of the many by the few', according to John Stuart Mill—in order that commerce could reveal itself to be, in Cobden's words, 'the grand panacea, which like a beneficent medical discovery, will serve to inoculate with the healthy and saving taste for civilization all the nations of the world'.[23]

Cobden had so much faith in the benefits of domestic reform and free trade that he rejected orthodox balance-of-power policies as well as the liberal-crusading rhetoric associated with Lord Palmerston: as already noted, he called for 'no foreign politics' and an absolute commitment to the principle of 'non-intervention'. Mill also believed in non-intervention as a general principle, although his recognition of a right of intervention to enforce this general principle was to be used, as already noted, to justify crusading.

Many 'internationalist' predictions came true, as was pointed out in 1912 by one of Cobden's British disciples, G. H. Perris:

Trade, travel and intellectual intercourse bring [states] constantly closer together. They copy each other's institutions; and, to strengthen their

common interests, they have built up a series of common institutions—
international unions to govern postal, railway and telegraphic com-
munication, conferences and conventions to regulate affairs both of
property (such as copyright) and labour; international law courts (at the
Hague and elsewhere) supported by a network of Arbitration and other
treaties; a sort of World-Duma, in the periodical Peace Conferences at the
Hague; and last but not least, the growing international organization of the
Labour and Socialist movements. That is one picture: national peace and
the beginning of a Union of nations; in a rudimentary form, the United
States of Europe is an accomplished fact.

Yet, as Perris recognized, other predictions had failed; and 'bitter
mutual suspicion and even hostility' persisted between certain
states.[24] Since the peak of early Victorian optimism in which
internationalism had found fertile soil, particularly in Britain and
the United States but also among the nascent liberal movements of
Europe, new tensions—nationalist, industrial, and imperial—had
emerged which worked in opposition to the integrating factors he
had identified. It could no longer be believed that commerce, plus
certain domestic reforms, would be enough. As a result, greater
stress began to be laid on improving the capacity of international
law to resolve conflicts between states. The American peace
movement was particularly keen on arbitration treaties and attached
great significance to the Hague conferences of 1899 and 1907,
although the second of these proved a considerable disappointment.[25] What is striking, however, is that before 1914 so
very little thought was given to the enforcement of international
agreements.

(b) Confederalism. The shock of the First World War almost
instantaneously converted liberals to the view that a confederal
institution was needed for the management of international
relations. They did not use this term 'confederal', however; and in
many cases they also failed to understand that the 'league of nations'
to which all were committed could have very different approaches
to the provision of security for its members. At one extreme, it could
aspire only to impose a cooling-off period on its members. At the
other, it could attempt to defend the status quo by means of its own
international police force. It was thus inevitable that the League of
Nations eventually set up in 1920 would dissatisfy a number of
liberals.

In the event, however, it dissatisfied a very large number indeed because of its association with the territorial settlement embodied in the unpopular Treaty of Versailles. Some liberals—particularly in the United States, which stayed out of the League—called for its reform. Others—particularly in Britain—felt that such doubts had to be concealed in an attempt to make the League work. But well before the outbreak of the Second World War it was evident to all that this was impossible: those continuing after 1936 to support 'collective security through the League of Nations' were in effect advocating the pre-1914 policy of rearmament and alliances directed against Germany that the League had been intended to supersede. After the war, moreover, it was soon apparent that the confederal organization which replaced it, the United Nations, was not going to fare any better. A few former League supporters managed to convince themselves that NATO was itself a development of the liberal tradition: even Philip (later Lord) Noel-Baker argued in 1949 that 'the Atlantic Pact is a measure of collective security . . . not an old Power politics alliance against Russia' and that it would 'help us abolish all war'.[26] But most had already come to the conclusion that it was federalism alone which was, in C. E. M. Joad's words of 1940, 'the logical development of the liberal tradition'.[27]

(c) Federalism. The third and most drastic version of liberal pacific-ism, which flourished from the very end of the 1930s to the beginning of the 1950s, argues that the only way to control the irrational forces of nationalism is wholly to remove from each state the control of its foreign—though not its domestic—policy, and hand it to a democratically elected federal government.

Federalism can be criticized on theoretical and practical grounds. The theoretical objection is that it appears to contradict the basic liberal assumption about the international system: that it is, if only latently, harmonious. If so fundamental a reform as the abolition of every state's external sovereignty is required, as federalists claim, does it make sense to describe the international system as in any sense harmonious? The practical objection is that, in view of the fact that confederal bodies such as the League of Nations and the United Nations have failed because their successful operation makes excessive demands on the sovereignty of states, federalism stands little chance of ever being implemented. As *United Nations News* inquired in September 1947: 'What conceivable reason is there for daring to suggest that the forces which were working against the United Nations (admittedly with disastrous effect) will suddenly disappear when confronted with something infinitely more offensive to them?'

Yet in the early 1940s the international system seemed fluid enough for suggestions of this sort not to appear utopian. And in the second half of the decade it was possible for a while to believe that the atomic bomb would so increase the fear of war as to make a real world organization practicable. 'Therein lies our hope', wrote Reinhold Niebuhr just a fortnight after the destruction of Hiroshima.[28]

By the early 1950s it had become apparent that the international system was not going to be reformed; and by the middle of the decade the federalist movement was visibly in decline. Some 'functionalists' continued to assert that federation could be achieved gradually through an extension of technical co-operation; some 'Europeans' hoped that a regional economic community could evolve from a squabbling autarkic bloc into a United States of Europe; and a few utopians have remained loyal to the full federalist case. Yet by 1974 Wolf Mendl could uncontroversially tell his fellow Quakers that the 'heyday' of this tradition was over: 'International organization is no longer seen as a straight path to world government.'[29]

(d) Transnationalism. It seemed for a time in the 1970s that academic theorists of 'transnationalism' and 'interdependence' were returning to a Cobdenite analysis of the international system, in reaction to the dominant realist school. It soon became clear, however, that they did so without the same optimism: most, like Robert O. Keohane and Joseph S. Nye, were careful to stress that they were very 'cautious about the prospect that rising interdependence is creating a brave new world of cooperation to replace the bad old world of international conflict'.[30] And in the 1980s it has been a striking feature of anti-nuclear propaganda how few thinkers have concluded that it is necessary to abolish the nation-state.[31] It seems that, after more than a century as the dominant strand of peace-movement thought, liberal pacific-ism has shot its bolt.

ii. Radical pacific-ism

Second only to liberalism as a historically important source of pacific-ism, and surpassing it in the nuclear era, is radicalism. It was radical pacific-ism which Michael Howard was describing when in 1983 he criticized

those leaders of the Peace Movement who believe, as have their predecessors for two hundred years, that the problems of power in international relations would not exist if it were not for the vested interests of the governing classes that created them; that weapons-systems are not created to serve real security needs but only to gratify the interests of 'militarists' and their industrial backers; and that popular pressure can sweep away the whole tangled web of international rivalries and suspicions like so many cobwebs left over from the past.[32]

Howard did not use the term 'radicalism', however; and not only is this (or any other) label rarely employed, the viewpoint he was describing is rarely recognized as a distinct theory. It is often regarded instead as merely a hybrid of liberalism and socialism which combines the former's attack on the power of the feudal élite with the latter's view that capitalism too generates a harmful élite. On closer inspection, however, this is an oversimplification: radicalism does not put its main trust in liberal panaceas for the ills of the international system; nor does it share socialism's hostility to capitalism or 'bourgeois democracy'. It differs also, as already noted, from another centre-left ideology, social democracy: radicals are sceptical about the latter's étatism because they believe that any state tends to be dominated by an 'establishment'—a classically radical concept—which is likely to be at best blinkered and self-serving and at worst corrupted by anti-social interests such as the 'military-industrial complex'—a term popularized by radicals, though not invented by them. Before analysing the pacific-ism to which it gives rise, it is thus necessary to say a few words about radicalism as an ideology.

(a) Radical ideology. This is best described as an anti-authoritarian form of populism, and has four main distinguishing features. The first is its belief in popular rule as an all-purpose panacea, on the assumption that only the common people have the sense and decency instinctively to see the truth and prescribe the remedy. As the historian D. C. Watt has pointed out, it is the concept of the

people as 'dumb, inarticulate, managed by the self-promoted élites who govern them, at once innocent, positively good, primevally naïve' which forms the stock in trade of the 'radical tradition', although he makes the telling point that this 'tradition is usually voiced not by the people themselves but by the *déraciné*, alienated intellectuals at the fringes of the ruling élites'.[33]

Its second assumption is that all élites are blinkered and corrupt. As the radical MP (and courtier's son) Arthur Ponsonby put it in 1915, with the British Foreign Office in mind: 'A small number of men, associating with others of their own class, and carrying on their intercourse in whispers, cannot fail to have a distorted perspective, a narrow vision and a false sense of proportion.' According to the successful British writer J. B. Priestley in 1957, the category of 'sensible men and women . . . excludes most of those in the *V.I.P.-Highest-Priority-Top-People Class*, men so conditioned now by this atmosphere of power politics, intrigue, secrecy, insane convention, that they are more than half-barmy.' And in the more recent and blunter words of the radical American journalist I. F. Stone: 'Every government is run by liars, and nothing they say should be believed.'[34]

A third characteristic is that, whereas most reforming ideologies are theories of progress, radicalism as often looks backwards as forwards: it believes that the popular rule for which it strives once existed in a golden age before political and social corruption permitted the élites to bring it to an end. British radicals, for example, long looked back to alleged Anglo-Saxon freedoms which had been lost under the Norman yoke since 1066. And the French Radical Party announced in the summons to its founding conference in 1901: 'The deliberations will not be concerned with the establishment of a new programme. Our programme is known. It was fixed by our fathers.'[35] Where the golden age is kept in being or restored, radicals can thus be more conservative in domestic policy and patriotic in foreign policy than is usual for reformers. 'Patriotism, a *culte de la patrie*, is a basic Radical principle . . .', a historian of the French Radical Party has observed. 'Radicals have been especially insistent in claiming that their party "represents more than any other the profound instinct of the Nation, its vital instinct" and in stressing the "certain identity of radicalism and French continuity".'[36] Indeed, of all the pacific-ist ideologies, radicalism has the strongest element of particularism: while in principle believing in 'the people' everywhere it often dwells on the particular merits of those in its own state; and although certain of its policies have a universal currency (such as its attack on arms traders as a war-fomenting vested interest), its political practice tends to differ markedly from state to state.

A fourth feature of radicalism is its spontaneity. It is more a dissenting cast of mind than a fully elaborated system of ideas; and its dislike of institutional structures causes it to prefer loosely structured single-issue campaigns to permanent organizations. Distinctively radical parties were a temporary phenomenon of the late nineteenth and early twentieth centuries. The radical movements in both Belgium and the Netherlands set up distinctive organizations in the late 1880s, although these had collapsed by the end of the next decade.[37] A short-lived Populist Party was active in the United States during the early 1890s, although it was an explicitly agrarian protest against the powerful interests generated by industrialization and gave no indication of the true strength of American radicalism, which had become an influential part of the dominant political culture. In late-Victorian and Edwardian Britain there was a self-styled radical wing within the Liberal Party. And in France, where (unlike the United States) fear of political counter-revolution died hard, a major Radical party was formed which from 1902 to 1936 was the largest and most influential in national politics.

Radicalism has often flourished in combination with other ideologies inside other parties. At first it tended to attach itself to liberalism. In France, where the latter was relatively weak and failed to sustain a separate party of its own, the Radicals were free to make use of the liberal rhetoric of progress, even though this jarred with their instinctive conservatism. The same was true in the United States, where, thanks to the efforts of Woodrow Wilson in 1912 and 1916, Populist radicalism and Progressive liberalism were fused into a single ideology, which, though primarily associated with the Democratic Party in domestic politics, 'has become the dominant tradition' (to quote D. C. Watt) in American thinking about international relations.[38]

It is increasingly common for radicalism to combine with socialism. Right from its foundation in 1900 the British Labour

Party was more radical than socialist, particularly in its foreign policy: Clement Attlee acknowledged that on the latter issue it initially 'shared the views which were traditional in radical circles'.[39] Although the party officially espoused socialism in 1918, it recruited more radicals during the 1920s as the Liberals declined; and its socialism took on a distinctively radical hue. Indeed one of Labour's most prolific theorists, G. D. H. Cole, not only described himself as 'a radical individualist as well as a socialist' but insisted that Labour's socialism depended on its radicalism.[40] It is notable that many leaders of the Labour left have leavened their socialism with a strain of traditional radicalism. This was true of Aneurin Bevan, whom Harold Macmillan privately described in June 1957 as 'by nature a Radical rather than a Socialist . . . who 50 years ago would have been Lib./Lab.—anti-church, anti-landlord, anti-Royalty and anti-military';[41] true also of Bevan's disciple Michael Foot, son of a radical Liberal MP and himself a Liberal while at Oxford, and of Tony Benn, a socialist proud of his radical ancestry.[42]

Even Britain's Trotskyist ultra-left has at times shown similar traces of radicalism; these can clearly be detected, for example, in the answer given in 1983 by David Widgery of the Socialist Workers' Party to the question whether defence of national territory was ever a legitimate goal:

The awful upper-class England of warm gin and tonics in the Members' Enclosure and Advance Commodity Speculators and Harley St face-lifts has got to go. But I'd defend the vulgar, eccentric and unruly country of John Ball's Kent and Wat Tyler's Maidstone and Tom Paine's Norfolk because those values travel beyond frontier and through history. I'd fight for the Cap of Liberty, the Charter, the Suffragettes and the Slough Soviet (and their equivalents in every language and climate of the globe).[43]

When radicalism is thus blended with socialism, élites and vested interests tend to be seen not as autonomous actors but as expressions of capitalism. By the same token, when it is blended with either ecological (that is, 'green') or feminist thinking, as it has been in the contemporary western-European peace movement, these can be seen to be expressions of industrial or patriarchal power.

(b) Radical views on war and peace. Now that radicalism has been expounded as an ideology, it is possible to examine its contribution to the war-and-peace debate. Because of the variation between states

which has already been noted, it is easiest to do this with reference to just one: Britain.

The radical-pacific-ist slogan of early twentieth-century Britain was 'democratic control'—enabling the will of the people (or at least of Parliament) to prevail over secretive diplomats, arms traders, the jingo press, imperialists, financiers and so on. Like liberals, radicals were disappointed at the failure of states to become more pacific as they became more influenced by capitalism and the bourgeoisie. But, instead of looking to improvements in international law, radicals persisted with their populist critique, arguing that capitalism and middle-class rule had generated their own élites, over which popular control had yet to be asserted. A leading radical theorist, J. A. Hobson, exonerated Cobden and his generation for failing to 'foresee how . . . the rush for lucrative investments overseas was destined to stimulate fierce conflicts between strong business groups capable of being transferred first into diplomatic, and afterwards, in extreme cases, into military and naval struggles'. Turn-of-the-century radicals saw themselves not as rejecting Cobden's ideas but as bringing them up to date—'because we have sixty more years history behind us', as L. T. Hobhouse, an admirer like Hobson, loyally put it. Their new synthesis was summed up early in 1914 by H. N. Brailsford: 'Let us admit at once that war is a folly from the standpoint of national self-interest; it may nonetheless be perfectly rational from the standpoint of a small but powerful governing class.'[44] Like other radicals influenced by socialism, Brailsford (who had joined the ILP in 1907) tended to perceive and indict a homogeneous 'governing class'. Those whose radicalism was purer pinned the blame more narrowly on particular individuals and groups acting autonomously. But both advocated the same policy (although for socialists it was only an interim one): to bring the selfishly bellicose under democratic control. Hence the name of the first peace society to be established in the First World War: the Union of Democratic Control. It catered above all for radical pacific-ists (for many of whom it proved an important staging-post on their journey from Liberalism to Labour), and supplied ideas both to President Woodrow Wilson, for his attack on secret diplomacy, and to the Russian Bolsheviks. The latter produced the purest expression of the radical assumption that diplomacy was unnecessary—Leon Trotsky's celebrated comment after becoming Commissar for Foreign Relations: 'All there is to do is publish the secret treaties. Then I will close the shop.'[45]

The tacit assumption about international relations made by the democratic-control movement was that Britain could and should opt unilaterally out of war. This was on not pacifist but neutralist grounds, of course, as the belated formation by radicals of a self-styled neutrality movement in the last days before British entry into the First World War was to show. By opting for a domestic explanation for the increased world tensions of the late nineteenth and early twentieth centuries, and ignoring the international reforms favoured by liberals, radicals had committed themselves to a strongly isolationist posture and often seemed as much concerned with improving the quality of public life at home as with improving the quality of international relations.

Between the two world wars, however, this posture became harder to sustain. Britain was committed to enforcing the European order which it had helped to lay down in the Versailles Treaty; and air power made the country unprecedentedly vulnerable to attack from the Continent. Since Britain would find it even harder to stay out of such a conflict than it had done in 1914, its radical pacific-ists were thus compelled for the first time to formulate a policy that would forestall a new European conflict. Since they pinned fewer hopes than liberals did on the League of Nations, they chose to call for the revision of the Versailles Treaty and for the appeasement of Germany—a policy also advocated by certain pacifists, socialists, liberals, defencists, and even militarists, but adopted earliest and most enthusiastically by the Union of Democratic Control. In doing so, it implicitly viewed the Versailles Treaty as another instance of incompetent secret diplomacy, and extended its analysis of the deficiences of Britain's policy-making élite to include that of France.

Since the Second World War British radical pacific-ism has been preoccupied with the cause of nuclear disarmament. Although, as in the case of appeasement, it has enjoyed no monopoly of this policy, radicalism has contributed more to anti-nuclear campaigning than has any other theory. In his celebrated *New Statesman* article which has already been mentioned as helping to launch CND, J. B. Priestley wondered:

Why should it be assumed that the men who create and control such monstrous devices *are* in their right minds? They live in an unhealthy mental climate, an atmosphere dangerous to sanity. They are responsible to no large body of ordinary sensible men and women, who pay for these weapons without ever having ordered them, who have never been asked anywhere yet if they wanted them. When and where have these preparations for nuclear war ever been put to the test of public opinion? The whole proceedings take place in the stifling secrecy of an expensive lunatic asylum.

And he appeared to imply—which is again reminiscent of pre-1914 radicals—that the implementation of his desired reform, in this case unilateral nuclear disarmament, would also rescue British public life from 'sour, cheap cynicism'. Similarly, Canon John Collins, though moved in part by a moral rejection of violence which had at times in his life brought him close to pacifism, was to a large extent sustained throughout four arduous years as CND's chairman by dislike of 'the Establishment' and a conviction that politicians 'do not hesitate to deceive the people. Under the intimidating influence of their military and security advisers, governments are particularly prone to this habit when questions of defence are at issue.'[46] For his part, A. J. P. Taylor, historian of the radical tradition of dissent from British foreign policy and himself an archetypal radical, found his greatest political fulfilment as a leading CND orator from 1958 to 1961.

Another distinguished historian of British radicalism, E. P. Thompson, has played a similar or greater role in CND's second coming (post-1980) and in the founding of a complementary campaign for European Nuclear Disarmament (END). Having recently distanced himself indisputably from his former Marxism, Thompson can clearly be identified as a radical. For example, his response to the calling of the June 1983 General Election was to issue a pamphlet, 'Published for the Defence of the Common People of this Nation' and incorporating a reference to Thomas Paine, explaining that his reason for doing so was anger at the power of authority and vested interests:

The democracy of Britain finds itself once more, as it has done so often in the past, with a whole set of rules and laws like locked doors between it and full access to the democratic process, and with money like water-hoses playing with full force against its face. And CND finds itself, as George Cruickshank's 'Freeborn Englishman' found himself in 1820, with a padlock through its mouth.[47]

Such a critique has not been confined to the movement's public figures. For example, the main preoccupation of *Living On The Front Line*, a booklet produced in 1981 by CND's local branch in Aberdeen, was 'the threats to democracy embodied in the steps already taken to ensure that the state survives the people'; and it concluded: 'Not only are the public excluded from Home Defence, "Home Defence" is itself a threat to democracy. Who is defending whom?'[48] But when so senior and distinguished a former government scientific adviser as Lord Zuckerman could argue that defence scientists ('the alchemists of our times, working in secret ways that cannot be divulged, casting spells which embrace us all')[49] were fomenting the arms race, it was scarcely surprising that the radical critique was commonly heard. Indeed the evident influence on the superpowers' weapons-procurement decisions of politically unaccountable scientists, military experts, defence bureaucrats, and arms manufacturers, and the near absence for many years of public discussion of the topic could have been tailor-made for it.

It is on the issue of nuclear weapons, moreover, that the radicalism of many of Britain's socialist politicians has been most pronounced. Tony Benn is a good illustration: during Labour's 1957 conference debate on nuclear disarmament he invoked the rhetoric of democratic control, warning of the need 'to re-establish the supremacy of Parliament . . . We are drifting towards disaster because we have not yet asserted popular control over the hydrogen bomb'; at the public launching of END in April 1980 he claimed: 'The *real danger* of nuclear weapons is that in the guise of defending people against a foreign threat, they place control of political action in the hands of the domestic military establishments'; and a year later he told an interviewer that he had become a unilateralist because 'if a country has nuclear weapons it destroys parliamentary democracy by having them'.[50]

From diplomats to defence bureaucrats, arms traders to the military-industrial complex, there is thus a sufficiently clear line of continuity running through the campaigns of the British peace movement for radical pacific-ism to be recognized as a highly influential, if somewhat negative, theory of war and peace.

iii. Socialist pacific-ism

Socialism is defined for the purposes of this study as the belief that capitalism is now the primary source of social evil, including war. (In former days the source was feudalism, a more primitive manifestation of class rule, capitalism then being a relatively progressive force.) All socialists thus believe that lasting peace is possible only after either evolution or revolution has brought socialism to the world. It is probable that the proportion of pacific-ists is smaller among socialists than among adherents of other reforming ideologies: this is because socialism has not only a crusading minority, as already noted, but a pacifist minority too, as the next chapter will show. Even so, the vast majority have always taken the pacific-ist view that a socialist world must be created by constitutional means.

The focus of socialist pacific-ism has from the start been on what all but the most optimistic of these have admitted to be a far-off goal: a socialist world. In this it differs from the liberal variety, which initially believed moderate reforms (internationalism) would abolish war and came only gradually to realize that profound changes (federalism) were in fact needed. It differs also from radicalism, which is vague about long-term goals and usually content to think about its campaign of the moment. As a result, socialist pacific-ists have always had to concentrate their efforts on devising an interim policy that would frustrate capitalism's aggressive drives while they wait for its distant demise. But, socialism being primarily a remedy for domestic problems, they have experienced considerable difficulty in formulating—let alone implementing—policies that are both practical and distinctively socialist. Yet the belief in 'a socialist foreign policy', dies hard on the left and has so far produced at least five interim policies: socialist patriotism, war resistance, the people's front, socialist internationalism, and positive neutralism.

(a) *Socialist patriotism.* The first is the policy of identifying the interests of international socialism with the defence of a particular state or group of states. In most cases, of course, it is simply the expression in socialist-pacific-ist terminology of a policy which is really derived from a defencist analysis. Socialist patriotism was invoked most persuasively after the establishment of the Soviet Union, since it could plausibly be claimed that the defence of the first 'workers' state' was a truly socialist activity. But it had originally been invoked in respect of non-socialist states. During the Wilhelmine era German socialists were urged to defend their homeland on the grounds that it 'belongs to us the masses as much and more than to the others', as August Bebel argued in 1891. In capitalist states, however, it has always been unclear how socialist patriotism differs from an act of defencism. In three circumstances, however, a case can be made for regarding them as distinct. The first is when the likely national enemy is ideologically reactionary: Bebel's case was thus based on the duty of socialists to resist 'Russia, the champion of terror and barbarism'.[51] The second is when the homeland to be defended can be represented, though capitalist, as of special ideological merit none the less: when on 29 July 1914, for example, the French socialist Gustav Hervé abandoned his plans for war resistance it was, he insisted, because 'international socialists like us know only one duty: to defend the birthplace of liberty . . . Long live republican and socialist France!'[52]

The third circumstance in which socialist patriotism can be distinguished from a policy inspired by defencism is one in which the professional standing army has been replaced by a popular militia. The latter would constitute 'an essential guarantee for the prevention of aggressive wars, and for facilitating the removal of differences between nations', according to a resolution passed at the Second International's Stuttgart conference in 1907. The socialist case for a popular militia was developed most memorably in a book by the French socialist Jean Jaurès, *L'Armée nouvelle*, published in 1910; and it also received support at this time from the idiosyncratic British Marxist H. M. Hyndman, and the Australian advocate of universal military training (and future prime minister) Billy Hughes. In general, however, English-speaking socialists condemned it, so strong was their belief that any form of conscription was 'militarist'. Indeed, the first English translation of *L'Armée nouvelle* was brought out during the First World War as part of a personal campaign against the peace movement by the irascible Cambridge historian G. G. Coulton.[53] In the event, the anti-war reaction after the First World War discredited both socialist patriotism in general and the popular militia in particular. The Spanish Civil War revived some interest in the latter—its virtues were extolled, for example, by Tom Wintringham, a Marxist who had commanded the British battalion of the International Brigade and later trained Home Guard units during the Second World War[54]—as did the exploits of Mao and Che Guevara; but it was not until the 1980s, when it could be represented as a constructive piece of alternative-defence thinking, that a significant number of western socialists again began to see some socialist merit in the idea.[55]

(b) War resistance. This policy assumes that even supposedly defensive wars are really fought for capitalist objectives and that the workers are cynically used as cannon fodder. Any attempt by a capitalist government to go to war should be resisted, therefore, if necessary by a general strike. This idea was first discussed at meetings of the Second International in the 1890s, but did not receive serious attention until the years before 1914, when it was strongly supported by veteran British socialist Keir Hardie and by the syndicalist element within French socialism. Yet no war-resistance agreement was ever in sight, mainly because of the hostility of the German SPD. And, when the First World War broke out, either socialist patriotism prevailed among the left in all belligerent countries (with the insignificant exception of the United States)[56] or there was a mass conversion to defencism. From 1914 onwards those advocating war resistance knew that such a policy would in future most likely have to be practised unilaterally rather than multilaterally.

Just as socialist patriotism is easy to confuse with a defencist policy, so war resistance is easy to confuse with a pacifist policy. (This is especially true when the pacifism is itself deduced from socialist principles, as will be seen in the next chapter.) Of course, to the discerning socialist, whether pacifist or pacific-ist, there are notable differences between the two positions.[57] War resistance is purely a tactic (its sole justification being its political effectiveness), whereas pacifism is a theory (its central proposition being that one should abstain from war whatever the practical consequences of so doing). And war resistance is itself a form of coercion, whereas pacifism preaches reconciliation. Yet since both involve an if necessary unilateral refusal to fight, they have frequently and understandably been confused by the socialist rank and file.

During the 1920s and first half of the 1930s, in particular, many socialists believed that war resistance was, with hindsight, the correct policy to have followed in 1914 (on the grounds that the First World War proved to be an imperialist war). They tended to assume that this made them actual pacifists. As a result, socialist pacific-ists were slower than they might otherwise have been to realize that they would not necessarily resist all wars: as soon as socialism took control of a state, they would—however reluctantly— need to defend it. The establishment in 1917 of the Bolshevik regime in Russia should have made clear straight away that socialist patriotism was more than ever a possibility; but it had surprisingly little impact. In the 1920s and early 1930s, the French left, reacting against its socialist-patriotic participation in the 'Union sacrée' of the First World War, became strongly committed to war resistance; and in Britain the Labour Party, though normally favouring the liberal-pacific-ist policy of supporting the League of Nations, endorsed war resistance in intermittent moods of political aliena- tion, such as those experienced at the times of its conferences of 1920, 1922, 1926, and 1933.

For a minority of socialists the commitment to war resistance was so strong that it long survived the advent of Hitler. This was particularly true in France; and in the United States the Socialist Party was so committed that even after the attack on Pearl Harbor it was unable to offer more than 'critical support' for the war effort. In Britain, George Orwell, who had fought against fascism in Spain, believed until late in August 1939 that for Britain and France to fight Germany would be a merely imperialist act; and his party, the Independent Labour Party (ILP), continued to preach war resistance throughout the Second World War, being joined for the duration of the Nazi–Soviet pact by the communists.

But Hitler forced most socialists who had embraced war resistance to rethink their position, even if this proved in some cases a painful process. In France, the Communist Party abandoned war resistance in 1935, the year of the Franco-Soviet agreement; and in the same year the British Labour Party advocated military sanctions against Italy for invading Abyssinia. But it was Franco's rebellion against Spain's popular-front government in 1936 which proved the most decisive watershed in socialist attitudes to war: it greatly reduced the confusion between socialist pacifism and socialist pacific-ism by almost entirely destroying the former and severely undermining the latter's belief in war resistance. Yet, though recognizing the need for a new interim policy to replace war resistance, most socialists were anxious to make clear that they had not simply reverted to socialist patriotism.

(c) The people's front. The policy they adopted instead was half-way between war resistance and socialist patriotism. It has no generally agreed name; but since it was associated with the popular front in domestic politics which communists and left-wing socialists called for after 1935, it is here called the 'people's front'. It accepts that 'people's wars' exist, but unlike socialist patriotism refuses to support the capitalist defence effort unconditionally. This policy explains the refusal of the British Labour Party to vote for the government's arms estimates (though in 1937 it switched from outright opposition to mere abstention). It also explains the party's somewhat half-hearted support for the Second World War at its outbreak, when it declined to join the government and when one of its leading intellectuals, Professor Harold Laski, favoured mediation by President Roosevelt: not until the 'phoney war' ended did Labour enter the government and most socialists endorse socialist patriotism. It was only in June 1940 that Laski was converted to the view that 'the objective facts of the situation make a victory over Hitler a victory for socialism'.[58]

A people's-front policy differs, too, from the collective security favoured by liberals: the principle which distinguishes it from defencism is not confederalism but anti-fascism. In the late 1930s advocates of the people's front thus argued that the participation of the Soviet Union was crucial and that there was a qualitative difference between the progressive capitalism of Britain and France and the fascist capitalism of Germany and Italy. For a time, however, some socialists—notably Sir Stafford Cripps—insisted that an anti-German alliance including Britain would become a true people's front only when a Labour government came to power; until this occurred, they argued, it was necessary for socialists to remain war resisters. Yet eventually most of them came to the conclusion which Kingsley Martin, editor of Britain's leading socialist weekly, the *New Statesman*, had arrived at by March 1938. In that month he admitted privately to Cripps that, whereas he had 'always tried to make a distinction between a war we ought to risk which would be genuinely in the interests of socialism in Spain, and a war for the British Empire' it had now become 'obvious that they would be the same thing'; and, though finding this 'an almost intolerable position to take up', he saw no alternative but to drop his opposition 'to war because it was capitalist'.[59]

(d) Socialist internationalism. The defeat of fascism, the emergence of the Soviet Union as a superpower, and the political progress made by the left in western Europe's first post-war elections: all raised for a time the prospect that there would be a sufficient number of socialist states for the most satisfactory interim strategy of all to be put into effect: socialist internationalism. This assumes that socialist governments can have a major influence on international relations if they work harmoniously together and receive the support of those socialist movements which do not yet enjoy office. The socialist-internationalist slogan of 1945 was: 'Left understands Left; but Right does not'—a phrase used by British foreign secretary Ernest Bevin at the 1945 Labour Party conference with particular reference to Anglo-French co-operation, but on other occasions with reference to British relations with the Soviet Union.[60]

These hopes proved premature, however. In western Europe the democratic-socialist cause not only failed to make progress but suffered a major setback with the collapse of left-wing unity in France and Italy in May 1947. And in eastern Europe the Soviet Union discredited socialist internationalism by using its rhetoric to justify its creating for strategic reasons a sphere of influence. Even as rhetoric, moreover, socialist internationalism was later to be further tarnished after the late 1950s by the growing Sino–Soviet rift and after 1979 by the outbreak of wars between Marxist-Leninist states (North Vietnam fighting both China and Kampuchea).

In the west most socialists reverted to socialist patriotism following the Czech coup of February 1948 and the Berlin blockade of June 1948 to May 1949. In Britain, for example, Labour back-bencher Richard Crossman, leading light of the 'Keep Left' group of protesters against Bevin's foreign policy during 1946–7, not only endorsed the North Atlantic Treaty in 1949 but came to insist in the early 1950s that 'we must not think it is un-Socialist to be strong or that the Socialist thing to do is to "abolish power politics" '.[61]

(e) Positive neutralism. The final and most tentative interim strategy is positive neutralism: this differs from negative neutralism in aspiring not merely to opt out of the cold war but also to bring it to an end. The idea of Europe's democratic socialists and progressives constituting a 'third force' to mediate between the American and Soviet blocs had a strong appeal in the period around

1947—after Soviet intransigence had already ruled out a full policy of socialist internationalism, that is, but before the left had resigned itself to socialist patriotism. Thereafter hopes of European neutralism lost ground for thirty years without, however, disappearing altogether. A weak form of the third-force idea—weak because it did not involve rejection of the Atlantic alliance—can be found in the arguments used by French socialists for supporting what became the European Economic Community: they believed economic integration could reduce western Europe's dependence on the United States and improve its relations with the Soviet bloc.[62] And, although during CND's first phase of activism its supporters were interested almost exclusively in protesting against Britain's own deterrent,[63] the movement officially campaigned for positive neutralism in the early 1960s, as already noted.

But positive neutralism was gaining ground outside Europe. In Japan, for example, the Socialist Party committed itself to neutralism in 1949 (a decision which split the party for a time).[64] More significantly, many former colonies adopted it as their policy on achieving independence. That the attitudes of the underdeveloped world constituted the 'most important factor today in the struggle for peace'[65] was a conclusion which the 'Keep Left' group had reached by 1950. Five years later, moreover, Britain's most committed third-force advocate, Labour's far-left MP William Warbey, was insisting:

What the world needs today is an India in Europe. Britain—if possible together with other Western European countries—can fulfil that role. We can act as the mediating third party whose intervention can alone bridge the gulf which divides the two main antagonists. With just sufficient arms, including maybe the hydrogen bomb, to convince other nations that they could not rob the hive without getting stung, and with our existing economic strength and our power of influencing world opinion, we could bring a great accession of strength to the group of uncommitted nations.[66]

But, as the example of India illustrates, it was far from clear what was distinctively socialist about positive neutralism. De Gaulle's policies, for which many on the left and in the peace movement had a grudging admiration, was later to make clear that it could be also conservative, nationalistic, and linked to an independent nuclear deterrent. But, even if this objection was overlooked, the policy posed other problems. One was an unwitting neo-colonialism—the danger that some European socialists favoured colonial liberation because they saw themselves as the natural leaders of a non-aligned bloc and the Third-World states as the natural rank and file. Certainly, it was the fear of being thought to have succumbed to 'great-power chauvinism' of this sort which in 1957 produced that rarest of events, a defeat for the Executive at a congress of the Communist Party of Great Britain.[67] Another problem was what came to be called 'Third Worldism':[68] a state of mind in which more attention is paid to national-liberation struggles than to more authentically socialist campaigns in the developed world.

In the 1980s, however, positive-neutralist hopes began to focus on Europe again for the first time for three decades. The NATO decision to install cruise and Pershing-2 missiles produced not merely a revived nuclear-disarmament movement but one which was far more Europe-focused than ever before. In 1980 a campaign for European Nuclear Disarmament (END) was formed to urge the dissolution of both NATO and the Warsaw Pact and the creation of a Continental nuclear-free zone. But although the European left is agreed that neither END nor the nuclear-disarmament movement in general is socialist—they have already been classified here as primarily radical, as has its leading theoretician, E. P. Thompson— some socialists believe that they must give it their enthusiastic support. Thus Ken Coates, a prominent socialist active in END, has warned of the dangers of the peace movement's 'populism' but insists nevertheless that 'there must be a coming together' of it and the socialist movement. He argues that the risk of nuclear war is so great that it must be confronted directly through explicitly anti-militarist campaigns, as well as indirectly through socialist ones, and points to military conflicts between Communist states as evidence that 'while anti-capitalism will be a necessary component of a strategy for a peaceful world, it does not eliminate all belligerent tendencies, nor all danger of war'.[69]

To the far left, however, socialism is sufficient as well as necessary, and radicalism a dangerous, opportunist distraction. According, for example, to the May 1981 issue of *Socialist Standard* ('the official journal of the Socialist Party of Great Britain and the World Socialist Party of Ireland'):

Capitalist society generates war, because it is based on competition . . . No amount of petitions and protests by pacifists and CNDers can alter the fact that this is how society works. Such protests leave untouched the root cause of war. This is the problem that working people have to understand, and to sidetrack them from this understanding is to do them a grave disservice.

Similarly in 1984 two socialist academics, Brian Jenkins and Günther Minnerup, condemned what they called the 'empty "Euro-peanist" abstraction of the END appeal' for being 'wide open to be filled with the hard currency of "third force" European imperialism—a new version of Gaullism minus the *force de frappe*'. But they in effect deny that any interim strategies—or 'shortcuts', as Jenkins and Minnerup dismissively call them[70]—are available to the left. Although by the mid-1980s many socialists were admitting that they had neglected the international arena, were calling for the bringing 'under political control' of the international economy, and had started to discuss afresh the relationship between socialism and war,[71] socialist pacific-ism appeared to have little to offer the war-and-peace debate in either the short or medium term.

iv. Feminist pacific-ism

With two of the three major pacific-isms—those based on liberal-ism and socialism—in decline, the peace movement has been increasingly dependent on two more recent and vigorous varieties. The first, which blames war on men or patriarchy, grew initially out of the female-suffrage campaign. 'Woman suffrage means peace' became a 'monotonous motto' at the start of the twentieth century, in the words of a historian of the American peace movement.[72] When the First World War broke out, many suffragists endorsed it; but some joined the peace movement—the first major political outlet, incidentally, for women apart from their own campaign for the vote. In 1915, for example, Holland's first woman doctor and leading suffragist, Aletta Jacobs, declared: 'Woman suffrage and permanent peace will go together . . . Yes, the women will do it. They don't feel as men do about war. They are the mothers of the race. Men think of the economic results, women think of the grief and the pain.'[73] A Women's International Congress met at the Hague in April 1915 in an attempt to end the war; and its efforts were carried on by an international society, the Women's International League for Peace and Freedom.

When, however, war failed to disappear even after women became a majority in the electorate of many states, feminist pacific-ism almost completely faded from the scene for half a century. Its second flowering did not begin until the early 1970s, when a women's liberation movement developed. Initially its attention was confined to domestic politics and society; but, with the onset of the second cold war a decade later, attempts were made to apply its feminist ideas to international relations as well. Characteristic of such attempts were assertions such as that made in 1981 by Lucy Whitman and Ruth Wallsgrove, members both of the *Spare Rib* editorial collective and of the explicitly feminist anti-nuclear group WONT (Women Oppose the Nuclear Threat):

To be aggressive, even violent, not be put off by worries about the effect of one's actions on other people or the earth, to pursue single-mindedly one's own ambitions and never, never, admit to weakness—that in our society is the idea of a Real Man. And Real Men are the people who have brought us to the edge of nuclear devastation.[74]

What has all too often been left unclear by feminists, however, is what exact relationship between masculinity and war is being alleged. Sometimes an explicitly biological theory is strongly implied, if not actually asserted. American feminists protesting outside the United Nations building in New York during the General Assembly's June 1982 special session on disarmament used the slogan: 'War is Man-Made'; and a major demonstration organized by the women's peace camp at Greenham Common on 12 December 1982 featured a banner declaring: 'War is Menstrual Envy'. Slogans must, of course, oversimplify, and may merely poke fun; but similar language is to be found in more considered writings. American campaigner Ynestra King has asserted, for example: 'We say to everyone who will listen that there will be no peace without feminism for in this world war is man-made.'[75] And British journalist Jill Tweedie may have been at least partly serious when she wrote:

How many other men, including those with their fingers on nuclear buttons, including our own Minister of Defence, unconsciously see nuclear weaponry as an integral part of their sexuality constantly under challenge from other male tribes? How many feel their virility dependent on aggression, their emasculation threatened by conciliation? Rape is grievous bodily harm under the guise of sex. Could nuclear war be planetary rape, sex under the guise of grievous bodily harm? Is it mere coincidence that missiles are phallic like the rockets of the space 'race'? Once upon a time, naked apes waggled their penises at each other in threatening gestures. Then they waggled guns, and now they waggle warheads.[76]

Similarly, although the decision to exclude men taken in February 1982 by the Greenham Common peace camp was prompted at least in part by practical and tactical grounds (the need to attract publicity and exclude troublemakers) it could be interpreted in theoretical terms as symbolizing the masculine gender's particular responsibility for war. If this biological theory is correct, the only way to preserve peace is to exclude men from political power.

But some feminists, such as Marcia Yudkin, have rejected 'hairy ape scenarios or theories of testosterone poisoning' and have made clear that their critique is not 'biological' but 'cultural':

Thus, by calling war a male institution, I mean that as a matter of social and historical reality there exist structures, patterns of behaviour, customs, practices, and organizations into which males, as a matter of social and political reality, have been socialized. In our society, men have been the actual and potential perpetrators of war; men have been shaped and moulded since birth to be capable of wielding political power, of identifying their interests with those of the nation-state, of destroying life; men have been in the position to prepare for war, declare war, and wage war. Any women who have fit [sic] into the mould have been anomalies, and any women who have participated centrally into the institution of war have been tokens.[77]

The cause of war is thus the cult of masculinity on which society is based—often called 'patriarchy' for short. The remedy is a new set of values which, though in a sense 'feminine', are also more rational ones for men to follow.

In both its biological and cultural versions, feminism is an ideology in its own right and therefore the inspiration for a distinct pacific-ism. But a number of avowed feminists do not take this view: some define feminism in an explicitly non-ideological way,[78] while others claim that feminism entails socialism, thereby implying patriarchy to be an aspect of capitalist conditioning rather than an autonomous factor. 'Secondary' feminists, as these can be called, do not claim to offer a distinctively feminist view of the causation of war, but merely to identify certain obstacles to getting *any* form of pacific-ism (or, for that matter, pacifism) across to the public. A clear example of a secondary-feminist peace campaigner is Penny Strange. Her anti-masculine rhetoric is as powerful as that of primary feminists: she insists, for example, that 'all who work for peace must uproot from their own lives the sexual dominance and hierarchical thinking that breed wars'; and she condemns male dominance because its 'thinking has led to the acceptance and approval of violence, and thus lies at the root of the arms race'. But she gives precedence to liberal- and radical-pacific-ist thinking about war-prevention: she states that the 'two major causes of the arms race [are] the *external* force of nation state rivalry and the *internal* force of the military/industrial/technological complex', and that patriarchy is but one factor reinforcing these forces, albeit a 'significant' one. 'The common belief that women are by nature non-aggressive' she condemns, moreover, as 'itself part of the feminine stereotype of passivity, the complement to the idea that violence and war are natural to men'.[79]

It seems likely that secondary feminism is more influential than primary feminism, although the ambiguity of much feminist discourse makes it hard to be sure. Indeed, despite a considerable output of recent writing by the women's movement, feminist pacific-ism remains a surprisingly underdeveloped body of ideas, the vitality of its contributon to the war-and-peace debate having so far undoubtedly exceeded its coherence.

v. Ecological pacific-ism

If the Greenham women have done most to inspire the 1980s peace movement in Britain, it is the ecologists or 'greens' who have recently done most to inspire the peace movements of western Europe (and particularly that of West Germany). The emergence of ecologism as a distinct pacific-ism has, however, been hindered by ambivalences similar to those affecting feminism.

Ecologism attributes the problems of human existence primarily to the ceaseless quest for economic growth and its concomitant over-exploitation of the environment. This upsets 'the balance between the human race and the rest of nature'—to borrow a phrase from 'The Joint Declaration of European Green Parties' issued for the 1984 European Assembly elections. The ecological critique seems applicable only to the industrial era; but, with this reservation, it can be recognized as a distinct pacific-ism, providing as it does a distinctive and all-embracing interpretation of man's predicament. This is particularly apparent in the view of nuclear weapons taken by CND's ecological section, Green CND: these, it insists,

> are not a nasty mistake in an otherwise healthy world. They are the logical outcome of the kind of society we have created for ourselves . . . That is why, alarmed though we all may be by nuclear weapons, we must not give way to the temptation to treat them as the root cause of the problems we face.

The true root cause is the 'logic of industrialism'—the belief that 'wealth and welfare will derive from producing more and consuming more'—and the remedy is quoted from E. F. Schumacher: 'Only by a reduction of needs can one promote a genuine reduction in those tensions which are the ultimate causes of strife and war.'[80]

Some enthusiasts for green politics, however, seem to be 'secondary' ecologists, either viewing damage to the earth as but one instance of the harm done by industrial capitalism, or regarding themselves as either eco-feminists (like the network which founded the Greenham peace camp, Women for Life on Earth) or eco-anarchists (like those in Watford who launched a magazine called *Green Anarchist* in July 1984). While it is perfectly reasonable thus to interpret ecologism either as merely a concern for environmental issues or as part of a broader ideological hybrid, rather than as a distinct and independent theory, its impact as a new form of pacific-ism is thereby reduced.

For all the vigour of the 1980s peace movement, pacific-ism still faces the difficulties which have beset it since the early 1950s when the cold war and nuclear deterrence undermined its more 'constructive' traditions—those based on liberalism and socialism. Since then, it is the largely negative radical tradition, and the still tentative feminist and ecologist critiques, which have flourished. If this trend continues and pacific-ism ceases to appear a positive and practical though idealistic creed, it will lose its advantage over the final and most utopian theory to be examined: pacifism.

7

Pacifism

The final theory to be discussed holds all participation in or support for war to be wrong. Although virtually two thousand years old,[1] this absolutist theory was handicapped for many centuries by the lack of an agreed name. When expounded by Christian sects such as the Mennonites and the Quakers, it tended to be called 'non-resistance'. After 'pacifism' and its etymologically more correct variant 'pacificism' were coined at the start of the twentieth century, it came instead to be most commonly described as 'extreme pacifism' (or 'extreme pacificism'). It was not until the mid-1930s, as already noted, that it became known simply as 'pacifism', having very largely captured that word from what is here called the pacific-ist movement (although it has never to this day managed to make its conquest total). Like the war-and-peace debate's other absolutist theory, militarism, pacifism tends to locate the cause of war in man himself more than in political or institutional structures. Unlike militarism, however, it not only regards man's propensity to go to war as a wicked or irrational aspect of human behaviour, but also believes that his conscience can be persuaded of this.

As already noted, however, pacifists differ among themselves as to the likelihood of such persuasion being successful in the foreseeable future. Optimistic pacifists view the international system as already at least latently a community: they therefore believe that a dedicated minority can at once trigger off a revolutionary change in human awareness and that pacifism is thus practical politics. Mainstream pacifists treat the international system as only a society but one capable in the foreseeable future of evolving into a community: they therefore believe that, although their faith is not yet practical politics, they can as a second-best support the anti-war campaigns of pacific-ists in the expectation of converting them to pacifism in the long term. Pessimistic pacifists view the international system as a vale of tears for the foreseeable future: they therefore believe that any change in human awareness will come only gradually and that until it does pacifists should opt out of political life.

These different types of pacifism are fostered by different conditions, both political and strategic. Optimistic pacifism needs, first, a free and stable domestic environment in which minority political and religious views are tolerated and domestic conflict has been brought sufficiently under control for it to be assumed that the same is possible in international affairs; and, second, a secure strategic situation in which the risks of practising pacifism will be less apparent than in more vulnerable states. It requires, in other words, far greater political and strategic confidence than mainstream pacific-ism does. This is rarely achieved in practice, though there is one clear example: the United States in the 1830s and 1840s was a haven for Christian-pacifist sects from Europe, and its freedom from external threat meant that, before the Civil War complicated the issue, an unusual proportion of the American peace movement explicitly rejected defensive wars as well as aggressive ones. Optimistic conditions of this sort have their drawbacks for pacifists, however. As already noted, ability to opt out of war can encourage mere escapism rather than efforts to prevent war. And, even where it does not, detachment from war and international quarrels can encourage crusading and utopian pacific-ism, as well as optimistic pacifism.

Mainstream pacifism requires conditions which are not quite so liberal and secure as those that give rise to optimistic pacifism. The degree of political and strategic confidence must be insufficient to encourage the expectation that pacifism will work straight away, but sufficient nevertheless to encourage the expectation that pacific-ism can immediately be implemented, and that pacifism will eventually supplant it. Mainstream pacifism thus requires conditions very similar to, albeit slightly more optimistic than, those which also foster pacific-ism. As a result, the latter tends to overshadow it.

Pessimistic pacifism is nourished by very different conditions. Its first requirement is a repressive political environment in which pacifists are forced into confrontation with the state. The maintenance of the pacifist tradition for a millennium and a half after Constantine made Christianity the official religion of the Roman Empire in 313 was largely due to the intermittent emergence, in times of social crisis, of small but influential sects which rejected the societies in which they found themselves; and modern anarcho-pacifism originated in the repressive environment of Tsarist Russia, in which the novelist Leo Tolstoy became converted to unconditional non-resistance to evil. Pessimistic pacifism's second requirement is a vulnerable strategic situation in which little hope is placed upon war-prevention. Only where there is peacetime conscription can pacifism easily distinguish itself from pacific-ism; and only when war is looming or has already broken out can it become politically salient. But the conditions in which pessimistic pacifism flourishes also have their disadvantages for the peace movement: they encourage militarism rather than pacifism in strong states, and defeatism rather than principled anti-war activity in weak ones.

In order to flourish, a pacifist movement needs all three political tendencies: optimists to set up pacifist societies and undertake propaganda work over long periods of time, a mainstream to hold the balance between the two extremes and forge alliances with the far stronger pacific-ist movement, and pessimists to maintain a pacifist witness even in periods of adversity. But this means that it requires contradictory conditions, which explains why it has always been a minority theory: indeed, in the modern times with which this book deals it has achieved much less support than pacific-ism within the English-speaking world,[2] and until recently at least has barely existed outside it. Only in Britain in the late 1930s were confidence and fear combined in the right proportions to produce a pacifist movement of even modest political importance. The Peace Pledge Union (PPU), founded in May 1936 by the charismatic Anglican clergyman H. R. L. (Dick) Sheppard, achieved a respectable membership of 136,000 at its peak in April 1940; and in the Second World War Britain had 60,000 conscientious objectors, most of whom were pacifists. It is thus inevitable that this chapter is illustrated by Anglo-American examples in general, and those from inter-war Britain in particular. Nevertheless, there are some recent signs of pacifism spreading its geographical base, as states without a pacifist tradition acknowledge their vulnerability to nuclear weapons and observe how this strengthens the case for pacifism, albeit of the pessimistic variety.

It is often assumed that, though of limited appeal, pacifism has at least the merit of simplicity. This, however, is far from true, as this chapter proposes to make clear. To start with, it will show that considerable care is required to distinguish pacifism from various non-pacifist absolutisms. Then it will turn to the distinctions which have to be made between different types of pacifism: these vary according to the particular aspect of war which is objected to and the degree of absoluteness with which that objection is maintained, according to the justification or 'inspiration' which is advanced for the objection, and according to the approach or 'orientation' to political activity which the objection is held to require.

1. Non-pacifist absolutisms

In order to make clear what distinguishes pacifism, at least four other absolutist anti-war positions must briefly be discussed.

i. Nuclear, biological, and chemical 'pacifism'

It is a pity that those who absolutely reject all nuclear weapons, but not conventional weapons, are commonly described as 'nuclear pacifists', since this wrongly implies that theirs is a type of pacifism. This usage is too well established to be discarded; but it is worth observing that 'anti-nuclear absolutism' would be a more accurate label. There are also a very large number of 'chemical pacifists' (or 'gas pacifists')[3] and 'biological pacifists'—although by the same token they ought to be described as anti-chemical and anti-biological absolutists respectively.

ii. Eccentric or fastidious defencism or pacific-ism

As was noted in chapter 5, a number of defencists and pacific-ists come very close to pacifism, either because they have idiosyncratic notions about the efficacy of limited defence measures or because they adhere so absolutely to the just-war tradition as to rule out not merely all nuclear but virtually all conventional wars too. But they are clearly eccentric or fastidious defencists or pacific-ists, rather than pacifists, in so far as they do not reject all military force but believe that it still has some justifiable uses. An example, already mentioned, is Sir Stephen King-Hall: even while he advocated non-violence as the best defence policy (and it should be noted that by 1962 he had compromised a little on this policy),[4] he always accepted the need for a token conventional army; he is best classified as an eccentric defencist.

iii. Extreme pacific-ism

It has been seen that pacific-ists believe that even some defensive wars are unjust because they hinder the political reforms on which the abolition of war depends. For this reason some have on occasion claimed to be conscientious objectors, although states are much less willing to grant this status to pacific-ists than to pacifists. ('Selective' objections of this kind not only are unlikely to be viewed by governments as truly conscientious but are also based explicitly on political beliefs, which governments always find more suspect than religious ones.)

Some pacific-ists have set very stringent tests for the justice of a war. For example, the British writer Hugh Ross Williamson, a prospective parliamentary candidate for the Labour Party from 1937 until the spring of 1939, argued that the Second World War failed to satisfy the traditional *jus ad bellum* criteria, and managed thereby to secure recognition as a conscientious objector. He argued that the 'sovereign authority'—the people—had not authorized the war, that a competent supra-national authority—the Pope—had not been appealed too, and that the Poles had refused to arbitrate the Danzig dispute. He made clear, however, that his objection was not pacifist but pacific-ist, since it was explicitly based on socialism—although it may be observed that this was of a type not far removed from national socialism. Soon after the British guarantee to Poland, of which he was a bitter critic, he had thus asserted:

I do not see why we should destroy civilization in a war fought on behalf of the great capitalists, the Communists, and the Jews . . . I am an English socialist and no pacifist. I would fight for England and would fight for Socialism. But neither of them is in question here.[5]

Other pacific-ists are even more stringent in the tests they require wars to meet and much less precise about whether they think a just war is still possible. But although 'extreme pacific-ists' of this variety may in practice be hard to distinguish from pacifists, the distinction is easy enough to make in principle.

iv. Exemptionism

Some opponents of war refuse absolutely to fight (or kill or use force) but do not believe other people necessarily should do the same. They are convinced that it is wrong for them, the élite or the elect, to participate in the defence of the state; but they believe either that it does not matter whether those of lesser sensibility or spiritual worth do so or not, or—even more controversially—that it is desirable that they do so. They are thus concerned with self-preservation, self-exculpation, or personal salvation, rather than with saving the world from the evil of resorting to war.

'Exemptionism'[6] is easiest to identify when it occurs in secular form because then it is so obviously unprincipled and because such an 'exemptionist' does not earn his exemption by undertaking a more onerous way of life—although the creative artists who have formed a sizeable proportion of secular exemptionists might disagree with this latter point. A clear example is the member of the Bloomsbury group who, to justify his refusal to fight in the First World War, is said to have argued: 'Madam, *I* am the civilization they are fighting for.'[7]

But, when it is religious, exemptionism is harder to distinguish from pacifism, since it is itself a matter of conscience and normally related to a self-denying sectarian life-style. It is easiest to identify in the case of religious objections which are not to war (or force or killing) as such but to the incidental difficulties which military service poses for those of unorthodox beliefs. According even to some Christian-pacifist scholars, for example, it was primarily the idolatrous oath of loyalty to the Emperor required of soldiers in the Roman Army to which the early Christian church objected.[8] And it is a refusal to be 'unequally yoked with unbelievers' in the army which explains the conscientious objection in modern times of sects like the Exclusive Brethren.[9] If armies were of the correct religious persuasion, such exemptionists would be willing to fight in them.

But even objections which are both religious and to war itself can be exemptionist if they are available only to the elect or the true believer and not to all human beings. 'It is not immediately obvious why, if war is wrong for the Christian, it should not also be wrong for the ungodly as well', as a British theologian, Neil Summerton, has pointed out. This apparent double standard is sometimes defended, however, with reference to the idea of the 'vocation', which, in Summerton's words, 'must be acknowledged as holding a long and honourable position in the tradition of the church'. This asserts that men are called to *different*—rather than higher or lower —forms of service to God, and that these involve different obligations in respect of war. To recognize the need for a priesthood and to grant it exemption from military service is thus not to deny that the ordinary layman, who has no such privilege and is expected to fight, can be a good Christian. Sects such as the Jehovah's Witnesses have used this vocational argument to claim conscientious objection on the grounds that they are ministers of religion.[10] But the vocational argument is not convincing if those with a pacifist vocation are *pleased* that there are others with a non-pacifist vocation to defend them and maintain order and justice. 'There seems here to be a grave risk of trying to have one's theological cake and eat it at the same time', as Summerton observes of those who are relieved that the majority does not share their pacifist vocation.[11] Although the true pacifist respects the vocations of others, he not only believes they are all morally capable of sharing his views but also desires that they should do so. To recapitulate: what identifies the exemptionist, secular or religious, is that he either does not care whether or not others bear arms, or—even less justifiably—believes that they should do so.

2. What is objected to

Pacifism is a more demanding position than these other absolutisms; but it is itself a spectrum of at least five positions of varying stringency. Its most extreme variants object not merely to war but to force or killing; and its more moderate versions object only to modern war, or war in the nuclear era.

i. 'Force' pacifism

The most stringent version holds force to be wrong: it objects to war only because it is a particular instance, albeit a major one, of the use of force. Tolstoy believed that the true Christian 'will always prefer to be killed by a madman rather than to deprive him of his liberty'. While admitting this to be a utopian goal, he was firmly opposed to 'the compromise in theory, the plan to lower the ideal of Christ in order to make it attainable', and wrote: 'I consider the admission of force (be it even benevolent) over a madman . . . to be such a theoretical compromise.'[12] Logically, force pacifists must object not only to the detention of convicted criminals but also to the forcible restraint of would-be suicides or those about unwittingly to walk off the edge of a cliff—unless, that is, they introduce further distinctions such as those between different types of force or between the innocent and non-innocent.

ii. 'Killing' pacifism

A slightly less strict type of pacifism believes that it is taking life (or, in a less stringent version, human life) that is always unjustified: it objects to war as part of a general objection to killing. To be consistent, killing pacifism entails also vegetarianism and, even in the less stringent version, also the rejection of capital punishment, euthanasia, and abortion—unless, once again, the argument is further refined (so as to distinguish murder from lawful killing, for example).

iii. 'War' pacifism

For most pacifists the objection is to war as such. Since war is not easy to define—for a legalistic definition may exclude civil wars fought with a savagery exceeding that of many international wars— what makes this particular human institution uniquely objection-able is not wholly self-evident. But, implicitly, war-pacifists seem to regard warfare as either the least legitimate or qualitatively the worst form of force and taking life—or, of course, both.

The illegitimacy argument against war is as follows: man has not introduced sufficient order into his international relationships to be permitted to use those forms of coercion which properly constituted states, by civilizing their domestic behaviour, have earned the right to employ as punishments of last resort (including, in an extreme case, the armed suppression of a rebellion). It follows that if a proper world-state existed, its judicial penalties would be as legitimate, and therefore as acceptable to pacifists, as those of any well-ordered polity.

But how, it must be asked, does this view differ from the liberal-pacific-ist view that measures which when used by a state would be dismissed as warlike are transmuted into acceptable 'police measures' when authorized by an international organization? The answer seems to be that, unlike liberal pacific-ists, pacifists refuse to accept that the modest developments in international law and order which have been achieved by bodies such as the League of Nations or the United Nations are sufficient to legitimize killing and force. In particular, whereas liberals have implied that the legitimacy of coercion arises from the (international) quality of the authority applying it, pacifists have implied that it depends on the (judicial) quality of the coercive process itself. For example, Mulford Sibley, a leading American pacifist, argued in 1944 that 'true police work is . . . basically preventive and non-violent; and in the marginal instances where physical force can be used constructively, the force is carefully controlled, employed discriminatingly as between and among individuals, and strictly subordinated to law.'[13] In a true world-state the police analogy would be appropriate, since criminals would be brought to book and punished as individuals. But in any international system which retained the identity of the state (or similar intermediate political unit) the process of retribution might have to be directed indiscriminately against a whole state for collective offences for which the citizens could not in any normal judicial sense be shown to be individually responsible. To pacifists it is the indiscriminate coercion of whole nations which makes war illegitimate even when it purports merely to be 'military sanctions'.

During the inter-war period in particular, however, many pacifists were prepared to advocate economic and other forms of non-military coercion against whole states. The justification for this was rarely spelled out, probably because it would have been controversial; but it indicates that it was the nature of the force employed, rather than its legitimacy, which was uppermost in the minds of many pacifists. And pacifist propaganda has at all times placed great emphasis on the qualitatively distinct horror of military force, the technological advances of this century turning this into far and away the most commonly expressed objection to war.

iv. 'Modern-war' pacifism

Some pacifists profess an objection not to war as such but only to modern war: they argue that just wars were once possible but are no longer so in view of the indiscriminate destructiveness of modern technology. 'My belief in absolute pacifism is limited to the present time,' Bertrand Russell wrote in 1936, 'and depends on the destructiveness of air power.'[14] Even in the nuclear era, some of those who convert to pacifism do so from an aversion to modern conventional weapons. An example is provided by Andrew Wilson, a long-serving defence correspondent of the *Observer*. He had already, in 1981, become a nuclear pacifist out of a conviction that 'the innovation of nuclear "war-fighting" weapons had so undermined the system by which we sought to make nuclear war impossible that [he] could no longer believe in it.' A mere eighteen months later he announced his arrival at the full pacifist position: 'For I cannot now see how one can reject nuclear weapons and accept the morality of modern war fought with today's huge array of indiscriminate *non*-nuclear weapons, of which we recently saw a limited demonstration in the Lebanon.'[15]

Modern-war pacifism is truly pacifist because it rules out all future wars on the grounds that they are bound to use unacceptable modern technology.

v. 'Nuclear-era' pacifism

A special case of modern-war pacifism asserts that it was not modern but nuclear technology which made it impossible ever again to expect a war to be justified. It assumes, in other words, that in the nuclear era the risk of escalation is so great as to render even conventional war illegitimate. In the recent words of Pat Arrowsmith, an indomitable stalwart of the British nuclear-disarmament movement:

I call myself a pacifist, and I'm one of those people . . . who decided that they were not going to support the idea of armed conflict for whatever purpose—good, bad, or indifferent, for social rights or anything else—because the potential end-product of any armed conflict was the use of nuclear weapons. I thought that many years ago, and I still think it today. There are certain armed conflicts whose goals I support, like many liberation movements, but I don't support the use of armed conflict because the potential outcome of this is the use of weapons of mass destruction.[16]

Unfortunately, like some other writers,[17] Arrowsmith calls this position 'nuclear pacifism', which is confusing since the latter term is more commonly reserved, as already noted, for the belief that nuclear weapons are anathema but conventional weapons acceptable. For all its slight clumsiness, the alternative prefix 'nuclear-era' removes the ambiguity.

Surprisingly few people have become nuclear-era pacifists,

however. Pacifists have argued that this is because an individual refusal to fight is thought to be irrelevant in the era of the nuclear bomb and missile.[18] By the late 1950s the veteran pacific-ist Sir Norman Angell was putting it down to the development of a 'cleaner' and more controlled nuclear bomb, which was 'almost a conventional weapon'.[19] But the lack of an obvious threshold between conventional and nuclear weapons could be interpreted in two ways. It could indeed be used, as Angell assumed it implicitly was, to argue that nuclear weapons were acceptable because conventional weapons were acceptable. But the fact 'that nuclear weapons are now becoming—if they are not already—conventional weapons in any conflict between the nuclear powers'[20] was given by Sir Stephen King-Hall as a reason for also rejecting conventional weapons. A more likely reason for the weakness of nuclear-era pacifism is that it tends to be overtly pessimistic—it accepts that pacifism involves severe political risks, albeit lesser ones than nuclear defence involves—whereas a considerable element of optimism is needed to launch a peacetime pacifist movement. Yet it seems in the 1980s that sections of the public may be coming to terms even with the pessimistic case.

3. Unqualified or contingent?

To complicate matters further, each of the above five variants of pacifism can in principle exist in both an unqualified and a contingent version. In practice, however, the first two types tend almost always to be unqualified, and the last two contingent. Only war pacifism is commonly found in both versions; and it is on this alone that the ensuing discussion will therefore focus.

Unqualified war pacifism asserts that no conceivable war is ever justified. This commits it to the extreme proposition that, even if a state fought an extraordinarily successful and apparently costless war (in which by simply mobilizing its army and firing a few shots it scared off a depraved and tyrannical invader), it would nevertheless have committed an impermissible act and would have done better to have submitted stoically to assured butchery and enslavement.

Contingent war pacifism—which is found more commonly in philosophical literature than in the arguments of pacifist activists—

believes 'that while there is in principle the possibility of a war being justified, this is in practice a possibility so remote that we can disregard it.'[21] It accepts that a near-miraculous low-cost war of the sort described above would indeed be justified, but insists that such an eventuality is so improbable as not to necessitate the modification of the rule of thumb that all wars should be resisted without exception. Contingent pacifism is pacifist in so far as it recommends behaviour indistinguishable from unconditional pacifism—in so far, that is, as the contingent pacifist pledges himself not to reconsider his judgement when a war breaks out.

If, however, he does not look at the war on its merits when it occurs, but sticks resolutely instead to his guess about what it will be like, he can be criticized for dogmatism. If, on the other hand, he does re-open his mind, he is not really a pacifist: either he is an eccentric or ultra-fastidious defencist or pacific-ist, who has a hunch that any war would require a violation of the just-war tradition as he understands it, but who is committed to checking the military and ethical circumstances each time to see whether this is in fact the case; or he is an extreme pacific-ist, who expects that any war will have reactionary political effects, but who is obliged to see whether or not his political prediction was accurate. In practice, this dilemma applies only to individuals, of course: a contingent-pacifist state would have disarmed and thus be in no position to offer resistance, even if it were to change its mind.

4. Inspirations

Different types of pacifism advance different arguments and draw on different inspirations. The unqualified version, for example, is normally found among those whose pacifism is, in philosophical language, deontological (as distinct from consequentialist)—in other words, based primarily on an assessment of the quality of an act itself (and not of the likely balance of its consequences). As a statement by the American Friends Peace Committee put it in 1940: 'Pacifism is an obligation, not a promise. We are not guaranteed that it will be safe. We are sure that it is right.'[22] The most extreme deontological pacifists can give the impression of disapproving of those claiming good political consequences for their faith. After his conversion to a position close to nuclear-era pacifism, Stephen

King-Hall was irritated to discover 'pacifists of the hundred per cent variety who actually criticize proposals for unilateral nuclear disarmament because they are declared by their authors to be "expedient" or "common sense" *and* moral'; he condemned them as 'perilously close to making pacifism an end in itself and not a means to the end of promoting moral behaviour'.[23] But, however much it may irritate non-pacifists, this is the most durable kind of pacifism, since it cannot be undermined by adverse events. In 1944, for example, a leading Methodist pacifist, the Revd Donald (now Lord) Soper, had come to admit that many of the arguments he and others had used in the previous decade—in his case merely to supplement deontological arguments—had been misguided: 'The utilitarian argument for non-violence breaks down under the overwhelming pressure of brute fact . . . I am alone sustained by the Christian faith which assures me that what is morally right carries with it the ultimate resources of the universe . . .'[24]

Like Soper, most deontologists do not simply assert on their own authority that the use of force, killing, or participation in war is intrinsically wrong. They insist that the latter is the correct inference to be drawn from a particular religious, political, philosophical, or humanitarian doctrine.

i. Religion

The oldest and most durable type of doctrine from which pacifism has been inferred is religion. Although oriental faiths such as Buddhism have also been invoked and there are even instances of Islamic pacifism,[25] far and away the most influential source of religious pacifism has been Christianity—mainly of the Protestant variety.

The early Christian Church was either pacifist or exemptionist; but from Constantine's conversion onwards pacifism was kept alive only by a series of Christian sects. From the nineteenth century, however, pacifist minorities began to develop in the major Churches, starting with the nonconformist denominations, spreading into Anglicanism after the First World War, and beginning to penetrate Roman Catholicism during the nuclear era. The debate between Christianity's pacifist minority and non-pacifist majority was long bedevilled by an assumption that it could be resolved by finding spiritual texts relating to force or war; these were often quoted out of context and with scant regard to the technical problems of translation. By the 1930s, however, the leading figures on each side of the debate had come increasingly to accept that the Christian attitude to war had to be inferred from the essential spirit of Christianity and its approach to the political world in general, rather than located in any explicit and definitive biblical reference.

In consequence, the debate was increasingly seen to depend on different theological assumptions. For example, in a symposium published in 1984 on Christian attitudes to war, a non-pacifist Christian, Sir Frederick Catherwood, was concerned above all to argue that 'the minority tradition of pacifism, represented by Quakers and Mennonites, has been strongly reinforced by mainstream Humanism' and to complain that the latter, which 'does not recognize the inherent power of wickedness', 'now controls the intellectual assumptions of most Protestant countries, and is now beginning to affect Roman Catholic countries too'.[26]

Christian pacifism has thus done best when the liberal, immanentist view which presupposes God's presence everywhere within the 'secular' world is in fashion. And it has lost ground when theologians prefer the transcendentalist view, according to which the secular and sacred are entirely separate; man is sinful; and God is superior to, and independent of, the universe. It is unlikely that the issue will ever be resolved, since any attempt to distil so complex a blend of differing historical, cultural, and doctrinal traditions as Christianity into a pure and agreed essence seems doomed to failure. But some observers believe that the tide is currently running in pacifism's favour. For example, one of Britain's most articulate Christian defencists, the Revd Richard Harries, has recently been troubled by 'signs that official church bodies are slipping almost unwittingly into a crypto-pacifism'.[27]

ii. Politics

Since the late nineteenth century, pacifism has also been deduced from political doctrines, notably anarchism and socialism.

(a) Anarchism. Pacifism's closest political counterpart ought in principle to be anarchism, which is here defined broadly, so as to encompass the full range of libertarian and communitarian thought. As the philosopher Bernard Williams has recently argued:

Absolute pacifism rests on the view that no state should ever use violence against another state, even in self-defence or in defence of others; alternatively and even more radically, no person should ever use violence on any other person. It follows from either of these positions that no state should ever use violence on any person. But if the state is not permitted to use violence on any person then there is no state, because a state necessarily has a monopoly of violence which it can legitimately deploy against persons. From this it follows that a pacifist is an anarchist.[28]

Some pacifists have always accepted this view. For example, a short-lived American pacifist group founded in 1838, the New England Non-Resistance Society, took an anarchist position under the influence of William Lloyd Garrison, later more famous as a stern campaigner against slavery. One of its members wrote: 'All preparations for war, in this nation, are begun at the ballot box. Voting is the first step . . . a bullet is in every ballot.'[29]

But those attracted to pacifism less by puritan zeal than by fear of war have, until recently at least, been reluctant to accept such arguments. In many cases this was because their domestic-political views were highly orthodox: indeed British pacifists in the 1930s were commonly criticized by anarchists and socialists for 'isolating' war from the many evils inherent in the state or capitalism to which they turned a blind eye. But 'conservatives' of this kind were more likely than other pacifists to abandon their pacifism as the Second World War approached. Those British pacifists who retained their faith needed to devise a means of living as a 'sect' within a state at war; and many of them became attracted to the idea of pacifist communities (which, if agricultural, could also satisfy the military-service tribunals). As a result, a number began to recognize their affinities with non-violent anarchists.[30] The late 1940s and early 1950s saw a fusion between the Gandhian-pacifist and anarchist traditions, with the formation of groups such as Peacemakers (in the United States) and the PPU's 'Operation Gandhi' and its independent successor the Direct Action Committee (in Britain).

Another factor which had previously prevented pacifists from identifying with anarchists was the extent to which, before the Second World War especially, the latter accepted the use of violence not only in self-defence (as in Catalonia in 1936) but even as a means of advancing their cause. There were some non-violent anarchists at this time: Leo Tolstoy, whose no-force idealism has already been noted, and Bart de Ligt, the Dutch admirer of Gandhi who wrote two books on non-violence in the mid-1930s, were notable examples. But they were a tiny minority within an anarchist movement which was itself tiny.

In the Second World War, however, anarchists were forced to make common cause with pacifists, since the latter were the major force opposed to war and conscription. More of them came to believe that non-violence was one of the anarchist virtues; and their use of peace rhetoric was further encouraged both by the atomic bomb which ended the war and by the cold war which followed it. By 1947 Herbert Read could argue that non-violence was one of three fundamental anarchist beliefs (the others being personal freedom and mutual aid), although this assertion did not meet with universal approval within the movement.[31] In the next two decades, moreover, the convergence between anarchism and pacifism made further progress. In the words of Geoffrey Ostergaard, himself a pacifist as well as an anarchist: 'In the 1950s and 1960s anarcho-pacifism began to gel, tough-minded anarchists adding to the mixture their critique of the state, and tender-minded pacifists their critique of violence.'[32] In 1963 one of Britain's most prominent anarchists, Nicolas Walter, argued: 'Pacifism is ultimately anarchism, just as anarchism is ultimately pacifism.'[33]

But anarchism's 'apocalyptic' strain and cult of 'heroic violence', as April Carter has described them,[34] revived in the 1970s with the activities of the Angry Brigade in Britain and the Weathermen in the United States. In that decade the British journal *Anarchy* carried articles supporting both these organizations as well as the Red Army faction ('Armed resistance is both possible and necessary in the advanced capitalist countries') and the IRA ('Up the Provos!').[35]

But the fundamental reason why pacifists have for the most part been slow to recognize their affinities with anarchism is, of course, that the latter is too weak and unpopular a political force to be worth laying claim to. They have instead preferred to appeal to the far more important socialist tradition, which if converted would represent a massive accession of strength for pacifism.

(b) Socialism. Such a conversion was initially not implausible: before political power was in prospect the socialist movement had an influential and respected pacifist minority—particularly in the English-speaking world, where nonconformist Protestantism was

more influential than Marxism. During the First World War the leading socialist pacifists tended to be those whose politics was either an extension of their Christianity (as in the case of Norman Thomas, who joined the American Fellowship of Reconciliation—a Christian-pacifist body—before the American Socialist Party, of which he was soon to become the major figure), or a complete substitute for it (as in the case of two prominent members of Britain's Independent Labour Party, Clifford Allen and Fenner Brockway, both of whom had lapsed from devoutly Christian backgrounds).

But, as socialism acquired vested interests that were worth defending—for example, the Soviet Union and the Spanish Republic—and as it came also to confront fascist regimes bent on suppressing labour movements altogether, so its pacifist minority was sharply reduced. By 1939 it had become clear that the debate on war reflected a deep-seated disagreement among socialists about the nature of politics itself. Non-pacifists took an orthodox view: they believed that socialism could be built at the level of social, economic, and political structures. Pacifists were committed to the much more esoteric doctrine that socialism could be achieved only at the level of individual consciences: as Norman Thomas put it in 1940, they 'had nothing to offer . . . except for a religious faith'.[36]

Although a socialist-pacifist faith which could survive the Spanish Civil War was normally able to survive the Second World War too, the old guard which had espoused the faith in pre-fascist times died out in the 1950s and 1960s; and no new generation was recruited to replace them. Since the Second World War socialist pacifism has to all intents and purposes been moribund.

iii. Utilitarianism

Many deontological pacifists argue that their faith has good consequences, even though this is not the primary reason why they are committed to it. In addition, other pacifists use exclusively consequentialist arguments. This is true notably of modern-war and nuclear-era pacifists.

Those converted to modern-war pacifism in response to the suffering and unintended dislocation caused by the First World War, and in anticipation of the far greater havoc the bomber was expected to wreak in a Second,[37] were the first to believe that it was possible to show, on a utilitarian calculation of the likely pros and cons, that no future war could ever be worth fighting. In 1925, for example, Arthur Ponsonby, a radical-turned-pacifist, claimed in his book *Now is the Time* that 'the most damaging criticism to be brought against war is . . . its failure to achieve a single desirable object, whatever the gigantic cost may be'.[38] Ten years later, moreover, Bertrand Russell argued in *Which Way to Peace?* that 'war, as it has now become, is not a method by which any good thing can be preserved'.

As a philosopher, Russell made his utilitarian assumptions explicit:

The problems we are considering do not, of course, arise for those who, on religious grounds, believe that all participation in war is wicked. For them it is not necessary to weigh pros and cons, since they enjoy a certainty which I envy them, but cannot share . . . The evil of war is quantitative, and a small war for a great end may do more good than harm.

Because of its destructiveness and adverse effect on civil liberties, however, the harm done by a modern war was practically certain to be greater than the good done, however 'great' its end. Russell was explicit that his pacifism was a contingent objection on consequentialist grounds to modern war: 'What is right and what is wrong depends, as I believe, upon the consequences of actions, in so far as they can be foreseen; I cannot say simply "War is wicked", but only "Modern war is practically certain to have worse consequences than even the most unjust peace".'[39]

But, once their apocalyptic expectations of air warfare were toned down in the light of the fighting in Spain and China, and their estimate of the costs of submission were scaled up in the light of Nazism, many utilitarian pacifists no longer felt the balance-sheet of consequences to be quite so one-sided as they had supposed. They came to accept that they had really been making a value judgement rather than a scientific calculation. In *Which Way To Peace?* Russell had revealingly observed that the pacifist movement should not 'be viewed primarily as political, but rather as a matter of personal conviction, like religion'.[40] This was the only one of his books which he refused to republish: he later claimed that it was 'unconsciously insincere' even at the time of writing, and that, while professing that his pacifism was strictly 'quantitative', he had all along 'allowed himself more of a creed than scientific intelligence can justify'.[41] In other words, instead of objectively assessing the balance of consequences, he had assumed one set of consequences (the damage which war would do to European civilization) to be infinitely harmful, so that no other consequences (not even the damage Hitlerism could do) could ever outweigh it. But, even if it was not the objective pacifism he had intended it to be, Russell's 'creed' was a new and distinct type nevertheless, since it deduced the wrongness of war not from an established religious or political doctrine, but from a more informal and humane one. Here it will be called humanitarian pacifism.

iv. Humanitarianism

For some (including Russell), the belated realization of their pacifism's creed-like quality caused them to renounce it; but those who had been aware of this when they first became pacifists proved in many cases as durable as their religious colleagues. Aldous Huxley had always known that his absolutist rejection of war was a 'faith' even though he initially believed it to have the 'double merit' of being 'strictly practical and business-like' as well as 'morally right'.[42] Humanitarian pacifism continued to attract converts, moreover, even after hope of preventing the Second World War had been abandoned. Christopher Isherwood became a pacifist as late as January 1939, when he realized that he would be unable to kill his German ex-lover, Heinz, and began to wonder: 'Was not every German somebody's Heinz?'[43]

Humanitarianism was the dominant pacifist inspiration by the late 1930s. As a leading Christian pacifist observed in July 1938: 'Of genuine pacifism, outside the Christian church, the greater part is motivated simply by humanitarianism'; and the leading historian of conscientious objection in Britain during the Second World War observed on the basis of personal experience as well as careful research that 'the typical PPU objector was broadly humanitarian, broadly moral, broadly ethical', rather than strictly religious or political.[44]

With support for consequentialist pacifism having crumbled as the Second World War became imminent, and having failed to revive as strongly as might have been expected in the form of contingent nuclear-era pacifism, the pacifist movement has been remarkably united since the late 1930s in its opinion that pacifism is a faith. (Those taking a different approach tend either not to join the movement in the first place, or to leave it after a short time, as will shortly be noted.) Religious pacifists have talked of the element of the divine present in man's soul, political pacifists of a brotherhood of men, and humanitarians of the unity of mankind; but all have been conscious of expressing the same belief, albeit in the particular language of their respective moral traditions. This explains why they all co-operated so well together in their heyday, disagreements within the pacifist movement over doctrinal inspiration being rare. Indeed such disputes as have occurred have usually been attributed not to doctrine as such but to the slightly different orientations towards political action which different doctrines tend to favour.

5. Orientations

The most divisive and enduring problem for pacifists—already acknowledged in the distinction between optimistic, mainstream, and pessimistic pacifism—is their orientation towards the problems of preventing war and participating in a society which believes in defence.

First, how should they try to prevent war? Should they, as the optimists among them claim, insist that total disarmament and a refusal to fight are the most practical way of ensuring peace? Or should they, as the mainstream has normally suggested, adopt an intermediate position and endorse pacific-ist reforms which, though not pacifist, are preferable to existing policies? Or, again, should they follow the pessimists' advice and abandon all political activity in order merely to bear witness to values which cannot be implemented for the foreseeable future?

Second, what attitude should they take towards the society in which they live, in view of the fact that it is almost certain to be preparing for war if not actually fighting one? Should they act defiantly, as the optimists want, look for compromise solutions, as the mainstream suggests, or withdraw into themselves as far as possible, as the pessimists urge?

i. Preventing war

(a) Non-violence. All pacifists by definition believe that their stance yields better results than war. But only the optimists, who regard the international system as essentially not just a society but a

community, believe that these results will be better *in conventional political terms* and that pacifism is an effective policy in the world as it is. This was the tenet of Donald Soper, who asserted in 1934: 'I hold that pacifism can be applied as a solution to most of the world problems of the day.' It is 'the safeguard of practical good as well as of eternal verity', he reaffirmed in 1982[45] (although during the Second World War he had retreated somewhat from this view, as already noted, and had accepted that pacifism was the safeguard of the practical good only in the long term).

This view that non-violence 'works' in international relations is based on a belief in the efficacy of either moral deterrence or non-violent resistance. Moral deterrence is the belief that an invader will not invade a disarmed state. Some pacifists have been prepared to assert this explicitly. In 1937, for example, John Middleton Murry claimed that it 'was probably as near to a certainty as human reckoning can attain that against a Pacifist England, a Fascist Germany would be completely incapable of making war'.[46] But in general even pacifists have not liked to rely on moral deterrence alone. Thus, although in April 1940 the great Indian exponent of non-violence, Mohandas K. Gandhi argued, 'A non-violent man or society does not anticipate or provide for attacks from without. On the contrary, such a person or society believes that no one is going to disturb him', he believed that pacifists had nevertheless to reckon on 'the worst' occurring.[47]

The vast majority of those believing that non-violence 'works' thus assume that, if a disarmed state is attacked, it can non-violently resist the invader's forces. As developed by Gandhi, a creative and eclectic rather than systematic thinker, this belief blended Tolstoyan and Hindu idealism with such political techniques as passive resistance and the boycott which had become familiar during the nineteenth century. Gandhi called it *satyagraha*: literally 'holding to the truth', but commonly translated 'soul-force'.

In particular, western peace movements welcomed the theory of *satyagraha* or non-violent resistance as the answer to their prayers for a distinctively pacifist means of ensuring political justice. Some of them went so far as to suggest that non-violent interventionism might be possible: during the 1931–2 Manchurian crisis a group of British pacifists, led by Dr Maude Royden (and including Donald Soper), recruited 800 volunteers for a 'Peace Army' of British pacifists to interpose itself between the Japanese and Chinese armies, although in the end no such force was sent.[48] In the 1930s several major studies of non-violence were published: by the Dutch anarchist Bart de Ligt; by Richard B. Gregg, an American Quaker and labour lawyer whose writings attained cult status within the early PPU; and by the Indian writer Krishnalal Shridharani, whose work prompted the formation in the United States of a Non-Violent Direct Action Committee in 1941. After Gandhi's assassination in 1948 *satyagraha* was kept alive by disciples such as Vinoba Bhave in India, by civil-rights groups such as CORE (the Congress of Racial Equality) which had been founded by American pacifists in the early 1940s,[49] and by campaigners such as Gene Sharp, an American whose writings include an impressively compendious survey of non-violence in theory and practice.

This orientation has worried many pacifists for both principled and practical reasons. Their principled objection is to the view that non-violence is (as a pioneering bibliography on the subject has assumed) 'a technique of action, not a dogma'.[50] This view has become the dominant one: as a British pacifist admitted in 1972, there has been 'a strong swing within the nonviolent movement away from principled nonviolence and pacifism towards trying to propagate nonviolence as a technique which can be used by anyone without any philosophical or ethical basis for that nonviolence'.[51] In order to attract the mass support on which their technique depends, its leading advocates have deliberately distanced themselves from pacifism. Gene Sharp, for example, has insisted that non-violence is

not synonymous with pacifism . . . [It] has often been practised, and in a vast majority of the cases led, by non-pacifists who saw it only as an effective means of action. The popular idea that only pacifists can effectively practise nonviolent action—a view sometimes pressed with considerable conceit by pacifists themselves—is simply not true.[52]

The pacifist retort is that, although any form of non-violence is preferable to violence, it is never fully satisfactory when practised by non-pacifists. For deontological pacifists, it is the moral intuition from which it arises, and not its effectiveness, which gives non-violence its value. They worry that, unless rooted in an absolutist faith, techniques of non-violence will prove to be merely 'a type of coercion' and 'not permanent proofs of a loving temper', as Reinhold Niebuhr warned in 1932,[53] or 'no more than a different method of getting your own way', as a PPU member put it three decades later.[54]

It was in an attempt to pre-empt such objections that Gandhi had described his policy as one of enlisting the adversary's participation in a search for truth. Richard B. Gregg invoked psychological theories to explain this idea to a western readership:

The non-violent resister seeks a solution under which both parties can have complete self-respect and mutual respect; a settlement that will implement the new desires and full energies of both parties. The non-violent resister seeks to help the violent attacker re-establish his moral balance on a level higher and more secure than that from what he first launched his violent attack.[55]

But even sympathetic writers have come to admit that Gandhi was not always able to avoid coercion. In 1939, for example, Krishnalal Shridharani argued not only that *satyagraha* depended for its very effectiveness on 'this element of compulsion', but even that it 'seems to have more in common with war than with Western pacifism'.[56] And more recently Gene Sharp has made no bones about regarding 'coercion' as a legitimate non-violent strategy.[57]

Some consequentialist pacifists, though accepting that efficacy is the criterion by which non-violence must be judged, believe that only those for whom it is rooted in a deeply held moral commitment will in practice have the dedication to practise it successfully. As a thoughtful advocate of non-violence, H. J. N. Horsburgh, has admitted: 'Non-violent defence presupposes steadfast adherence to the fundamental principles of Satyagraha . . . only those communities which satisfy certain exacting conditions can hope to defend themselves effectively by non-violent means.'[58]

But the main objection to non-violence is practical: it takes too utopian a view of the enemy. As Richard B. Gregg was honest enough to admit in 1934, the 'basic assumption' made by non-violent resisters 'is that their opponents, no matter how forbidding externally, or no matter what their past history, are at bottom decent and have in their hearts at least a spark of good spirit which can eventually be aroused and strengthened into action.'[59] Where their adversaries are indeed relatively sympathetic or humane, as were those faced by Indian nationalists and black Americans, campaigners may be better advised to play on the guilt of the oppressor than to attempt violence. Even in domestic struggles, however—and it is with these, significantly, that the literature of non-violence is overwhelmingly preoccupied—it is questionable whether this assumption always holds good: in South Africa, for example, racial supremacism is proof against moral challenges from those whom it considers to be its inferiors.[60]

Advocates of non-violence tend to imply that it will do well in all circumstances. In 1938, for instance, Gandhi told German Jews not only that they had in the Indian *satyagraha* campaign 'an exact parallel', but also that, if they followed its example, 'Herr Hitler will bow before the courage which he has never yet experienced in any large measure in his dealings with men' (although Gandhi did somewhat casually accept that there was the risk of a 'general massacre').[61] This is true even where they explicitly acknowledge that their strategy is helped by certain special conditions. In 1957, for example, Gene Sharp admitted: 'The Indian culture provided a favourable environment for the first major experiments with this method. India's opponent was a State which, however brutal at times, was not as ruthless as totalitarian regimes would have been.' But he none the less went on to insist: 'These observations . . . do not affect the general validity of non-violent resistance: its basic application and methods seem to be applicable with modifications and varying difficulty in application, in widely differing circumstances.'[62]

In struggles between states, moreover, there are two reasons for doubting whether non-violent resistance will work. The first is technical: it presupposes face-to-face encounters between the resisting population and occupying troops. Although some non-violent theorists such as Gregg were swift to recognize the possibility that an invading army which met effective non-violent resistance might evade such encounters by resorting to 'poison gas, either of a disabling or lethal kind, or bomb attacks by aeroplanes', they did not regard this as an objection: in 1934 Gregg simply asserted that this would 'add so many sympathizers to the ranks of the non-resisters from among their own people, that a very complete and effective trade boycott and strike of domestic or industrial work could be organized'.[63] In 1974 two left-wing observers complained that 'nowhere in the literature of non-violent defence does one find

anything remotely like a strategic analysis of the confrontation
which results when military occupation is countered by non-violent
resistance'.[64]

The second doubt about the applicability of non-violence to
international relations is whether, other than in highly exceptional
circumstances, the requisite degree of community exists between the
resisting population and the violent attacker. Gandhi urged the
Czechs in 1938 and the British and Indians during the Second
World War to put their trust in non-violent resistance; but he
expressed sympathy for the Polish decision to fight in 1939 (as will
shortly be noted), and admitted in 1942 that pacifists 'might be
unable to bring about peace outright' and could expect to produce
results only 'in due course'.[65] The claims which had been made for
non-violent defence early in the 1930s were thus subtly toned down
during the Second World War. Success was often claimed if non-
violence was even attempted at all, despite the fact that the invader
was not thereby repulsed but at worst slightly inconvenienced. Thus
in the post-war edition of his book Richard B. Gregg claimed that
the Danes had practised non-violent defence 'not perfectly, yet
effectively against the ruthless Nazis' and 'resisted non-violently and
successfully for two and a half years until the warring British
government persuaded them to use violence'.[66]

The revival of interest in non-violence in the late 1950s and early
1960s—when Stephen King-Hall took it up, as already noted, and
academics such as Adam Roberts began seriously examining its
potential—was posited not on the goodness of the adversary but on the
absence in the nuclear era of a more rational alternative. According to
H. J. N. Horsburgh in 1965: 'New methods of international struggle
must emerge if deterrence is to be successful and there seem to
be reasons for believing that these may be non-violent.'[67] Such
arguments are open to the objection, however, that what is rational is
not necessarily possible. Furthermore in so far as 'new methods of
international struggle' seem to be emerging, they seem to be those of
the terrorist, the guerrilla warrior, or the people's militia practising
'territorial defence' with the aid of the latest precision-guided
munitions, rather than those of the *Satyagrahi*. Whereas the argument
that non-violence is the best policy once meant that it was an effective
defence policy, it now tends to mean that there is no such thing as an
effective defence policy in the nuclear era.

Most of those who become pacifists do so in order to prevent war; hence they are normally drawn first to the non-violent orientation, since it is the most optimistic and seems to hold out the greatest hopes of political efficacy. But, by the same token, once they come to appreciate the difficulties involved in both moral deterrence and non-violent resistance, they are more likely than those drawn to the other orientations to abandon pacifism altogether in disillusion.

(b) Collaboration. The pacifist mainstream has been insufficiently optimistic to believe in the efficacy of non-violence, but insufficiently pessimistic to believe that practical efforts to prevent war should be abandoned. Its orientation is one of collaboration with non-pacifist remedies on the grounds that, though in the long term only palliatives, they have a far better chance of being implemented in the short term than pacifism does. Collaboration is, of course, easiest in the case of policies—for example, neutralism, appeasement, and war resistance—which involve no military action, although pacifists can be embarrassed to find themselves thereby endorsing the special interests of conservatives, fascists, or communists. Support for collective security is more controversial, of course: many pacifists have refused to collaborate even with economic sanctions, although a number have been prepared to give political support to an international army, while admitting that they would themselves refuse to serve in it.

The collaborative orientation has normally been adopted instinctively; and the few pacifists who have been aware of what they are doing have found it hard to justify.[68] The most persuasive vindication has come from those who have used the vocational argument, which has already been discussed in the context of exemptionism. Those using it have mainly been Christians, but not exclusively so. When, for example, in 1935 the well-known socialist academic G. D. H. Cole began to give political support to collective security while remaining personally a pacifist, he explained: 'I cannot try to force the *consequences* of my views upon fellow-Socialists who do not share my *reasons*.'[69] Cole, however, was shortly to abandon his pacifism altogether and become a pacific-ist; and it may therefore be doubted whether in 1935 he was sincere in wishing non-pacifist socialists to abandon collective security and convert to pacifism, since if they had done so the short-term prospects of war prevention would have been made worse. It is possible to be similarly sceptical about the views of other collaborative pacifists; and, if such doubts are justified, then much of what purported to be collaborative pacifism has really been exemptionism.

(c) Sectarianism. Pacifism's most durable loyalists and most distinguished theorists—particularly those of deontological inspiration—have been pessimists. Believing that the dictates of conscience bear no necessary relation to the requirements of politics in the conventional sense, they have not expected pacifism to prevent war—indeed it may even hasten it. They thus see no point in participating in the mainstream of political life: pacifists should be content to keep their distinctive values alive and uncontaminated.

This orientation is 'sectarian' in the sense that it was characteristic of the sects—other than the Quakers, who have often favoured a collaborative orientation—to which the pacifist tradition owes so much. For example, as the pacifist tradition's leading historian, Peter Brock, has pointed out, virtually all the historic peace sects in early-nineteenth-century America

were opposed to participation in the political life of the state, which they regarded as hopelessly entangled with the apparatus of violence . . . They found no need to devise a blueprint for a successful pacifist policy. Wars and violence were probably inevitable in this world . . . Theirs was the witness of a suffering love, a testimony to a higher way which, however, only a handful would find the strength to follow. Their pacifism, in short, was a sectarian pacifism . . . which made little attempt to reach out to the world with the message of peace and non-violence.[70]

But modern 'sectarians' have been reluctant to adopt a wholly quietist and individualist attitude which appears simply to abandon society to its fate, and have insisted that they too are working constructively to prevent war. From the late 1930s, when they came under attack for being negative and individualistic and for isolating war from other political problems, sectarian pacifists began to claim that they were really engaged on the task of building a non-violent society. Thus a group of seven American conscientious objectors stated in 1943: 'Western pacifism has too long depended on individual conscience. We must now develop group non-violent action to effectively build a peaceful society.'[71] Pacifists admit that their approach is inevitably slower to attain its goals than that of those who think in terms of conventional politics, but argue that this is because they are working at the deeper level at which the real roots of war are to be found. Thus, although one of the PPU's post-war mainstays, Myrtle Solomon, has recently acknowledged that pacifism 'cannot offer a blueprint for a solution to our predicament', she was careful also to insist: 'Nor is it a dream outside reality; it is a way of saying "give peace a chance", that moving call to open doors on a new world which would concentrate less on the balance of weaponry or the debate on defence, and more on learning to live.'[72]

The sectarian orientation became relatively dominant in the late 1930s, when the difficulties of war-prevention had become un-mistakable. Its strength and its weakness are the opposite of those of the non-violent orientation: it is immune to political disappoint-ments but lacking in appeal to the practical-minded.

ii. In wartime

The same three orientations towards war prevention apply also to the problem of how pacifists should behave in a state at war: believers in non-violence defy the war effort; advocates of col-laboration favour a policy of service to society; and sectarians set up separate communities where possible.

(a) Defying the war effort. The option favoured by optimists—with the support, as already noted, of the anarchist movement—is to make no concessions to a tolerant society. This involves efforts to halt the fighting and hinder the war effort.

This option was, for example, adopted early in the Second World War by the Forward Movement which was set up to urge the PPU 'to be more active in stopping the war'. Its tacit assumption was, however, that an acceptable peace could be worked out if the two sides simply reasoned together. But such an eventuality ceased to be realistic after the fall of France in 1940—as Storm Jameson pointed out soon after recanting her pacifism at this time: 'The way of reasoning together is not open to us. What is open to us is submission, the concentration camp, the death of our humblest with our best, the forcing of our children's minds into an evil mould'[73]—and this orientation suffered a dramatic loss of support. When in 1943 a Peace Now Movement was launched in the United States, most pacifists shunned it because of its pro-fascist implications.[74]

To stop the war implies taking as obstructive and absolutist a stand in relation to conscription as is compatible with pacifist principles. This is easiest to do, paradoxically, in repressive states: even though it may require considerable moral and even physical courage, the pacifist can go to prison or submit to any other punishment inflicted by the state in the knowledge that he is being true to his conscience and resisting the war effort. Moreover, apart from deciding how far to co-operate with the prison authorities, he has no other political decisions to worry him.

It was thus not despite but because of their often harsh treatment that Britain's conscientious objectors of the First World War enjoyed both high morale and a favourable reputation with liberal opinion. They had 'gained in inner strength and in intensity of support from the persecution [they] had to meet', as one of the most courageous of their number, Fenner Brockway, later admitted to a gathering of their counterparts during the Second World War.[75] But the latter were demoralized and isolated, a state of affairs which can only partly be attributed to the fact that Hitler was a more dangerous and evil enemy than the Kaiser. Their intellectual problems were paradoxically the greater for their having in most cases been exempted on acceptable terms and thus left free to wrestle with their consciences whilst at the same time feeling that they owed a debt of gratitude to their fellow citizens—especially those risking their lives to import the food that sustained them. As a British conscientious objector of 1940, David Morris, later put it: 'A little less kindness and understanding, a little more obvious hatred and persecution would have made the "conchie's" life much easier.'[76] It is noticeable that in the United States, where there was less reason for pacifists to feel themselves a burden upon society and where hostility to them was anyway stronger, there was a greater tendency—particularly later in the war when victory was in sight— for pacifists to be defiant.[77] In Britain, however, even the incorrigibly intransigent were reduced to complaining at being 'diddled' by the state's 'ingenious' tolerance, which itself represented an 'extraordinary extension of totalitarianism'.[78] But most had long since abandoned any thoughts of defiance, and had tried to adopt a more moderate position.

(b) Serving society. Mainstream pacifists who adopt the collaborative orientation towards war-prevention face a problem when a war breaks out which most of their pacific-ist colleagues believe to be just.

Having once supported war-prevention proposals such as the creation of an international police force, can they similarly endorse military resistance to aggression while remaining personal pacifists? Even Gandhi, in addition to supporting recruitment for the British war effort during the First World War, took an indulgent view of Polish armed resistance to Hitler in 1939, as already noted.[79] And in the Second World War a senior British pacifist, the Revd Cecil Cadoux, expressed both the view that, although non-violent resistance was the ideal policy, resistance to Hitler was 'relatively justified', and the hope that the war against him would be won.[80]

This meant, Cadoux argued, that pacifists should undertake humanitarian service and ignore the argument which had weighed heavily on them in the First World War: that they were thereby assisting the war effort. Most conscientious objectors in Britain and (especially at the start of the war) in the United States agreed with him. The problem with such an orientation, however, was that, although it helped pacifists to claim they were helping society, it failed to make clear how they differed from ordinary air raid wardens or welfare workers. Roy Walker, one of the PPU's most intelligent activists, did not make himself popular with its 1941 annual general meeting when he pointed out that there was 'no difference between a cup of tea handed out by an air raid warden and a cup of tea handed out by a pacifist relief worker'.[81] As in peacetime, in other words, the collaborative orientation was sensible and popular, but did not bring out the distinctiveness of the pacifist position. For this reason many of the movement's leaders preferred instead to try to demonstrate that pacifism could be the basis of a unique social experiment.

(c) Withdrawing into communities. It is the sectarian approach to war prevention which adapts best to wartime: having made no claim to be able to prevent or resist war, it therefore suffers fewest disappointments when it breaks out and pacifists are unable to stop it. Although liable to feel guilty towards a society that takes risks to feed them, sectarian pacifists have attempted to cope with this by forming communities to undertake agricultural work—an activity which in Britain had the additional advantage of satisfying the conditions commonly imposed by military-service tribunals. Above all, the community idea enabled pacifists to claim that they were laying the foundations for the non-violent society: on 14 March

1941 *Peace News* launched a monthly 'Community' supplement in the expectation that 'so soon as the grim period of war is over, it will be revealed as the forerunner of the new society'. For all its intellectual appeal, however, the community idea often proved a disappointment: most pacifists were simply too individualistic to work harmoniously together.[82] Sectarian pacifists were for the most part solitary individuals who adhered to their faith without benefit of any belief that it was of political relevance for the foreseeable future.

Pacifism has never been strong; and such strength as it achieved in the English-speaking world in the 1930s was all but destroyed by the Second World War. The optimistic and mainstream versions suffered most severely: those who remained pacifists were those who had concluded that pacifism was a faith rather than a policy for preventing war. This meant that the pacifist movement was of little appeal to the casual war-hater. Admittedly, non-violence was sufficiently interesting as a possible technique for promoting social justice to attract successive cohorts of young optimists into the pacifist movement, as already mentioned. But for the most part these new converts resigned as soon as they realized that for them non-violence was a means—and not necessarily the most effective one—to promote political goals that had no necessary connection with pacifism, whereas for the old guard of the pacifist movement it was an end in itself. More durable converts to pacifism tended to be those, like the political theorist R. V. Sampson in 1956, who espoused pacifism as a reaction against the view that war prevention was 'essentially a political issue . . . The issue of war and peace, I came to realize, is not of this order, and can never be rationally resolved on this plane; the issue is always a religious issue, and can be correctly resolved in no other way.'[83] And those taking so exigent a view were understandably few in number. Its revival in the nuclear era has been surprisingly slow; yet there are some signs that the next intellectual development in the war-and-peace debate will be a revival of pacifism—or, more precisely, of consequentialist, contingent, and sectarian nuclear-era pacifism.

8

The determinants of the debate

If the war-and-peace debate is a contest between the ideological options set out in the last five chapters, it must now be asked: what determines its outcome?

To some extent, of course, it is the current international situation which determines the ebb and flow of the debate within each state. A world crisis, for example, will not only make the war-prevention issue more salient and intensify the debate; it will also have some effect on which theories seem most plausible at the time. Illustrations are plentiful: the First World War and its embittered aftermath discredited militarism and for a while defencism too in many states; Japan's occupation of Manchuria in 1931 did much to undermine liberal pacific-ism among the leading member states of the League of Nations; Hitler's military victories during 1940 did much to destroy pacifism; North Korea's attack on the South in 1950 was a blow to socialist pacific-ism in the free world; the NATO Council's decision of 12 December 1979 to install a new generation of Euromissiles stimulated radical pacific-ism, particularly in western Europe; and the shooting down by the Soviet Union of a South Korean civil airliner in September 1983 helped to increase support in the United States for President Reagan's crusading-tinged defencist hard line. But it is hard to detect any very precise relationship between a particular international situation and a particular war-and-peace debate: increased tension sometimes helps peace movements and sometimes helps their opponents. And it is impossible to use the international situation to explain why states respond differently to the same crisis.

The same, of course, is true of domestic politics: although a particular internal crisis may suit one party's approach more than another's, the outcome of political competition can only partly be explained in such terms. Yet in domestic politics other, more important determinants can readily be identified: the relative popularity of the various ideologies can to a considerable extent be linked to the relative strength of the various social classes and economic interests. For example, where both a class-conscious proletariat and a strong trade-union movement exist, socialism will be well supported.

It is here argued that the war-and-peace debate has equivalent determinants. Just as the social culture of a class predisposes its members towards particular views of domestic politics, so a state's political culture—by which is meant simply the complex historical accretion of values and assumptions governing its political activity —predisposes its citizens towards certain views of international relations. And, just as his particular location within the economic system gives an individual a selfish reason to favour a particular ideology, so a state's strategic situation—in other words its degree of vulnerability to or security from attack—gives it a special interest in certain ways of organizing the international system.

These points are obvious enough in themselves, of course. Yet they have never been developed into a systematic explanation of the variation in war-and-peace debates. To remedy this deficiency comprehensively would take a whole book, however; this chapter can merely suggest how to begin. It offers a simplified scheme of classification according to the degree of liberalism in a state's political culture and the degree of security in its strategic situation.

1. Political culture

If war-and-peace debates are ideological, it is evident that they will be influenced by a state's subjective outlook as well as by the objective realities of the world situation. Thus militarism will automatically be strong in political cultures in which fascism is influential, whatever the external conditions. Admittedly, a state's political culture is itself a product of its strategic situation: that is why a strong correlation will be observed between insecurity and illiberalism. But political culture is nevertheless an autonomous factor, as can be illustrated with particular clarity by comparing two island states: Japan, where militarism once flourished, and Britain, where it has always been negligible. This stark contrast in their war-and-peace debates cannot be explained by their respective strategic situations, since both enjoyed a reasonable measure of security. Although imperial Japan felt itself vulnerable economically, its geographical location was particularly favourable, as Robert E. Ward has pointed out:

> geography has endowed Japan with a degree of national security unique in the history of the greater states. It is approximately 130 miles across the Straits of Tsushim to Korea, Japan's closest continental neighbour. It is about 475 miles across the Yellow Sea to the Chinese coast. Japan's safety from invasion from the continent is thus far greater than that of Great Britain, lying 20-odd miles from the shores of France. Prior to 1945, no one had successfully invaded Japan since the ancestors of the present Japanese race did so in prehistoric times.[1]

Only contrasting political cultures can thus explain the differences between the imperial Japanese and the British war-and-peace debates.

A political culture is complex and multi-faceted. Except where it is imposed by the government (as in communist states, which officially have a pure-socialist political culture), it consists of a pluralistic mixture of values. In virtually all states, in other words, virtually all ideologies are to some extent represented, albeit in different strengths. Judged by ideal-types standards, moreover, these mixtures vary only marginally between states. A complete discussion of the influence of political culture on the war-and-peace debate would thus take the entire range of ideological variables into consideration. For example, it is impossible to understand the Indian contribution to the theory of non-violence without understanding the contribution of Hinduism to its political culture. For the sake of simplicity, however, this chapter will assume the primacy of one ideological variable: the strength or weakness of liberalism. It will represent war-and-peace debates as varying according to whether the political culture is 'illiberal', 'non-liberal', 'semi-liberal', or 'liberal'.

i. Illiberal cultures

One example of an illiberal state has just been noted: imperial Japan, where liberalism was a foreign import and consequently under suspicion. It is particularly striking that its tiny and impotent peace movement was wholly a product of Christian and socialist ideas imported from the west.[2] The development of a truly indigenous peace movement has been a symptom of the extent to which post-war Japan has accepted western liberalism, even if the movement has certain features—notably a particularist strain emphasizing the uniqueness of Japanese experience as the one state to suffer nuclear attack—which can perhaps be traced to a pre-liberal era.[3]

The only illustration to be considered here in detail, however, is Germany from its unification in 1871 to its defeat and partition in 1945. To British and American liberals in particular, the 'German problem' was at root caused by the fact that their opposite numbers in Germany had in the mid-nineteenth century, when liberalism was in the ascendant elsewhere, sold out to Prussian autocracy. Instead of insisting on full representative government (not achieved until the end of the First World War and abandoned fifteen years later) and economic freedom, German liberals settled instead for the national unity Bismarck had achieved by military means and for state-sponsored industrialization. As a result the major challenge to defencism came not from pacific-ism or even crusading, but from militarism.

Germany had developed a small peace movement by the Wilhelmine period; and in Karl Holl's words it stood 'close to the left-wing of liberalism'. But its efforts 'in support of the Anglo-American trend in favour of the establishment of international arbitration' remained weak and half-hearted; and liberal pacific-ism received no support from either the National Liberals, who 'were much in favour of imperialist colonial policy and the massive armaments policy, in which they were deeply involved economically, or from the [Roman Catholic] Centre Party, which disliked liberalism in any form'.[4] With liberalism weak and compromised, 'the only factor that lent even a faint aura of credibility' to the peace movement was, as Roger Chickering has pointed out, the powerful Social Democratic Party (SPD), which, being officially Marxist, talked the language of socialist pacific-ism. But even the SPD's bark was worse than its bite: it in practice consistently refused to consider war resistance (its support for war credits in 1914 coming as no surprise to the Second International); and a section of its revisionist wing openly favoured imperialism.[5] And, there being (in Holl's words) 'no stimulus of the kind given by religious dissent, e.g. by the Quakers and Mennonites in the U.S.A. and in England', since in Germany this was 'of secondary or of no importance at all',[6] pacifism was non-existent.

Nor did this situation change greatly when Germany became a democracy in 1918. Although peace societies, such as a League of Nations Union, flourished, they accepted much of the nationalist case against the Versailles Treaty; and where they did not their influence was negligible.[7] Despite these compromises, however, such societies were strongly criticized for being, in Hans Rühle's words, 'politically naïve, unmanly, weak, even morally inferior, and unpatriotic' and for lacking the more 'positive connotations' of their counterparts in other states.[8] The coming of the Third Reich put an end to all peace campaigning.

Since 1945, of course, defeat, division, and democratization have enabled West Germany to enter the liberal mainstream. As a result, although its organized peace movement remained comparatively weak for many years, there have been intermittent upsurges of anti-war feeling. The first was in opposition to the rearmament required by the NATO powers in the early 1950s: indeed West Germany might have opted for permanently disarmed neutrality (as the best means of securing reunification) had the Christian Democrats not been the government party during the new regime's crucial first decade. The second upsurge was in late 1957 and early 1958, moreover, when a 'Campaign Against Nuclear Death' (*Kampf dem Atomtod*), prompted by NATO's deployment of the newly developed tactical nuclear weapons, seemed to be developing in step with CND in Britain. It was, however, nipped in the bud in the summer of 1958 by Khrushchev's activation of the Berlin crisis[9]—a further example of the effect of the international situation on the war-and-peace debate. In 1959, moreover, the SPD formally renounced Marxism and neutralism and in effect espoused social democracy and defencism.

The third and most important upsurge has taken place in the 1980s. To some extent it reflects changes both in the international situation (the second cold war) and in Germany's strategic position (to be noted later). But it reflects domestic changes too. As Peter Graf von Kielmansegg had noted in explanation of the contrast between the second and third upsurges:

Between the late fifties and the early eighties lie the sixties and the seventies. This is not just a statement of the obvious. It is an allusion to the profound change of consciousness that took place in that interval: Western industrial society began to question itself, became alienated from itself.[10]

Although disillusionment affected all western societies, it has been particularly marked in West Germany. One factor has been the intensity of the latter's inter-generational conflict: this cannot be attributed solely to the fact that youth was reacting against a generation tainted with Nazism, since, as Peter Merkl has pointed out, 'recurrent generational tensions and youth revolts' have been so marked a feature of German life throughout this century that 'there can be no doubts about the explosive recurrence of the phenomenon that appears to be rooted in German culture'.[11] The economic miracle has enabled young protesters to make a big issue of West German materialism: to such people, Hans-Joachim Veen has argued,

the prevailing ethos of the state is the national economy, which supports a huge apparatus of welfare services. Despite all the material riches this system produces, its moral foundation is poor. There is no community spirit of libertarian and humanitarian vein to be found, no historically-informed tradition of cultural identity and political self-responsibility.[12]

Those taking this view have been forced by the growing moderation of the SPD, particularly after it became a party of government in 1966, to find a new political outlet. This, and the high level of industrial pollution West Germany suffered as the price of its economic growth, have led to the emergence of 'green politics', as already noted, on a scale unequalled in other states. Even the Christian churches have outspoken dissenting minorities, which use slogans such as 'Would Francis of Assisi be with the Greens Today?' and 'Today the Lord Jesus would live in Kreuzberg' (the alternative-culture section of Berlin), and which are attributed by some observers to sectarian impulses within the Lutheran tradition.[13]

Thus, despite West Germany's acceptance of liberal democracy, its peace movement has in the 1980s been notably different in ideological inspiration from those in traditionally liberal states. According to an unsympathetic observer, Clay Clemens:

Today's peace movement is heir not only to traditional tendencies towards *Angst* and romanticism, but also to the perspectives which those basic impulses have shaped: social anti-modernism, political illiberalism and anti-dogmatic Christianity. The same despairing, pessimistic uncertainty and radical rejection of reality which generated dissent in Germany's past are at work in the current peace movement.[14]

The peace movement's critics have voiced the fear that its hostility to the western alliance could turn into a nationalist campaign for reunification. They warn, in Jeffrey Herf's words:

Germany does not need yet another national identity grounded in romanticism and anti-Western sentiments. The Federal Republic is a welcome break with German illiberalism. Only a search for national identity firmly rooted in the liberal traditions of democracy and individual liberty can avoid the errors and illusions that caused so much grief this century.[15]

ii. Non-liberal cultures

Whereas liberalism is positively unpopular in illiberal cultures, in non-liberal cultures it simply plays a minor role. France is the best example. Its war-and-peace debate is now conspicuously out of line with those of other liberal democracies. As Christian Mellon, one of the country's relatively few Roman Catholic peace activists, has recently admitted: 'It is well known that organizations working for peace and disarmament are weaker in France than anywhere else in western Europe.'[16] The weakness of its peace movement reflects the fact that, for all its importance in the development of Enlightenment thought, France did not develop a liberal tradition as here defined. Being a Roman Catholic country which lagged behind in industrialization and urbanization, it lacked the nonconformist conscience and free-enterprise enthusiasms from which liberal pacific-ism was forged in the Anglo-Saxon states. Though granting asylum to foreign radicals, it has no tradition of tolerating pacifist sects; and its political culture is noted for the general weakness of its cause groups.

France has, in consequence, been notably unmoralistic in its approach to foreign policy. Whereas Britain's role in the Hoare–Laval plan of 1935 (which would have handed Abyssinian territory to Italy) and the Suez invasion of 1956 produced major moral outcries from its own people, the French role in the same events passed off with little other than the normal partisan criticism. Similarly, its independent nuclear deterrent arouses so little domestic opposition that its rationale has been explained by some observers as more to build a domestic political consensus than to defend the country. Even its own anti-nuclear movement refused to support an international protest against France's first nuclear test in 1960 because such a protest was anti-French. It tests its warheads in the atmosphere without significant domestic dissent, while opinion polls indicate that its public felt that *raison d'état* could even justify the sinking of the Greenpeace ship *Rainbow Warrior* in Auckland harbour in July 1985.

Such peace campaigning as has taken place in France, moreover, has tended to be avowedly non-moralistic. It is wholly characteristic that a leader of the anti-nuclear minority, the ecologist Brice Lalonde, should insist on making clear his disapproval of the attitude of British CND: 'It is a purely moral position and like any moral position it is well-meaning but it forgets one thing: the appearance of weakness is the cause of war.'[17]

Above all, French anti-war campaigning has been political, being an extension initially of radical and then of socialist and communist partisanship. It has thus been severely handicapped by the left's tradition of Jacobin nationalism. Although strongly opposed to militarism, it has always felt the need to defend the achievements of the French Revolution, notably republicanism, against foreign attack as well as aristocratic reaction.

The peace movement was originally identified with the radical movement, as Roger Chickering has pointed out:

In France, the peace movement was inextricably connected to the groups associated with Radicalism—Masonic lodges, societies of *libres penseurs*, and local political committees of the Radical Party. Particularly with the growth of Radicalism after the turn of the century, then, the peace movement became increasingly visible in French politics.[18]

Radicalism was indeed strongly anti-militarist, and played a major part in the vigorous but unsuccessful attempt to prevent the period of conscription being extended to three years in 1913. But it nevertheless wished to defend the Third Republic against its enemies at home and abroad, and was in many respects more patriotic than the far right. Indeed by the First World War, according to David E. Sumler: 'In their attitudes toward international affairs, the Radicals . . . were nationalists and even imperialists.'[19] Thus, for all radicalism's political success, its challenge to defencism was minor.

As the major source of peace activity, radicalism was gradually replaced by socialism, though the latter's desire to impede the defence effort has usually been less than its rhetoric might suggest. Theodore Zeldin has claimed: 'Anti-militarism developed in close association with socialism';[20] and it is indeed the case that the language of war resistance was adopted in France by many socialists, strongly influenced by Marxism and syndicalism, and trade unionists, whose anti-militarism was reinforced by hatred of the army for its role in breaking strikes. Yet the French socialist movement adopted a strategy of socialist patriotism: Jean Jaurès had been pressing for a citizen army; and even the Marxists refused in 1914 to regard defence of the Republic as merely a capitalist war.

Only from disillusionment with the First World War did the left come, for a generation, to support war resistance. The powerful Communist Party, formed in 1920 when the Socialist Party split, took this line at first, but began to advocate a 'people's front' instead when the Soviet Union entered the League of Nations in 1934 and signed a pact with France the following year. The Socialist Party adopted war resistance too, but lacked the Communists' facility for reversing their policies and was in the second half of the 1930s painfully divided between war resistance, outright pacifism, support for the League of Nations, and socialist patriotism. The demoralization of French foreign policy at this time and the abject collapse of 1940 cannot, however, be attributed to the strength of socialist or any other sort of pacific-ism. The failure of the late 1930s was a failure of defencism: it could not make up its mind until too late whether defiance was feasible or whether accommodation was the most prudent policy for France to follow.

For most Frenchmen, the need to restore national security so as to prevent any repetition of the humiliation of 1940 (and perhaps also to compensate for domestic political instability), meant that there was no alternative to the western alliance, even though this involved some dependence on the United States as well as the rapid rehabilitation of West Germany. The Socialists reverted to wholehearted socialist patriotism, and became for the most part loyal Atlanticists too. Despite two disastrous colonial wars, defencism was thus unchallenged under the Fourth Republic, except by Communists. That the latter and their fellow travellers set up a Mouvement de la Paix in 1948—a blatant front organization, but the country's one significant 'peace society' until the 1980s at least—was a sign that they had been forced into a political ghetto as a result of the cold war and had little to lose politically.

France's development of an independent nuclear deterrent was, however, a more controversial question, particularly as it became identified with Charles de Gaulle's position of unprecedented political power as President of the Fifth Republic. The Socialists condemned the *force de frappe*; and it seemed for a while that the defence consensus was in jeopardy. But, as well as being an insurance against the slight risk of a renewed threat from Germany, the deterrent was skilfully turned into a symbol of republican independence from United States hegemony when in 1966 de Gaulle withdrew his country from the military command structure of NATO. Indeed, because it is thus associated with anti-Americanism, the *force de frappe* has been more popular with the Marxist left of the new Socialist Party, notably the CERES group, than it has with the more Atlanticist right.

As early as 1969, François Mitterrand's opposition to the deterrent was weakening; and in 1978 the Socialists finally came out in its favour. The Communists, for whom policy reversals were much easier to arrange, endorsed the deterrent in 1977.[21] These conversions clearly had a tactical element: being close to achieving office, the left undoubtedly needed to make clear that it was not soft on the Soviet Union. And it has been suggested that the Communist Party may have felt the *force de frappe* so to lack credibility that to devote resources to it rather than to the conventional defence of Western Europe is in the Soviet interest.[22]

But, whatever their motive, these switches of policy further weakened the peace movement. Although the Mouvement de la Paix did not follow the new Communist line slavishly, it nevertheless muted its criticism of the French deterrent. When the second cold war began, it was no longer a credible campaigning body, particularly after the formation of a left-wing government in 1981, which helps to explain why a new organization, CODENE (Comité pour le Désarmement Nucléaire en Europe), was formed in February 1982. Its main importance is that it is independent of the Communists and able to work as part of the END movement and to draw support from a wider range of opinion (including ecologists as well as some socialists) than is usual in French politics. But

CODENE remains by western-European standards a weak body, and a cautious one, since it does not demand unilateral nuclear disarmament.

In addition to the Jacobin and Gaullist traditions, at least three other cultural factors seem to explain the remarkable relative weakness of the French peace movement. The first is the absence of a strong 'alternative culture' among the young. The second is the conservatism of the Roman Catholic hierarchy, which has been rather more reluctant than its American counterpart to condemn nuclear weapons. And the third is the idiosyncratic isolationism of the nation's intellectual life, which caused it to come late to an awareness of the Soviet Union's human-rights violations. As E. P. Thompson put it, in some irritation, in 1984:

The final discovery of the Gulag came extraordinarily late, was passionate, was for a period of two or three years obsessional—at the expense of any other kind of analysis and concern—and led into a human rights movement in which there are very many former communist personalities who are still in a state of shock. This has to some degree captured the internationalist tradition.[23]

Thus post-war France remains the best example of a 'non-liberal' political culture: it does not feel threatened by the peace movement, as an 'illiberal' one would; it for the most part simply ignores it.

iii. Semi-liberal cultures

'Semi-liberal' political cultures are those in which conservative tendencies and liberal challenges are more or less equally combined. The former ensure a strong defencist tradition and prevent moralism from becoming so intense as to result in crusading. But the latter give rise to influential peace movements: indeed it will be seen that they are on balance the strongest in the world. The best examples of semi-liberal cultures are Scandinavia, the Netherlands, and England.

The strength of its liberalism has been a recognized feature of modern Scandinavia. T. K. Derry has argued that

by the outbreak of the First World War the individual Scandinavian citizen was among the most fortunate in the eyes of European liberals. This was in part due to the ease with which their small-scale societies were permeated by popular movements—such as co-operation, trade unionism, and social democracy—which originated elsewhere: the gap between the classes and the masses was relatively easy to bridge.

It is no coincidence that it was in this period that the peoples of Scandinavia began to become identified with

an impartial humanitarianism, leading to an ardent championship of the world peace cause as they understand it . . . Before 1914 they preached arbitration, and the Nobel Peace Prize awards began to exert an influence. Since then they have preserved their pacifist ideals, in spite of numerous disappointments over the turn of events and their own disillusioning experiences of the 1940s.[24]

A similar analysis can be applied to the Netherlands. A specialist on its foreign policy, J. J. C. Voorhoeve, has pointed out that 'the Dutch have a Northern Protestant mentality' and that their 'political culture has more in common with the Scandinavians and British than the French and Italians'. He stresses that it was above all their commercial activities—free trade being 'a sacred principle' after 1845—which made the Dutch 'rather cosmopolitan' and favourably disposed towards 'international idealism'.[25] The Hague became the world's peace capital, home of the official peace conferences of 1899 and 1907 which bear its name, of an international congress of women in April 1915, and of the Permanent Court of International Justice, set up in 1921. More recently it was the Dutch peace movement which inaugurated the successful campaign against the neutron bomb in 1977–8 and which played so prominent a part in the campaign against the Euromissiles that the critics of that campaign began to talk of 'Hollanditis' and 'Dutch qualm disease'.[26] Indeed, one rally, on 29 October 1983, was attended by no less than 550,000 people—4 per cent of the Dutch population.[27]

The best example of a semi-liberal political culture is that of Britain—or, more accurately, England, since Wales in particular has a somewhat different political tradition. For all its deeply rooted conservatism, English political culture has been strongly marked by Protestant Christianity (particularly that of the nonconformist minority) and *laissez-faire* political economy which fused together to form classical liberalism. Because England had enjoyed political progress without violence since the seventeenth century, moreover, it was encouraged to assume that the international system could also evolve peacefully. In 1876 the war-and-peace debate became a party-political issue. In that year William Gladstone, the Liberal leader, took up the issue of the atrocities against its Bulgarian subjects by Turkey—an ally which could not be condemned, defencists argued, because its support was essential for the protection of the gateway to India. Gladstone thus urged a moral alternative to the *realpolitik* of the Conservatives. From that point, the British party system offered a clear choice, in terms of rhetoric if not actual practice, between pacific-ism (mainly liberal, but later radical and even socialist as well) and defencism.

With the spread of democracy and free political discussion, pacific-ism expected to win the argument. According to the radical L. T. Hobhouse: 'Both the friends and enemies of democracy inclined to the belief that when the people came to power there would be a time of rapid and radical change at home combined in all probability with peace abroad—for where was the interest of the masses in any war?' The popularity of imperialism in particular was thus, as he put it, 'one of the surprises which play ducks and drakes with political prophecy'. The willingness of the working classes to imbibe invasion literature and jingoistic propaganda and to respond on cue to the periodic war scares meant that even radicals, with all their theoretical trust in the people, were complaining about 'the broad bestowal of a franchise, wielded by a people whose education has reached the stage of an uncritical ability to read printed matter'.[28]

But though not enjoying a political walk-over, liberal and radical pacific-ism permeated English thinking about war to an extent which alarmed defencists of all parties by the late nineteenth century. In 1883, for instance, the Cambridge history professor J. R. Seeley went out of his way to attack the current 'commonplace that the wars of modern England are attributable to the influence of the feudal aristocracy . . . whereas the trader just as naturally wants peace', insisting that history taught instead that 'England itself grew ever more warlike . . . as she grew more commercial'. His considered verdict was: 'Commerce itself may favour peace, but when commerce is artificially shut out by a decree of government from some promising territory, then commerce just as naturally favours war.' Ten years later Sir Charles Dilke (like Seeley a Liberal imperialist) was telling the House of Commons: 'Liberals should give up thinking of this question of natural defence as a hateful one, and as one against which they should close their eyes and ears.' And when in 1900 the military theorist Spenser Wilkinson, himself a lapsed disciple of Cobden's close colleague John Bright, looked back over the previous decades, he observed:

British public life and English literature, under the influence of that Liberalism of which Bright was one great exponent, were pervaded by a false and distorted view of war and regarded the exertion of force in support of right, not as something that might be necessary and for which the nation ought to be prepared, but as something altogether wrong.[29]

Propagandists habitually overstate their case. Yet it is undeniable that during the Victorian period 'Cobdenite' assumptions became so ingrained in English political culture that they were able to withstand the less favourable conditions of the twentieth century. This explains the strength between the wars of the League of Nations Union (which collected nearly 400,000 subscriptions in 1931), and the phenomenal success of the 'Peace Ballot' (a private referendum in support of the League in which 38 per cent of the adult population took part between November 1934 and June 1935).[30] It also explains the strength of the moral outcry at the Hoare–Laval plan of December 1935 (to placate which the foreign secretary, Sir Samuel Hoare, had to resign, even though he possessed the full confidence of his colleagues). Cobdenite assumptions contributed also to the comparative success of the PPU (the pacifist body founded, as already noted, in 1936). And even after the Second World War they help to account both for the strength of popular protests against the Suez invasion and British nuclear weapons, and for the propensity of the left in particular to call for 'collective security through the United Nations' (to quote Labour's 1984 defence statement), despite being fully aware that such a thing does not exist. There is thus at least a kernel of truth in the claim by the 1974 Spenser Wilkinson memorial lecturer, Correlli Barnett, 'that it is not a Wilkinsonian viewpoint which dominates British opinion at large but, however modified, the old sentimental Cobdenite illusions'.[31]

iv. Liberal cultures

Liberal political cultures are those which, lacking an indigenous feudal hierarchy and so enjoying a relatively egalitarian social order, have comparatively weak conservative and defencist traditions and comparatively strong radical movements. They are strongly drawn to the more extreme anti-war ideas—optimistic pacifism (the theory that non-violence will work) and the most utopian manifestations of pacific-ism (such as the belief that world government is feasible). But their liberal and radical moralism can sometimes take crusading form, which is why their peace movements are overall less strong than those of semi-liberal cultures.

The United States provides by far the best example of a liberal political culture. As well as the features which make it a 'typical' liberal state, it has at least four idiosyncrasies which further intensify its liberal character.

The first is its lack of either a class-conscious proletariat or a strong socialist movement. Admittedly, it has always had a strong radical tradition; but in so far as this has ever criticized American capitalism it has been for failing to live up to its free-market principles. Thus the mid-West's powerful small-farmer sector has a long history of denouncing the eastern-dominated railroad and finance companies, but only for forming trusts in restraint of trade. In countries where scepticism about capitalism as such exists, it acts as an inhibition on liberal self-righteousness. In the United States, clearly, such an inhibition is lacking.

The second idiosyncrasy is its legalism. Because of the unrivalled importance of written constitutions in political life and of litigation and lawyers in economic and personal life, American pacific-ism has had a strongly constitutionalist and legalistic flavour. In the inter-war period, for instance, there was considerably more enthusiasm in the United States for what might be called 'legal internationalism' than for the political variety of which the League of Nations was an embodiment. One illustration was the role American public opinion played in bringing about the Kellogg–Briand Pact of 1928, the signatories of which renounced (aggressive) war as an instrument of policy without accepting any corresponding obligations of any kind, such as to disarm, go to arbitration, or impose sanctions against a state breaking its word. Whereas European pacific-ists attached little importance to the pact, which its historian Robert Ferrell has subsequently described as the 'peculiar result of some very shrewd diplomacy and some very unsophisticated popular enthusiasm for peace',[32] their American counterparts took it very seriously indeed. Another illustration was the strength of the campaign (which, however, failed to overcome isolationist resistance) for persuading Congress to accept the jurisdiction of the 'World Court', as the Permanent Court of International Justice was commonly called in the United States. Subsequent historians have admitted that much of the campaign was 'incredibly obtuse' and have attributed its naïve faith in international law to 'the legal background of American life—the heritage, through American history, of Calvinism, Coke and the federal Constitution'.[33] The same point could be made about the federalist campaigns which began in the late 1930s and remained vigorous until the late 1950s: their explicit assumption was that if the states of North America could form a federation as early as the eighteenth century, the states of the world could do the same in the twentieth.

The third distinctive feature of American political culture is its suspicion of government. A primary aim of the United States Constitution was to place checks on the federal executive in particular; and this has been very effectively achieved. The separation of powers (which deprives the executive of the right to declare war or make treaties without the approval of Congress) and frequent elections (which have never been suspended even in wartime), along with weak party discipline (which makes it hard for the executive to control Congress even if it ostensibly has a majority) force the president and secretary of state continuously to secure the consent of Congress and public opinion to their foreign policy. To achieve this, the executive is often obliged to present its initiatives in moralistic terms even where its rationale is geopolitical. This helps to explain why, for example, the decision taken in 1947 that it was in the strategic interest of the United States to prevent Greece and Turkey passing out of the western sphere of influence was not presented to Congress in such terms but instead in the grandiloquent and principled language of the Truman doctrine, which smacked of the 'counter-crusade', as Hans J. Morgenthau soon pointed out.[34]

The fourth idiosyncrasy of American political culture is its conviction, attributable to its immigrant origins, that the United States is a uniquely valuable society. This belief can take either isolationist or interventionist form. (Which form it in fact takes is partly a question of region—the Middle West is traditionally more isolationist and the South more interventionist than the North-East and the West[35]—and partly of national mood.) Its isolationist form has been colourfully described by James Burnham:

It is the notion, not without its grandeur for all its falsity, that the United States is not as other nations are. It is the vision of a New World of new hope and new promise, taken naïvely, literally. It must draw its strength from its own rich, untainted earth; it must be shielded from those osmotic contacts through which the ancient infection might flow. Hence, America First and Unique, its own star not part of any constellation, its destiny unentangled with common human fate.[36]

Such a sentiment is obviously particularist, and might have given rise not only to a belief in Manifest Destiny but even to overt militarism had it not been for the other characteristics of American political culture just noted. Thus, instead of rejecting liberalism for failing to acknowledge the idea of national superiority, the United States was persuaded by its commitment to capitalism, legalism, and constitutionalism to take the view that its national superiority consisted of being itself the true source and embodiment of liberalism. This became apparent whenever the unique-value doctrine took its interventionist form and attempted to export American values. In the words of a perceptive historian of America's pre-1914 peace movement:

When Americans contemplated the prospects for international co-operation, few questioned the viability of their values and institutions for world politics; rather, Americans overwhelmingly assumed that they would extend them to the world. 'Internationalism' for these people represented merely an extension of their national faith.[37]

Because a particularist doctrine was thus metamorphosed into a universalist one, its effect has been to stimulate crusading and pacif-ism rather than militarism and defencism.

The result of a distinctive political culture is not only a distinctive domestic debate (in which the main ideological cleavage is between conservative liberals and radical liberals) but a distinctive war-and-peace debate which Europeans often find puzzling. Instead of a clear polarization between defencists on the right and pacif-ists on the left, the debate is a three-way contest, with defencists sandwiched uneasily between 'right-wing' crusaders and 'left-wing' pacif-ists. Geopolitical reasoning is thus attacked on two fronts, at the rhetorical level anyway: virtually every writer on America's approach to international relations has stressed the weakness of the Hamiltonian 'realist' tradition in relation to that of Jeffersonian 'idealism'. According the Hans J. Morgenthau, for example, writing during the Korean War: 'We have acted on the international scene, as all nations must, in power-political terms; but we have tended to conceive of our actions in non-political, moralistic terms.'[38] Although immigrants such as Henry Kissinger have helped the 'realist' tradition by bringing with them the central-European balance-of-power tradition, the strongly moralistic anti-Soviet feelings of Americans of eastern-European descent have more than countered this.

The vulnerability of defencism to attack from both crusaders and pacific-ists on account of its use of 'amoral' concepts such as national interest and the balance of power was illustrated by the hostility aroused by the *détente* policy formulated by Kissinger and President Nixon. Not only hawks such as Henry Jackson condemned its *realpolitik* assumptions, but also doves such as Jimmy Carter. As late as 1972 Stanley Hoffmann was still stressing the difficulty defencism faced in getting its basic concepts across to the American public:

The subtleties of the balance of power, the apparent coldness of a policy that gives up both the most extreme claims of force and those of evangelism, that tries to curb both disembodied idealism and the imperial strivings of a self-interest licensed by idealism are not likely to strike a particularly responsive chord.

Admittedly, there is some evidence, as was noted in chapter 4, that defencist thinking has been steadily gaining ground in the United States since the early 1950s. Coral Bell argued in the mid-1970s—in part on the evidence of approving references in American television's *Star Trek* series to the universe having a balance of power—that such concepts had already 'percolated down to the political grassroots . . . without exciting any particular revulsion'.[39] And in 1980 even an instinctive pacific-ist like President Carter could use the language of national interest when declaring, in the 'doctrine' now associated with his name: 'An attempt by an outside force to gain control of the Persian Gulf region will be regarded as an assault on the *vital interests* of the United States of America, and such an assault will be repelled by any means necessary, including military force.'[40] Even so, the United States remains an illustration of how in a powerful state a liberal political culture can suddenly overbalance from pacific-ism or pacifism to crusading.

2. Strategic situation

Like its political culture, a state's strategic situation is a complicated compound. Although the successive inventions of the aeroplane, the rocket, and the nuclear warhead have somewhat reduced the significance of its geographical location, this is still the most important component: the outlook of a relatively protected state, such as the United States or Switzerland, differs significantly from that of a highly exposed one, such as Poland during its period of true independence, or Germany. But, as imperial Japan's worries indicate, another element is the extent to which its economy is self-reliant or dependent. However, these two factors cannot explain why the United States is not vulnerable on its northern border and why no effort has been made in recent times to penetrate Switzerland's mountain fastness. An additional factor is thus a state's diplomatic situation: the United States is further protected by its good relations with Canada, just as Switzerland is by the mutual rivalry of its neighbours.

Although it is obvious that states can be strong in some components of security but weak in others, it will henceforward be assumed that their strategic situations can always be classified along a one-dimensional scale running from extreme insecurity to security, and also that there are only four gradations on this scale: 'extreme insecurity', 'moderate insecurity', 'moderate security', and 'security'.

i. Extreme insecurity

If a state has an extremely insecure strategic position it will take a sceptical view not only of pacific-ism but even of defencism, since extreme vulnerability makes the international system appear not merely unreformable but also too anarchic to be stabilized. It will thus be tempted towards extreme positions. (Whether or not it succumbs to them depends largely on its political culture.)

The extreme position towards which a state will be drawn will depend on its military capability. In the case of a strong state—such as Germany on the eve of both world wars—the temptation will be militarism, since it has the prospect of doing well out of an anarchical competition. In the case of a weak state—such as France in the late 1930s—the temptation will be either pessimistic pacifism or defeatism. Pessimistic pacifism was discussed in the previous chapter: it flourishes whenever the international system appears to confirm its image of the political world as a vale of tears in which nothing practical can be done to prevent war. But the notion of defeatism requires some explanation here. Its reason for not fighting or doing anything which might provoke the enemy is not principled but prudential. Or, to put it another way, it is not a theory but a policy. It is, moreover, a policy which even defencists believe it is often rational to adopt in situations of extreme insecurity. Many French defencists tacitly adopted it in the late 1930s, for example; and it is perhaps surprising that more of their West German counterparts do not do so today, in view of the likelihood that their state would largely be destroyed should it ever have to be 'defended' against a major invasion.

ii. Moderate insecurity

The more moderate degree of insecurity which most states experience is ideal for defencism. Moderately insecure states regard the international system as still too anarchic for idealism to be worth pursuing, and regard those who deny this as a menace to national security. But they accept that common interests exist not only with friendly states, on the basis of which alliances can be formed, but also to some extent with adversaries, on the basis of which informal understandings to respect spheres of influence, to operate a balance-of-power system, or to accept the logic of deterrence can be achieved. In other words, faced with a moderate degree of insecurity, most states feel that defence measures are not only necessary but likely to be effective.

A particularly clear example of a moderately insecure state is provided by post-war France. The partition of Germany and the American guarantee to Europe have dramatically improved its situation since the late 1930s, when it could have been classified an extremely insecure state. But the country remains too close to the Warsaw Pact for comfort; and the prospect of West German neutralism and eventual German unity remains a long-term worry.

iii. Moderate security

A situation of moderate security is ideal for both mainstream pacific-ism and mainstream pacifism, since these, as already noted, require the right combination of optimism and pessimism. A degree of security allows a state to perceive the international system as not merely an anarchical but a true society, and ensures a strong peace movement. But the security is only moderate. This ensures a sufficient awareness of the horrors of war to discourage it from expressing its moralistic view of international relations in crusading terms, even if it is powerful enough to contemplate this. And, above all, it does not permit a state simply to opt out of war: it risks being embroiled if one breaks out. It must always therefore work to prevent it.

Britain, Scandinavia, and the Netherlands have normally enjoyed moderate security of this kind. They have done so not only because—particularly in the British case—of their geographical location (on the periphery of Europe) but also—particularly in the Dutch case—because of their diplomatic good fortune (in being protected to a considerable extent by the workings of the European balance-of-power system). Their moralistic approach to international relations would be impossible without this measure of security. 'Disinterestedness is the luxury of the secure,'[41] wrote H. N. Brailsford in 1917: he was thinking of the oddity of the British attitude to international relations compared with that of most of Continental Europe. Two Swedish historians made a similar point in the 1930s in respect of their own country's attitude: 'In the long era of peace that has lasted ever since 1814 (now nearly 120 years) the outside world has almost forgotten Sweden. The Scandinavian peoples have grown accustomed to watching the upheavals on the Continent detachedly from their safe point of vantage.'[42]

Crusading is not an option for these states (although it will be seen that it almost was for nineteenth-century Britain): they lack not only the strength but the confidence that war will make things better. Nor is isolationism an option: to guarantee their own peace they have to make sure no war breaks out. They thus opt for pacific-ism or pacifism rather than escapism. Amry Vandenbosch has made this point in his study of Dutch foreign policy, noting that although one of the 'two currents' in the country's approach to international relations has been 'a timid neutrality', it has never been able to take this very far:

With an overseas colonial empire, an extensive merchant marine and a world-wide commerce but with relatively little military strength, the Dutch were a people whose every interest was served by peace. The Netherlands became the champion of the freedom of the sea, equality of the flag and the general development of international law. The Dutch became greatly interested in peace movements. They began to see that their national interests were advanced by the strengthening of the peace structure of the world.

Because it could not opt out, in other words, the second 'current' in its thinking, 'interest in the peace movement and the development of international cooperation',[43] prevailed over the neutralist one.

iv. Security

A secure strategic location predisposes a state to view the international system as not just a society but one that is either a community or fast developing into one. It gives rise to crusading, in states which have the military capacity to undertake it, to speed up this process of development: security encourages both impatience with the failings of the international system and ignorance of the unintended effects which fighting, however just the cause, can bring. It also fosters both pacifism of the optimistic type (which believes in the immediate practicality of non-violence) and the most utopian types of pacific-ism.

Security also engenders escapism. This, it should be made clear, is the view that it is easier simply to opt out of the international system than to try to reform it. It is, of course, a prudential rather than a principled position, being to the secure state what defeatism is to the extremely insecure one—a policy which defencists and others find rational under certain conditions. 'Excessive' security, like excessive liberalism, is thus on balance harmful to peace movements.

Secure states are rare. Nineteenth-century Britain was not far from this happy condition and thus manifested some of its characteristics. It was self-confident as well as strong enough, particularly during the Palmerstonian era, for crusading at least to be discussed as a foreign-policy option. It possessed one of only two pacifist traditions in the world of any significance (which was, moreover, optimistic in outlook), as well as a pacific-ist movement which hoped that the abolition of war was in sight. Moreover, so many of its citizens believed that the country could if it wished pursue a policy of 'no foreign politics' that anti-war feeling was to some extent distracted away from pacific-ism into escapism. The British peace movement was thus far less influential in the nineteenth century than in the twentieth, when fear of war made its ideas more salient. But even at the Victorian peak of its security the English Channel was too narrow for Britain to be able wholly to ignore the threat of blockade or invasion from Europe; and its government had consequently to keep a watchful eye on the Continental balance of power.

The United States, at least up to the late 1950s when it became vulnerable to missile attack, has been by far the best example of a secure state. As chapter 4 has emphasized, it has enjoyed both self-assurance and power in sufficient quantities sometimes to divert its anti-war moralism into crusading. It has had the world's other significant pacifist tradition (and one which includes a strong optimistic vein too—notable in its enthusiasm for non-violence—even though some of the older pacifist sects to which the United States gave shelter were quietist); and its pacific-ism has been utopian by international standards.

Moreover, its peace movement has been undermined by the easy appeal of escapism. For example, as one historian has pointed out: 'In the inter-war period pacifism was often popularly understood as being synonymous with isolationism.'[44] Indeed the confusion between principled and prudential arguments was such as to provoke the influential theologian Reinhold Niebuhr to condemn in scathing terms those 'who equated American neutrality with the Sermon on the Mount'.[45] Not only has a secure state no incentive to prevent war, its reform-minded citizens will regard international issues as less important than domestic ones. It has, for example, been observed of American peace campaigners around the turn of the century that 'few found the rather abstract idea of world peace capable of commanding their total devotion'; in consequence, the story of the peace movement was 'part of innumerable other stories'.[46] In other words, peace campaigning was treated as an extension of work for domestic reforms, such as temperance, the abolition of slavery, or female suffrage, rather than given priority as a distinct issue. (It is worth nothing that the same was true, albeit to a lesser extent, of the peace movement in almost-secure nineteenth-century Britain.) For much of the 1930s, moreover, pacifists in the United States were preoccupied more with the challenge to their beliefs from Marxists arguing that revolutionary violence was a legitimate way of redressing domestic wrongs—a response to the severity of the country's depression—than with the challenge from Hitler.

As suggested early in the chapter, political cultures and strategic situations tend to be found in predictable combinations: the degree of liberalism normally correlates with the degree of security. It is therefore possible to sum up this discussion of the determinants of the war-and-peace debate by setting out the four most common combinations of political culture and strategic situation and listing beneath each the theories (and prudential anti-war policies) which it specially favours:

Illiberal and extremely insecure	Non-liberal and moderately insecure	Semi-liberal and moderately secure	Liberal and secure
		mainstream	
MILITARISM	DEFENCISM	PACIFIC-ISM	CRUSADING
pessimistic PACIFISM			utopian PACIFIC-ISM
		mainstream	optimistic
DEFEATISM		PACIFISM	PACIFISM
			ESCAPISM

Epilogue

This book has argued that to a previously neglected extent thinking about peace and war is ideological, that it is best understood as a contest between five ideal-type theories or sets of theories, and that the outcome of this contest is considerably affected by the political culture and strategic situation of the state in which it takes place, as well as by the objective facts of the international situation. Its aim, as emphasized in chapter 1, has been analytical: to provide the basic concepts with which the structure and determinants of the war-and-peace debate can be properly identified for the first time. But, although thus devised to explain political behaviour rather than to guide it, the book may be thought to have certain prescriptive implications too; and it is with these that this brief epilogue is concerned. Its theme is simple: the need for greater self-awareness. It argues that, if we try to understand the biases of the political culture and the strategic situation within which we and everyone else have to operate and the ideological assumptions we and they have to make, we can perhaps improve the quality of our efforts to prevent war.

The subjectivism attributable to political culture and strategic situation has been discussed at length in chapter 8 and need not long detain us here. It is obvious that, since those in a liberal and secure environment will take a different view of the same international situation from those in a non-liberal and insecure one, everyone should make allowances for this fact. It is possible that, had such allowances duly been made, there would have been less tension both between the United States and the Soviet Union during the first cold war and between the United States and its western-European allies during the second.

Only a little more needs to be said about ideology. There is no point in trying to banish it from international politics: there is, after all, no reason to think this a significantly easier proposition than banishing it from domestic politics. This being so, it is better to try to make the role played by ideology as explicit as possible in order at least to reduce the dangers of muddled and naïve thinking.

Instances of dangerous ideological muddle were given in chapter 4, where it was seen that misguided acts of aggression (such as the Anglo-French invasion of Suez), which could be justified on neither crusading nor preventive-defensive grounds alone, have sometimes been committed for a confused mixture of the two. If those responsible—who can, of course, range from the decision-makers themselves to the public which makes demands on them—had known whether they were really crusaders or defencists, they would have been less likely to commit such acts.

But as well as the danger of muddle there is the danger of naïvety. It is possible to be sure which ideology one favours (even if one does not know it by the name given here), and still not understand its full implications. It seems very likely, for example, that many people who endorsed militarism—particularly those who did so in the years before 1914—were unaware of the assumptions about man and society on which the theory rested, and would have been horrified had they known. Indeed, it is here suggested that almost every war-and-peace theory would lose support if its ideological content were fully understood. It was strongly hinted in chapter 7 that the decline in pacifism was caused by a growing awareness that its optimistic version was unrealistic, its mainstream version inconsistent, and its pessimistic version politically irrelevant. It seems reasonable to assume that crusading would have even fewer exponents than it still has if it were generally known to require—except in the restricted form favoured by just-war theorists—both moral arrogance and ignorance of the real effects of war. And it is likely that many, if not all, varieties of pacific-ism would suffer similarly if their basic ideological assumptions were laid bare for all to see.

The ideology which stands up best to scrutiny is defencism—a judgement which will scarcely surprise the reader who recalls from chapter 1 that it is my own preference. As suggested in chapter 5, it provides the best combination of realism (in its explanation of how the international system works) and humanitarianism (in its opposition to all aggressive war). Admittedly, there are some reasons for querying whether its attempt to reduce just wars to defensive wars has been wholly successful. But greater ideological self-awareness would undoubtedly not lead many defencists to abandon their theory. Nevertheless it ought to make them modify their behaviour in certain respects. This is because, despite the fact that their ideology attaches importance to stability, prudence, and compromise, many defencists behave as if they valued military strength alone. They often devote considerable intellectual rigour and energy to trying to show, for example, that a military 'balance' is necessary at all the different points on a complex ladder of escalation. But they do not for the most part show the same commitment to making weaponry and tactics non-provocative. And even those defencists who recognize the need for stability and international negotiations have tended to be interested more in arms control than in the non-military dimension of security. As a result, certain important defencist doctrines—in particular, that of the special rights of great powers—have yet to be spelled out, let alone made the subject of an international agreement. Yet it can be argued that nothing would contribute more to the peace of the world than for the superpowers to come to an understanding concerning their respective privileges—the size of their spheres of influence and the degree of political control they are permitted over them. Defencists should try, in other words, to be more ideological.

Appendix

Wight's and Waltz's typologies

It is necessary to explain for the benefit of the reader familiar with the classifications suggested by two important scholars, Martin Wight and Kenneth N. Waltz, why they have not been made use of here.

In his lectures at the London School of Economics over many years —which, remaining largely unpublished, have received posthumous recognition through the efforts of pupils and colleagues (notably Hedley Bull)—Martin Wight expanded the realist/idealist distinction into three or four categories. Since he retained 'realism' as the first of these, his typology was based on the division of idealism into 'rationalism', 'revolutionism', and (sometimes) 'inverted revolutionism'. These labels were not well chosen, however: in particular, 'rationalism' was not a helpful description of some of the thinkers—Winston Churchill, for instance—to whom he attached it.

After a while, he renamed the first three categories after Machiavelli, Grotius, and Kant, respectively, although the fourth—being something of an afterthought—was left unchanged. But this alteration brought its own difficulties. Although Wight regarded his categories as 'paradigms'—'not even Machiavelli, for example, was in a strict sense a Machiavellian'[1]—to name ideal types after real thinkers is to invite political theorists to point out where these thinkers fell short of the ideal type. Just as some of them have argued that Hegel was not, on a strict reading of his views, a militarist,[2] so others have criticized the account given by Wight and his followers of Kant for having greatly exaggerated his 'revolutionism', at least when writing *Perpetual Peace*.[3] This approach can lead also to a running together of the views of similar but far from identical thinkers: in particular, the Wight school seems to regard Hobbes as virtually interchangeable with Machiavelli, despite the considerable differences in their thought; and its Machiavellian category includes also 'Bacon, Hegel, Treitschke, Spengler, Hitler, Freud, E. H. Carr and Hans Morgenthau'.[4] More trivially, the great-name approach cannot be applied to theories with which it is impossible to associate a theorist of sufficiently 'classical' stature: this may have been why 'inverted revolutionism' never became a full part of the typology.

Substantive objections can also be offered to all these categories, except the last, which coincides with pacifism—Wight's own position, incidentally, from the mid-1930s onwards. The first, Machiavellian realism, like 'orthodox' realism, covers all militarism and at least some defencism, as already indicated by the list of thinkers identified with it: revealingly, Wight sometimes subdivided it into aggressive and defensive strands. The second, Grotian rationalism—of which the other typical figures were 'Locke, Montesquieu, Rousseau (in regard to the *Project for Perpetual Peace*), Bentham and Burke' and, in another account, also 'Castlereagh, Gladstone, Franklin Roosevelt, and Churchill'[5]—lumps the residue of defencism with much pacific-ism: indeed Wight subdivided it into realist and idealist strands. While the third, Kantian revolutionism, appears to be identifiable mainly with crusading, it is defined in such a way ('The ultimate reality was the community of mankind which existed potentially, even if it did not exist actually and was destined to sweep the system of states into limbo')[6] as not to exclude pacific-ism: this accords with Wight's subdivision of it into revolutionary and evolutionary strands. In other words, Wight's typology is of little help without its subdivisions, which make it possible to identify militarism as aggressive Machiavellian realism (an exemplar being Hitler), and crusading as revolutionary Kantian revolutionism. But even so, the two most influential categories are spread across two subdivisions: defencism is identifiable as defensive Machiavellian realism (Carr, Morgenthau) plus realist Grotian rationalism (Churchill), although the difference between these is hard to grasp; and pacific-ism is a combination of idealist Grotian rationalism and evolutionary Kantian realism, the distinction again being difficult to justify. Wight's typology is thus unnecessarily complicated, as well as using labels which are neither readily understood nor easily memorable.

The other typology which must be considered is that adopted in the classic work by Kenneth N. Waltz, *Man, the State, and War*.[7] This identifies three 'images' of where the causes of war are to be found: in human nature, in the internal structure of states, or in the international anarchy of competing sovereign states. It is true that it is to some extent possible to fit the different theories discussed in the present work into this framework. Militarists and pacifists, for example, can be placed more comfortably in the human-nature image than in the other two. Yet the difference between them—militarists believe that man is essentially and eternally bellicose; pacifists that he has a latent peaceableness which can in the end be brought out—shows that further subdivisions of the image are needed (as, of course, Waltz realizes). It will also have been seen that radical pacific-ists mostly blame the internal structure of states for war, and that liberal pacific-ists indict the international anarchy. But no ideology, as here defined, accepts that its analysis is confined to one image: all believe that they have demonstrated that the three are complexly interrelated. Defencism, for example, can be said to regard human nature as the ultimate cause of war; but it believes that the right policies can mitigate at least some of the anarchic features of the international system and thereby enable man often to contain his warlike impulses; and it further takes the view that such modifications are more likely to be achieved by those taking certain views (conservatism, social democracy) of domestic politics. Moreover, socialist pacific-ism identifies the economic system (capitalism) as the real cause of war: this requires it to reform internal and international structures alike, which in turn are expected to have an effect on human behaviour. Waltz's distinguished book belongs to the category of philosophical works rather than those able to elucidate the everyday war-and-peace debate.

Notes

(Unless otherwise stated, the place of publication is London.)

Chapter 1: The war-and-peace debate

1. Lord Carver, *A Policy for Peace* (1982), p. 111.
2. Notable works falling into these four categories respectively are: A. J. R. Groom, *British Thinking About Nuclear Weapons* (1974), a compendious survey of the debate on one topic (and in one state); Michael Howard, *War and the Liberal Conscience* (1977), a highly perceptive series of lectures, but concerned only with what is here called pacific-ism; Ken Booth and Moorhead Wright (eds), *American Thinking About Peace and War* (Hassocks and New York, 1978), a single-country study; and W. B. Gallie, *Philosophers on Peace and War: Kant, Clausewitz, Marx, Engels and Tolstoy* (Cambridge, 1978), an account by a political philosopher of selected major theorists.
3. 'Revolutionary defencism' is sometimes used to describe the alternative to Lenin's 1917–18 policy of 'revolutionary defeatism'; but with this exception the author has never seen the term used.
4. Martin Ceadel, *Pacifism in Britain 1914–1945: The Defining of a Faith* (Oxford, 1980), esp. pp. 3–5.
5. Robert E. Osgood, *Limited War: The Challenge To American Strategy* (Chicago, 1957), p. 28.
6. Klaus Hildebrand, *The Foreign Policy of the Third Reich*, trans. Anthony Fothergill (1973), p. 3.
7. Michael Mandelbaum, *The Nuclear Revolution: Internatonal Politics Before and After Hiroshima* (Cambridge, 1981), pp. 17–19.

Chapter 2: Principles of classification

1. The term is used in Geoffrey Ostergaard, 'Resisting the Nation-State: the Pacifist and Anarchist Traditions', in Leonard Tivey (ed.), *The Nation-State: The Formation of Modern Politics* (Oxford, 1981), p. 172; and in the editor's essay, 'Pacificism: Sources of Inspiration and Motivation', in Peter van den Dungen (ed.), *West European Pacifism and the Strategy for Peace* (1985), p. 21.
2. F. H. Hinsley, 'Reflections on the Debate about Nuclear Weapons', in

David Martin and Peter Mullen (eds), *Unholy Warfare: The Church and the Bomb* (Oxford, 1983), p. 57.

3. David Fisher, *Morality and the Bomb: An Ethical Assessment of Nuclear Deterrence* (1985), p. 16.

4. Admittedly, Howard states that 'bellicism' regards war as not just a 'normal' and 'acceptable' but even a 'desirable' way of settling differences, thereby departing somewhat from the neutral meaning of the term used here. See his *The Causes of Wars and other essays* (1983), p. 21, and also his 'Weapons and Peace', *Atlantic Quarterly* 1 (1983), esp. pp. 50–1.

5. F. H. Hinsley, *Nationalism and the International System* (1974), p. 139.

6. Ian Brownlie, *International Law and the Use of Force by States* (Oxford, 1963), pp. 19, 66, 214, 424.

7. Cited in Robert W. Tucker, *The Just War: A Study in Contemporary American Doctrine* (Baltimore, 1960), p. 12.

8. James Turner Johnson, 'Toward Reconstructing the *Jus Ad Bellum*', *The Monist* 57 (1973), p. 487. See also his *Just War Tradition and the Restraint of War: A Moral and Historical Inquiry* (Princeton, 1981), p. 328, and his *Can Modern War Be Just?* (New Haven, 1984), pp. 21–2.

9. See, for example, Charles Beitz, *Political Theory and International Relations* (Princeton, 1979), p. 92, and Michael Walzer, *Just and Unjust Wars: A Moral Argument with Historical Illustrations* (Penguin edn, Harmondsworth, 1980), esp. p. 108.

10. Raymond Aron, *Peace and War: A Theory of International Relations*, trans. Richard Howard and Annette Baker Fox (1966), pp. 591, 592.

11. See, for example, Michael Mandelbaum and William Schneider, 'The New Internationalism: Public Opinion and Foreign Policy', in Kenneth A. Oye, Donald Rothchild, Robert J. Lieber (eds), *Eagle Entangled: U. S. Foreign Policy in a Complex World* (New York, 1979), esp. p. 44; and Ole R. Holsti and James N. Rosenau, *American Leadership in World Affairs: Vietnam and the breakdown of consensus* (Boston, 1984), esp. pp. 147–9, 209.

12. See, for example, the debate in the *New Statesman* in 1935, reprinted as Henry Brinton (ed.), *Does Capitalism Cause War?* (1935).

13. For example, *International*, July 1982, cited in Christopher Coker, 'Politics and the Peace Movement in Britain', in Phil Williams (ed.), *The Nuclear Debate: Issues and Politics* (1984), p. 51.

14. Letter, *Guardian*, 26 Mar. 1984.

15. See 'The Twilight of Reason', in *Challenge to Death* (1934), a book of essays which Storm Jameson edited anonymously. Her later observations are to be found in *Journey From The North: Autobiography*, vol. 1 (1969), pp. 326–8.

Chapter 3: Militarism

1. Gen. Friedrich von Bernhardi, *Germany and the Next War*, trans. Allen H. Powles (1912), p. 31.
2. According to Alfred Vagts, *A History of Militarism* (rev. edn, 1959), p. 17, militarism is 'not the opposite of pacifism; its true counterpart is civilianism'. And the two schools of thought identified in Volker R. Berghahn, *Militarism: the History of an International Debate 1861–1979* (Leamington Spa, 1981) both regarded it as a domestic phenomenon: 'those analysts who saw it in a political and constitutional framework and those who examined it as a socio-economic problem' (p. 10). There is some material on it as a war-and-peace theory, however, in Albert T. Lauterbach, 'Militarism in the Western World: A Comparative Study', *Journal of the History of Ideas* 5 (1944), pp. 446–78.
3. *Mein Kampf*, trans. Ralph Mannheim (1969), pp. 593, 597. *Hitler's Secret Book*, trans. Salvator Attansio (New York, 1961), pp. 8, 10.
4. Cited by Hermann Rauschning, *Hitler Speaks* (1939), p. 16.
5. Cited by Zeev Sternhell, 'Fascist Ideology' in Walter Laqueur (ed.), *Fascism: A Reader's Guide* (1979), p. 334.
6. John Raphael Staude, *Max Scheler 1874–1929* (New York, 1967), pp. 80–1.
7. Max Scheler, *Der Genius des Krieges und der Deutsche Krieg* (Leipzig, 1915), p. 46. No translation of Scheler's book exists; and, the syntax of this passage being incoherent, the present effort can be only an approximate one. I am grateful to my colleague John Cowan for his help.
8. Anthony Ludovici, *A Defence of Conservatism: A Further Text-book for Tories* (1927), pp. 253, 257. I owe this source to Gerry Webber.
9. Heinrich von Treitschke, *Politics*, trans. Blanche Dugdale and Torben De Bill (1916), vol. 1, p. 66. The first German edition appeared in 1897.
10. Speech at Munich, 13 April 1923, cited in Alan Bullock, *Hitler: A Study in Tyranny* (rev. edn, Harmondsworth, 1962), p. 399.
11. Bernhardi, *Germany and the Next War*, pp. 13, 14; Bullock, *Hitler*, p. 398.
12. 'The Curse of Militarism', *The Young Man*, May 1901, repr. in William Clarke, *A Collection of his Writings* (1908), pp. 119–20.
13. Sir Oswald Mosley, *The Alternative* (Ramsbury, Wilts., 1947), p. 84.
14. Cited in Robert Soucy, *Fascist Intellectual: Drieu La Rochelle* (Berkeley, 1979), p. 198 (for his being 'swept off his feet' by Nietzsche, see p. 45). Benito Mussolini, 'The Political and Social Doctrine of Fascism', trans. Jane Soames, *Political Quarterly* 4 (1933), pp. 344–5.

15. Bernhardi, *Germany and the Next War*, p. 39. Fritz Stern, 'Bethmann Hollweg and the War; the Limits of Responsibility', in Leonard Krieger and Fritz Stern (eds), *The Responsibility of Power: Historical Essays in Honor of Hajo Holborn* (1968), p. 268.
16. Roland N. Stromberg deals mainly with the purgative view in his impressively wide-ranging survey, *Ordeal by War: The Intellectuals and 1914* (Lawrence, Kan., 1982)—a study which, however, is weakened by a failure to distinguish between different types of enthusiasm for war.
17. Cited by Bullock, *Hitler*, p. 471.
18. Soucy, *Fascist Intellectual*, pp. 195–6.
19. Cited in George M. Wilson, *Radical Nationalist in Japan: Kita Ikki 1883–1937* (Cambridge, Mass., 1969), p. 98.
20. Cited in Nicholas M. Nagy-Talavera, *The Green Shirts and the Others: A History of Fascism in Hungary and Rumania* (Stanford, 1973), p. 115. I owe this source to Stephen Cullen.
21. Cited in Jonathan Haslam, *Soviet Foreign Policy 1930–33* (1983), pp. 48–9.
22. Cited (with the insertions) in Soucy, *Fascist Intellectual*, p. 176.
23. Robert Skidelsky, *Oswald Mosley* (1975), p. 483.
24. Cited in Rauschning, *Hitler Speaks*, p. 230.
25. Ibid., 229, 230.
26. *Hitler's Table Talk 1941–44: His Private Conversations*, trans. Norman Cameron and R. H. Stevens (1973 edn), p. 490.
27. Milan Hauner, 'Did Hitler Want a World Dominion?', *Journal of Contemporary History* 13 (1978), p. 25. *Hitler's Table Talk*, p. 489.
28. Bernhardi, *Germany and the Next War*, p. 48.
29. Jonathan Steinberg, 'The Copenhagen Complex', *Journal of Contemporary History* 1 (1966), p. 40.
30. Norman Stone, 'Army and Society in the Habsburg Monarchy, 1900–1914', *Past and Present* 33 (April 1966), pp. 108, 109.
31. Treitschke, *Politics*, vol. 2, p. 597.
32. Bernhardi, *Germany and the Next War*, pp. 18–19.
33. *Hitler's Table Talk*, p. 660.
34. José Antonio Primo de Rivera, *The Spanish Answer*, selected and trans. with an introduction by Juan Macnab Calder from the complete works, ed. Agustin del Rio Cisneros (Madrid, 1957), pp. 91–3.
35. See, for example, Howard, *The Causes of Wars and other essays*, p. 27.
36. Cited in Gaetano Salvemini, *Mazzini*, trans. I. M. Rawson (1956), pp. 81, 82.
37. See G. Gangulee (ed.), *Giuseppe Mazzini: Selected Writings* (1945), pp. 124–6.
38. Ibid., 18; see also pp. 13–14 and 90–1.

39. Gwilym O. Griffith, *Mazzini: Prophet of Modern Europe* (1932), p. 10.
40. Cited in Rauschning, *Hitler Speaks*, p. 229.
41. David Pryce-Jones, *Unity Mitford: A Quest* (1976), p. 208 and the facsimile reproduced on the back dustjacket.
42. Treitschke, *Politics*, vol. 1, pp. 69–70.
43. *Hitler's Table Talk*, p. 661. Albert Speer, *Spandau: The Secret Diaries*, trans. Richard and Clare Winston (1976), p. 144.
44. Lord Milner, *The Nation and the Empire, Being A Collection of Speeches and Addresses* (1913), pp. xxxii, xxxv; see also p. 152.
45. W. K. Hancock, *Argument of Empire* (Harmondsworth, 1943), pp. 76, 128, 152.
46. Cited in Charles DeBenedetti, *Origins of the Modern American Peace Movement 1915–1929* (Millwood, N.Y., 1978), p. 89.
47. *The Times*, 8 June 1931. On the same occasion Keith argued that 'race prejudice' worked 'for the ultimate good of the world'.
48. J. F. C. Fuller, *The Reformation of War* (1923), esp. pp. 1, 7, 130–1, 146–7.
49. Richard Hillary, *The Last Enemy* (1942), pp. 151–4, 206.
50. Mosley, *The Alternative*, p. 297.
51. Cited in Andrew Sinclair, *Guevara* (1970), pp. 87–8.
52. Cited in S. Neil MacFarlane, *Superpower Rivalry and Third World Radicalism* (1985), p. 111.
53. Peter Worsley, in *Peace News*, 18 Oct. 1963.

Chapter 4: Crusading

1. Walzer, *Just and Unjust Wars*, pp. 113–14.
2. Michael Walzer, *The Revolution of the Saints* (Cambridge, Mass., 1965), ch. 8.
3. Cited by R. J. Vincent, *Nonintervention and International Order* (Princeton, 1974), p. 67. (An important book.)
4. Burke's proposal is recognized as a crusade in Frank O'Gorman, *Edmund Burke: His Political Philosophy* (1973), pp. 112–13.
5. Walzer, *Just and Unjust Wars*, p. 108.
6. Cited by R. J. Vincent, 'Edmund Burke and the theory of international relations', *Review of International Studies* 10 (1984), pp. 210–11.
7. Walzer, *Just and Unjust Wars*, pp. 103, 104.
8. Hans J. Morgenthau, *In Defense of the National Interest: A Critical Examination of American Foreign Policy* (New York, 1951), p. 131.
9. Henry Kissinger, *The White House Years* (1979), p. 59.
10. Walter Lippmann, *Public Opinion and Foreign Policy in the United States* (1952), pp. 25, 26.
11. Wendell L. Wilkie, *One World* (UK edn, 1943), pp. 165, 166.

12. See Walter Lippmann, *U. S. Foreign Policy* (1943), esp. pp. 84–5. See also Ronald Steel, *Walter Lippmann and the American Century* (1981), esp. chs. 32, 34.

13. *Cavalcade*, 20 Oct. 1945, repr. in Barry Feinberg and Ronald Kasrils, *Bertrand Russell's America*, vol. 2: *1945–1970* (1984), pp. 312, 314.

14. *Observer*, 21 Nov. 1948, cited in Skidelsky, *Oswald Mosley*, p. 542. See also Ronald W. Clark, *The Life of Bertrand Russell* (1975), ch. 19.

15. John Middleton Murry, *The Free Society* (1948), pp. 39–40: a book written in December 1946 and January 1947 and sent to the press in September 1947.

16. Cited in John Lewis Gaddis, *The United States and the Origins of the Cold War 1941–1947* (New York, 1972), p. 245.

17. Samuel T. Francis, *Power and History: The Political Thought of James Burnham* (Lanham, Md., 1984), p. 85.

18. James Burnham, *The Struggle for the World* (1947), pp. 196, 198, 230, 236; and his *The Coming Defeat of Communism* (1950), pp. 30, 79, 113, 155.

19. This is the interpretation put foward by Richard H. Ullman in his three-volume study of *Anglo-Soviet Relations, 1917–21*, (Princeton, 1961–72).

20. Cited in Richard Little, *Intervention: External Intervention in Civil Wars* (1975), p. 21.

21. Cited in *Lord Riddell's Intimate Diary of the Peace Conference and After 1918–1923* (1933), p. 224.

22. Cited in Selwyn Lloyd, *Suez 1956: A Personal Account* (1978), pp. 238–9.

23. Jason Gurney, *Crusade in Spain* (1974), p. 188.

24. Osgood, *Limited War*, p. 22.

25. Hedley Bull, 'Intervention in the Third World', in Hedley Bull (ed.), *Intervention in World Politics* (Oxford, 1984), p. 147.

26. Robin Edmonds, *Soviet Foreign Policy: the Brezhnev Years* (Oxford, 1983), pp. 72, 194.

27. G. I. Tunkin, *Theory of International Law*, trans. William E. Butler (1974), pp. 427, 430, 435–6.

28. It is ironic that this term has been popularized by a peace researcher concerned to oppose 'direct' violence too: see Johan Galtung, 'Violence, Peace and Peace Research', *Journal of Peace Research* (Oslo) 6 (1969), pp. 167–91. Galtung defines structural violence as being 'present when human beings are being influenced so that their actual somatic and mental realizations are below their potential realizations' (p. 168).

29. Speech at Baylor University, 28 May 1965, cited in Richard J. Barnet, *Intervention and Revolution: The United States in the Third World* (1970 edn), p. 174.

30. Cited in Arthur Schlesinger, Jr, 'Foreign Policy and the American Character', *Foreign Affairs* (New York) 62 (1983), p. 5.
31. Vincent, *Nonintervention and International Order*, p. 167. Philip Windsor and Adam Roberts, *Czechoslovakia 1968: Reform, Repression and Resistance* (1969), p. 62.
32. Ruth B. Russell, *The United Nations and United States Security Policy* (Washington, D.C., 1968), p. 180.
33. Michael Akehurst, 'Humanitarian Intervention', in Bull (ed.), *Intervention in World Politics*, pp. 96, 97.
34. George F. Kennan, *American Diplomacy 1900–1950* (1952), p. 3.
35. Cited in Sinclair, *Guevara*, p. 34.
36. Stephen E. Ambrose, *Eisenhower*, vol. 2: *The President 1952–1969* (1984), pp. 34–5.
37. Speech at Columbia University, cited ibid. 39–40.
38. Ibid., 195.
39. Ronald W. Pruessen, *John Foster Dulles: The Road To Power* (New York, 1982), pp. 77, 154–5, 180, 186 ff.
40. David Rees, *Korea: the limited war* (1964), p. xi.
41. Lyndon Baines Johnson, *The Vantage Point: Perspectives on the Presidency 1963–1969* (1972), p. 201.
42. *Time*, 7 Nov. 1983, p. 150, cited in Jeff McMahan, *Reagan and the World: Imperial Policy in the New Cold War* (1984), p. 150.
43. Vincent, *Nonintervention and International Order*, pp. 197–8, 211.
44. Speech at Baylor University, 28 May 1965, cited in Barnet, *Intervention and Revolution*, p. 174.
45. Russell, *The United Nations and United States Security Policy*, p. 181.
46. *Facts on File* (New York) 28 Oct. 1983, p. 810.
47. Richard H. Ullman, 'At War with Nicaragua', *Foreign Affairs* 62 (1983), pp. 40–1.
48. Cited in Schlesinger, 'Foreign Policy and the American Character', p. 5.
49. *The Times*, 9 June 1982.
50. Holsti and Rosenau, *American Leadership in World Affairs*, p. 253.
51. Cited by P. H. Vigor, *The Soviet View of War, Peace and Neutrality* (1975) p. 71. (An impressive study.)
52. Ibid., 5–6; see also 54–5 and 156–7.
53. Cited in Milovan Djilas, *Conversations with Stalin* (Pelican edn, Harmondsworth, 1969), p. 90.
54. Cited in Daniel Yergin, *The Shattered Peace: The Origins of the Cold War and the National Security State* (Pelican edn, Harmondsworth, 1980), p. 166.
55. Cited in Michael B. Yahuda, *China's Role in World Affairs* (1978), p. 109.

56. William F. Gutteridge, 'Africa', in Kurt London (ed.), *The Soviet Union in World Politics* (Boulder, Col., 1980), p. 127.

Chapter 5: Defencism

1. Barry Buzan, *People, States and Fear: The National Security Problem in International Relations* (Brighton, 1983), pp. 157, 173.
2. *The Times*, 15 Nov. 1936, cited in Keith Middlemas, *Diplomacy of Illusion: the British Government and Germany 1937–39* (1972), p. 106.
3. Laurence Housman, *The Preparation of Peace* (1940), pp. 9–10.
4. Sir Ernle Chatfield to Warren Fisher, 4 June 1934, cited in David Reynolds, 'Competitive Co-operation', *Historical Journal* (Cambridge) 23 (1980), pp. 244–5.
5. See James Turner Johnson, *Ideology, Reason and the Limitation of War: Religious and Secular Concepts 1200–1740* (Princeton, 1975), esp. pp. 7, 26, 43.
6. Hedley Bull, *The Anarchical Society: A Study of Order in World Politics* (1977), pp. 17–18.
7. For an excellent discussion of the philosophical difficulties raised by this argument, see Gregory S. Kavka, 'Some Paradoxes of Deterrence', *Journal of Philosophy* lxxv (1978), pp. 285–302.
8. F. S. Oliver, *Ordeal By Battle* (1915), p. 250.
9. This is suggested in Simon Newman, *March 1939: The British Guarantee To Poland: A Study in the Continuity of British Foreign Policy* (Oxford, 1976), pp. 219–21.
10. Walter Lippman, *The Cold War: A Study in U.S. Foreign Policy* (1947), p. 42.
11. Secretary Shultz, 'Power and Diplomacy in the 1980s' (address before the Trilateral Commission, 3 Apr. 1984), Current Policy no. 561, US Department of State Bureau of Public Affairs, Washington, D.C. I owe this reference to Douglas Jehl.
12. For example, Hylke Trompe, 'Alternatives to Current Security Policy and the Peace Movements', in van den Dungen (ed.), *West European Pacifism and the Strategy for Peace*, p. 86.
13. Walzer, *Just and Unjust Wars*, pp. 82–5.
14. *The Times*, 13 Oct. 1983.
15. An Alternative Defence Commission was set up in 1982 by the Lansbury House Trust Fund and Bradford University's School of Peace Studies and has published two reports: *Defence without The Bomb* (1983), and *Without The Bomb: Non-Nuclear Defence Policies for Britain* (1985). Just Defence is a less pacifist-tinged organization of which the leading members are Frank Barnaby, Sir Hugh Beach, Anthony Kenny, and Stan Windass. 'Transarmament' was coined by Theodor

Ebert, according to Adam Roberts (ed.), *The Strategy of Civilian Resistance: Non-violent Resistance to Aggression* (1967), p. 29 n.

16. Bull, *The Anarchical Society*, pp. xiv, 24–6, 46–51.
17. *Guardian*, 2 Jan. 1984.
18. Franz Joseph Strauss, 'Peace—but not Pacifism', *The Times*, 19 Mar. 1984.
19. Michael Howard, 'The Concept of Peace', *Encounter*, Dec. 1983, p. 19.
20. Jean-François Revel, *How Democracies Perish* (1985), p. 360.
21. Hans J. Morgenthau, *Politics Among Nations: The Struggle for Power and Peace* (3rd edn, New York, 1962), pp. 4, 10.
22. Brian Crozier, *A Theory of Conflict* (1974), p. viii.
23. Michael Howard, 'Apologia pro Studia Sua', in his *Studies in War and Peace* (1970), p. 13.
24. Michael Howard, 'Is Winston Churchill Still Relevant?', *Encounter*, Apr. 1985, p. 25.
25. Michael Dummett, 'Nuclear Warfare', in Nigel Blake and Kay Pole (eds), *Objections To Nuclear Defence: Philosophers on Deterrence* (1984), pp. 28–9.
26. See their joint article, 'Nuclear weapons and the Atlantic Alliance', *Foreign Affairs* 60 (1981–2), pp. 753–68.
27. Stephen King-Hall, *Defence in the Nuclear Age* (1958) pp. 142, 159. His views were first published in the *King-Hall News Letter* of 24 Apr. 1957 and reprinted in *Peace News*, 10 May 1957.
28. Stephen King-Hall, *Common Sense in Defence* (1960), p. 4.
29. Baldwin to Arthur Ponsonby, 15 Dec. 1927, Ponsonby Papers, Bodleian Library, Oxford.
30. Michael Howard, 'Morality and Force in International Politics', in his *Studies in War and Peace*, p. 236.
31. Cited in Skidelsky, *Oswald Mosley*, pp. 426, 496.
32. Johan Galtung, *Peace: Research. Action. Education*, Essays in Peace Research vol. 1 (Copenhagen, 1975), pp. 91–4.
33. Joseph W. Bendersky, *Carl Schmitt: Theorist for the Reich* (Princeton, 1983), pp. 251–63.
34. Brian Crozier, *Strategy of Survival* (1978), pp. 9–10.
35. Howard, 'Apologia pro Studia Sua', p. 15.
36. Helmut Schmidt, *The Balance of Power: Germany's Peace Policy and the Superpowers*, trans. Edward Thomas (1971), pp. 15, 292.
37. Johan Galtung, *There are Alternatives! Four Roads to Peace and Security* (Nottingham, 1984), p. 23 (italics in original).
38. Michael Howard, *War and the Nation State* (Oxford, 1978), pp. 15–16.
39. Douglas Jay, *Change and Fortune* (1980), p. 505.
40. H. J. N. Horsburgh, *Non-Violence and Aggression: A Study of Gandhi's Moral Equivalent of War* (1968), p. 103.

41. See his paper 'France and Belgian Security', printed in Martin Gilbert, *Winston S. Churchill*, vol. 5 Companion Part 1: *The Exchequer Years 1922–9* (1979), p. 415. For his different views in 1921 see vol. 4: *1916–1922* (1978), pp. 608–9.

42. Cited by John Colville in Sir John Wheeler-Bennett (ed.), *Action This Day: Working With Churchill* (1968), p. 89.

43. Albert Resis, 'The Churchill–Stalin Secret "Percentages" Agreement on the Balkans, Moscow, October 1944', *American Historical Review* 83 (1978), pp. 368–87.

44. On 1953 see Anthony Glees, 'Churchill's Last Gambit', *Encounter*, Apr. 1985. The quotation is given in David Butler and Anne Sloman, *British Political Facts 1900–1979* (1980), p. 252.

Chapter 6: Pacific-ism

1. Lawrence S. Wittner, *Rebels against War: The American Peace Movement 1941–1960* (New York, 1969), p. ix.

2. Louis Mackay and David Fernbach (eds), *Nuclear-Free Defence* (1983), p. 23.

3. Alan Wilkinson, *Dissent or Conform? War, Peace and the English Churches 1900–1945* (London, 1986), p. 90.

4. *London Review of Books*, 2 Oct. 1980, p. 4; for Taylor's original usage see his *The Trouble Makers* (1957), p. 51 n.

5. David A. Martin, *Pacifism: An Historical and Sociological Study* (1965), p. 205. The distinction between being pacific (*pacifique*) and pacifist is also made in J.-B. Barbier, *Le Pacifisme dans l'histoire de France de l'an mille à nos jours* (Paris, 1966), pp. 11–12, although the former seems to include defencism in addition to pacific-ism.

6. Cited by Martin Gilbert, *Winston S. Churchill*, vol. 5 (1976), p. 776.

7. F. H. Hinsley, *Power and the Pursuit of Peace: Theory and Practice in the History of Relations Between States* (Cambridge, 1967), p. 1.

8. Hinsley, *Nationalism and the International System*, p. 71.

9. Howard, *War and the Liberal Conscience*, p. 32.

10. For a psychoanalytical approach see Edward Glover, *War, Sadism and Pacifism* (1933). Calendar reform is one of the odd theories noted by Norman Angell, *After All* (1951), p. 301. The dietary theory was how Lydia Landau, a disciple of the New Jersey therapist Dr E. K. Stretch, explained Hitler's invasion of Poland: see Paul Avrich, *The Modern School Movement* (Princeton, 1980), p. 291.

11. Majid Khadduri, *War and Peace in the Law of Islam* (Baltimore, 1955), pp. 45, 72–3, 141.

12. Cited in Gideon Rafael, *Destination Peace: Three Decades of Israeli Foreign Policy: A Memoir* (1983), p. 13.

13. The phrase is Michael Dummett's, from his *Catholicism and the Social Order: Some Reflections on the 1978 Reith Lectures* (1979), p. 31. This pamphlet is a reply to the criticism that Christians 'have adopted the moralities of secular political ideologies and promote them for what they think of as authentically Christian social ends' put forward in E. R. Norman, *Christianity and the World Order* (Oxford, 1979), p. 58. Dummett is doubtful whether the distinctively Christian political programme implied by Norman in fact exists, although he insists that Christianity requires a strict adherence to the just-war tradition.

14. G. H. Perris, *Our Foreign Policy and Sir Edward Grey's Failure* (1912), p. 197; Lord Grey of Fallodon, *Twenty-Five Years, 1892–1916* (2 vols, 1925), i. 91–2; 280 HC Deb., col. 377.

15. The title of a 1968 lecture by Robert Neild, cited in Nicholas A. Sims, *Approaches to Disarmament* (2nd edn, 1979), p. 11.

16. *New York Review of Books*, 18 July 1981, p. 14.

17. Salvador de Madariaga, *Disarmament* (1929), p. 8.

18. For the accidental/unintentional distinction, see Daniel Frei, with the collaboration of Christian Catrina, *Risks of Accidental Nuclear War* (Totowa, N.J., 1983), pp. 3–4.

19. Jonathan Schell, *The Fate of the Earth* (1982), p. 221.

20. *Peace News*, 26 Feb. 1938; George Lansbury, *My Quest For Peace* (1938), p. 55.

21. For example, C. A. W. Manning (ed.), *Peaceful Change* (1937), and C. R. M. F. Cruttwell, *A History of Peaceful Change in the Modern World* (1937).

22. The *Journal of Conflict Resolution* was founded in 1957.

23. Kenneth E. Miller, 'John Stuart Mill's Theory of International Relations', *Journal of the History of Ideas* 22 (1961), p. 500. Richard Cobden, 'Russia 1836' in *The Political Writings of Richard Cobden* (1886 edn), p. 36.

24. Perris, *Our Foreign Policy and Sir Edward Grey's Failure*, p. 193.

25. David Patterson, *Toward A Warless World: The Travail of the American Peace Movement 1887–1914* (Bloomington, Ind., 1976), esp. pp. 111–20.

26. House of Commons, 12 May 1949 (464 HC Deb., cols. 2121–3).

27. C. E. M. Joad, *What Is At Stake And Why Not Say So?* (1940), p. 100.

28. Cited in Wittner, *Rebels against War*, p. 140. See also p. 165.

29. Wolf Mendl, *Prophets and Reconcilers: Reflections on the Quaker Peace Testimony* (1974), p. 87.

30. Robert O. Keohane and Joseph S. Nye, *Power and Interdependence: World Politics in Transition* (Boston, 1977), p. 10.

31. One of the few to do so was Jonathan Schell at the end of *The Fate of the Earth*.

32. Howard, *The Causes of Wars and Other Essays*, p. 5.
33. D. Cameron Watt, *Succeeding John Bull: America in Britain's Place 1900–1975* (Cambridge, 1984), pp. 184–5; see also pp. 34–9.
34. Arthur Ponsonby, *Democracy and Diplomacy: A Plea for Popular Control of Foreign Policy* (1915), p. 66; J. B. Priestley, *New Statesman*, 2 Nov. 1957, pp. 555–6; I. F. Stone, cited by John Pilger in his preface to Crispin Aubrey *et al.*, *Nukespeak: The Media and the Bomb* (1982).
35. Cited in Theodore Zeldin, *France 1848–1945*, vol. 1: *Ambition, Love and Politics* (Oxford, 1973), p. 714.
36. Francis De Tarr, *The French Radical Party from Herriot to Mendès-France* (1961), pp. 6, 7.
37. E. H. Kossman, *The Low Countries 1780–1940* (Oxford, 1978), pp. 336–40.
38. Watt, *Succeeding John Bull*, p. 185.
39. C. R. Attlee, *The Labour Party in Perspective* (1937), p. 200.
40. *Political Quarterly*, July/Sept. 1949, cited in A. W. Wright, *G. D. H. Cole and Socialist Democracy* (Oxford, 1979), p. 274.
41. Macmillan to Charles Hill, 5 June 1957, cited in Harold Macmillan, *Riding the Storm 1956–1959* (1971), p. 299.
42. See Sydney Higgins, *The Benn Inheritance: The Story of a Radical Family* (1984).
43. Mackay and Fernbach (eds), *Nuclear-Free Defence*, p. 44.
44. J. A. Hobson, *Richard Cobden: The International Man* (1919), p. 406; L. T. Hobhouse, *Democracy and Reaction* (1904), p. 243; H. N. Brailsford, *The War of Steel and Gold* (1914), p. 163.
45. Adam B. Ulam, *Expansion and Co-existence: Soviet Foreign Policy 1917–73* (New York, 2nd edn, 1974), p. 54.
46. L. John Collins, *Faith Under Fire* (1966), p. 266.
47. E. P. Thompson, *The Defence of Britain* (1983), p. 15.
48. Aberdeen CND, *Living on the Front Line* (Aberdeen, 1981), pp. 5, 46.
49. Solly Zuckerman, *Nuclear Illusion and Reality* (1982), p. 106.
50. *Labour Party Conference Report 1957*, p. 174; *The Times*, 29 Apr. 1980 (emphasis added); interview by Robert McKenzie, *Listener*, 21 May 1981, p. 665.
51. Cited in James Joll, *The Second International 1889–1914* (2nd edn, 1974), p. 114.
52. Translated from Gustav Hervé, *La Patrie en danger* (Paris, 1915), pp. 25–6. For his previous views see his *My Country Right or Wrong*, trans. Guy Bowman (1910).
53. *Democracy and Military Service: An Abbreviated Translation of the 'Armée Nouvelle' of Jean Jaurès* (1916). Coulton also expounded Jaurès's views in his pamphlets *Workers and War* (Cambridge, 1914)

and *Pacificist Illusions* (Cambridge, 1915). For the British left's criticisms, see J. Ramsay MacDonald, *National Defence: A Study in Militarism* (1917), ch. 2.

54. See David Fernbach, 'Tom Wintringham and Socialist Defence Strategy', *History Workshop Journal* 14 (Autumn 1982), pp. 63–91.

55. See, for example, Peter Tatchell, *Democratic Defence* (1984).

56. See Jolyon Howarth, 'French Workers and German Workers: the Impossibility of Internationalism, 1900–1914', *European History Quarterly* 15 (1985), and Douglas J. Newton, *British Labour, European Socialism, and the Struggle for Peace 1889–1914* (Oxford, 1985), esp. ch. 10. For the United States, see Murray B. Seidler, *Norman Thomas: Respectable Rebel* (Syracuse, N.Y., 1961), pp. 41, 52.

57. See, for example, Lord Allen of Hurtwood in G. P. Gooch (ed.), *In Pursuit of Peace* (1933), pp. 20–1; Sir Stafford Cripps in Bertrand Russell *et al.*, *Dare We Look Ahead?* (1938), pp. 125–6; Martin Shaw, *Socialism against War: Remaking a Tradition* (Nottingham, n.d. [1981]), p. 3.

58. *Tribune*, 7 June 1940.

59. Kingsley Martin to Stafford Cripps, 18 March 1938, Cripps Papers, Nuffield College, Oxford.

60. *Labour Party Conference Report 1945*, p. 119. Although Bevin was referring to Anglo-French rather than to east–west co-operation he was reported the following month as saying: 'Russia would deal better and with greater confidence with a Labour Government than with the historical men of Munich. Left can speak to left in comradeship and confidence' (*Daily Worker*, 9 June 1945, cited in C. R. Rose, 'The Relationship of Socialist Principles to British Labour Foreign Policy 1945–51', unpublished D. Phil thesis, Oxford, 1959, p. 159).

61. R. H. S. Crossman and Kenneth Younger, *Socialist Foreign Policy* (1951), p. 11.

62. For example, André Philip; see Michael Newman, *Socialism and European Unity: The Dilemma of the Left in Britain and France* (1983), pp. 32–3.

63. For recognition by an activist of the limitations of first-wave CND's positive neutralism, see, for example, Nigel Young, 'The Contemporary European Anti-Nuclear Movement: Experiments in the Mobilization of Public Power', in *Peace and Change* 9(i) (Spring 1983), p. 8.

64. J. A. A. Stockwin, *The Japanese Socialist Party and Neutralism* (Melbourne, 1968).

65. A Group of Members of Parliament, *Keeping Left* (1950), p. 43.

66. *New Statesman*, 12 Mar. 1955, p. 357.

67. Stephen Howe, 'Anti-Colonialism in British Politics: The Left and the End of Empire, 1939–1964', unpublished D.Phil thesis, Oxford, 1985, p. 366.
68. This phrase is used, for example, by Ernest Mandel, 'The Laws of Uneven Development', *New Left Review* 59 (Jan./Feb.1970), pp. 20–1.
69. Ken Coates, 'The Peace Movement and Socialism', *New Left Review* 145 (June 1984), esp. pp. 117, 121. For a similar argument see Shaw, *Socialism against War*, esp. pp. 32–3.
70. Brian Jenkins and Günther Minnerup, *Citizens and Comrades: Socialism in a World of Nation States* (1984), pp. 138, 142.
71. Michael Mann, 'Nationalism and Internationalism' in John Griffiths (ed.), *Socialism in a Cold Climate* (1983), pp. 185, 197; see also Martin Shaw (ed.), *War, State and Society* (1984).
72. Patterson, *Toward a Warless World*, p. 58.
73. Cited by Jill Liddington, 'The Women's Peace Crusade: The History of a Forgotten Campaign', in Dorothy Thompson (ed.), *Over Our Dead Bodies: Women against the Bomb* (1983), p. 187.
74. *Spare Rib*, Dec. 1981.
75. *Spare Rib*, Feb. 1983; Lynne Jones (ed.), *Keeping the Peace: A Women's Peace Handbook (1)* (1983), pp. 62–3.
76. *Sanity*, Dec. 1981/Jan. 1982, repr. in Cambridge Women's Peace Collective, *My Country is the Whole World: An Anthology of Women's Work on Peace and War* (1984) p. 217.
77. Marcia Yudkin, 'Reflections on Woolf's *Three Guineas*', in Judith Stiehm (ed.), *Women and Men's Wars* (Oxford, 1983), p. 263 (originally published in *Women's Studies International Forum* 5 (3–4). I owe this source to Anne Summers.
78. For example Janet Radcliffe Richards, *The Sceptical Feminist: A Philosophical Inquiry* (1980). See also the distinctions made by Alison Jagger, 'Political Philosophies of Women's Liberation' in Mary Vetterling-Braggin, Frederick A. Elliston and Jane English (eds), *Feminism and Philosophy* (Totowa, N.J., 1977), pp. 5–21, and by John Charvet, *Feminism* (1982), esp. p. 130.
79. Penny Strange, *It'll Make A Man Of You . . .: A Feminist View of the Arms Race* (Nottingham, 1983) pp. 4, 20, 29.
80. Green CND, *Embrace The Earth: A Green View of Peace* (1983), pp. 15, 16, 22, 41.

Chapter 7: Pacifism

1. Peter Brock, *Pacifism in Europe to 1914* (Princeton, 1972), p. 3.
2. See Peter Brock, *Twentieth-Century Pacifism* (New York, 1970), esp. pp. 62–3, 104.

3. A term used in Anthony Kenny, *The Logic of Deterrence* (1985), p. 6.

4. He accepted the need to supplement non-violent resistance with a small international frontier police force 'armed with conventional weapons': see Stephen King-Hall, *Power Politics in the Nuclear Age* (1962), pp. 190–2.

5. Hugh Ross Williamson, *The Walled Garden* (1956), pp. 131–3, 192.

6. This is the position I described as 'quasi-pacifism' in *Pacifism in Britain 1914–1945*.

7. Cited in Michael Holroyd, *Lytton Strachey: A Critical Biography*, vol. 1 (1967), p. 416.

8. See, for example, Geoffrey Nuttall, *Christian Pacifism in History* (Oxford, 1958), p. 10.

9. John Rae, *Conscience and Politics: The British Government and the Conscientious Objector to Military Service 1916–1919* (1970), p. 74.

10. Mulford Q. Sibley and Philip E. Jacob, *Conscription of Conscience: The American State and the Conscientious Objector, 1940–1947* (Ithaca, N.Y., 1952), pp. 31–5.

11. Neil Summerton, 'The Just War: A Sympathetic Critique', in Oliver R. Barclay (ed.) *Pacifism and War* (Leicester, 1984), pp. 196, 198.

12. Cited in Brock, *Pacifism in Europe to 1914*, p. 464.

13. Cited by Paul Deats, 'Protestant Social Ethics and Pacifism' in Thomas A. Shannon (ed.), *War or Peace? The Search for New Answers* (Maryknoll, N.Y., 1980), p. 83.

14. Bertrand Russell, *Which Way to Peace?* (1936), p. 151.

15. Andrew Wilson, *The Disarmer's Handbook of Military Technology and Organisation* (Harmondsworth, 1983), pp. 306–7; for his joining CND see the *Observer*, 1 Nov. 1981.

16. See her contribution to Mackay and Fernbach (eds), *Nuclear-Free Defence*, p. 65.

17. For example, Donald L. Davidson, *Nuclear Weapons and the American Churches: Ethical Positions on Modern Warfare* (Boulder, Col., 1984), pp. 42–3.

18. For example, the Revd Eric Rees, *Pacifist*, Sept. 1964.

19. Norman Angell, *Defence and the English-Speaking Role* (1958), pp. 39.

20. King-Hall, *Common Sense in Defence*, p. 16.

21. Jonathan Glover, *Causing Death and Saving Lives* (Harmondsworth, 1977), p. 258, summarizing John Rawls, *A Theory of Justice* (Cambridge, Mass., 1971), section 58, from which the term 'contingent pacifism' is taken.

22. Cited in Wittner, *Rebels Against War*, p. 30.

23. King-Hall, *Power Politics in the Nuclear Age*, p. 209.

24. *Peace News*, 15 Dec. 1944.

25. John Ferguson, *War and Peace in the World's Religions* (1977), pp. 50, 136.

26. Sir Frederick Catherwood, 'A Case against Nuclear Pacifism', in Barclay (ed.), *Pacifism and War*, pp. 68, 69.

27. Richard Harries, 'The Christian Churches and the Pacifist Temptation', *World Today* 40 (1984), p. 327.

28. Bernard Williams, 'Morality, Scepticism and the Nuclear Arms Race', in Nigel Blake and Kay Pole (eds), *Objections to Nuclear Defence: Philosophers on Deterrence* (1984), p. 101.

29. Cited in Peter Brock, *Pacifism in the United States: From the Colonial Era to the First World War* (Princeton, 1968), p. 600.

30. Ceadel, *Pacifism in Britain 1914–1945*, pp. 307–8.

31. See *Freedom*, 17 May and 26 July 1947.

32. Ostergaard, 'Resisting the Nation-State', in Tivey (ed.), *The Nation-State*, p. 191.

33. Nicolas Walter, *Nonviolent Resistance: Men against War* (1963), p. 17.

34. April Carter, 'Anarchism and Violence', in J. Roland Pennock and John W. Chapman (eds), *Anarchism* (Nomos XIX) (New York, 1978), p. 337.

35. *Anarchy* 7 [1972] and 22 [1977].

36. Cited in Wittner, *Rebels against War*, p. 30.

37. Exaggerated expectations of warfare are most clearly expressed in the novels of the period; see Martin Ceadel, 'Popular Fiction and the Next War, 1918–1939', in Frank Gloversmith (ed.), *Class, Culture and Social Change: A New View of the 1930s* (Brighton, 1980).

38. Arthur Ponsonby, *Now is the Time: An Appeal for Peace* (1925), p. 137.

39. Russell, *Which Way to Peace?*, pp. 129, 151, 211–12.

40. Bertrand Russell, *Autobiography*, vol. 2 (1968), p. 191; *Which Way to Peace?*, p. 220.

41. Russell, *Autobiography*, vol. 2, p. 222.

42. Aldous Huxley, *What are You Going to Do about It? The Case for Constructive Peace* (1936), p. 26.

43. Jonathan Fryer, *Isherwood, A Biography of Christopher Isherwood* (1977), pp. 193–5.

44. Revd A. D. Belden, *Peace News*, 23 July 1938; Denis Hayes, *Challenge of Conscience: The Story of the Conscientious Objectors of 1939–49* (1949), p. 29.

45. *Friend*, 30 Mar. 1934, p. 284; *The Times*, 28 June 1982.

46. John Middleton Murry, *The Necessity of Pacifism* (1937), p. 114.

47. M. K. Gandhi, *Non-Violence in Peace and War*, vol. 1 (Ahmedabad, 1942), p. 265.

48. For an account of the Peace Army see Ceadel, *Pacifism in Britain 1914–1945*, pp. 93–7. For a defence of the proposal see Henry Brinton, *The Peace Army* (1932).

49. See Brock, *Twentieth-Century Pacifism*, ch. 6.
50. April Carter, David Hoggett, and Adam Roberts, *Non-Violent Action: A Selected Bibliography* (rev. edn, 1970), p. 5. See also the even more explicit comments in the first edition (1967), p. 5.
51. John Hyatt, *Pacifism: A Selected Bibliography* (1972), introduction (unpaginated).
52. Gene Sharp, *The Politics of Nonviolent Action* (Boston, 1973), p. 68.
53. Reinhold Niebuhr, *Moral Man and Immoral Society* (1933), p. 251.
54. Hilda von Klenze, *Pacifist*, June 1961.
55. Richard B. Gregg, *The Power of Non-Violence* (1935 edn), pp. 36–7.
56. Krishnalal Shridharani, *War without Violence: A Study of Gandhi's Method and its Accomplishments* (1939), pp. 15, 251.
57. Brock, *Twentieth-Century Pacifism*, p. 74. Horsburgh, *Non-Violence and Aggression*, p. 168. Sharp, *The Politics of Nonviolent Action*, pp. 707, 741–4.
58. Horsburgh, *Non-Violence and Aggression*, pp. 123–4.
59. Gregg, *The Power of Non-Violence* (1935 edn), p. 65.
60. On this, see Leo Kuper, *Passive Resistance in South Africa* (1956).
61. Gandhi, *Non-Violence in Peace and War*, vol. 1, pp. 161, 167–8.
62. Gene Sharp, *Which Way to Freedom?* (Cardiff, n.d.[1957]), p. 8.
63. Gregg, *The Power of Non-Violence* (1935 edn), p. 75.
64. Anders Boserup and Andrew Mack, *War without Weapons: Non-Violence in National Defence* (1974), p. 148.
65. Gandhi, *Non-Violence in Peace and War*, vol. 1, p. 381.
66. Gregg, *The Power of Non-Violence* (1960 edn), p. 30 (emphasis added).
67. Horsburgh, *Non-Violence and Aggression*, p. 198.
68. For examples, see Ceadel, *Pacifism in Britain 1914–1945*, pp. 160–1.
69. G. D. H. Cole, *The Simple Case for Socialism* (1935), p. 101.
70. Brock, *Pacifism in the United States*, pp. 445–6.
71. Cited in Wittner, *Rebels against War*, p. 78.
72. Myrtle Solomon, 'Alternative Defence: Nonviolent Struggle and Peace Building' in Thompson (ed.), *Over Our Dead Bodies*, p. 134.
73. Storm Jameson, *The End of This War* (1941), p. 25.
74. Wittner, *Rebels against War*, p. 57.
75. Fenner Brockway, *The C.O. and the Community* (n.d. [1941?]), pp. 3, 4.
76. David Morris, *China Changed My Mind* (1948), p. 27.
77. Sibley and Jacob, *Conscription of Conscience*, p. 466.
78. *Peace News*, 18 July 1941, 5 Apr. 1940.
79. See Peter Brock, 'Gandhi's Nonviolence and His War Service', in *Gandhi Marg* (New Delhi) 2 (1981), pp. 601–16.
80. C. J. Cadoux, *Christian Pacifism Re-Examined* (Oxford, 1940).

81. *Peace News*, 2 May 1941.
82. For entertaining accounts by two leaders of pacifist communities in Britain, see Ronald Duncan, *Journal of a Husbandman* (1944), and J. Middleton Murry, *Community Farm* (1952).
83. R. V. Sampson, *The Discovery of Peace* (1972), p. viii.

Chapter 8: The determinants of the debate

1. Robert E. Ward, *Japan's Political System* (Englewood Cliffs, N.J., 1967), p. 26.
2. Nobuya Bamba and John F. Howes (eds), *Pacifism in Japan: The Christian and Socialist Tradition* (Kyoto, 1978), p. xiv.
3. I learned much from J. A. A. Stockwin's lecture on 'Does Japan have a special attitude to peace?', under the auspices of the Oxford Project for Peace Studies, on 5 March 1986.
4. Karl Holl, 'The Peace Movement in German Politics 1890–1933', in Art Cosgrove and J. I. McGuire, *Parliament and Community: Historical Studies XIV* (Dublin, 1983), p. 179.
5. Roger Chickering, *Imperial Germany and a World without War* (Princeton, 1975), pp. 260–85. See also Roger Fletcher, *Revisionism and Empire: Socialist Imperialism in Germany 1897–1914* (1984).
6. Holl, 'The Peace Movement in German Politics 1890–1933', pp. 177–8.
7. Ibid., 183–7.
8. Hans Rühle, 'The Historical Perspective', in Keith Best, Geoffrey Warhurst, Hans-Joachim Veen and Ludger Eling (eds), *Playing at Peace: A Study of the 'Peace Movement' in Great Britain and the Federal Republic of Germany* (1983), pp. 25–6.
9. James L. Richardson, *Germany and the Atlantic Alliance: The Interaction of Strategy and Politics* (Cambridge, Mass., 1966), pp. 48–56.
10. Peter Graf von Kielmansegg, 'The Origins and Aims of the German Peace Movement', in Walter Laqueur and Robert Hunter (eds), *European Peace Movements and the Future of the Western Alliance* (New Brunswick, N.Y., 1985), p. 321.
11. See his essay, 'The West German Peace Movement', in Peter H. Merkl (ed.), *West German Foreign Policy: Dilemmas and Directions* (Chicago, 1982), pp. 83–4.
12. Hans-Joachim Veen, 'The Psychology and Sociology of the Peace Movement', in Best, Warhurst, Veen, and Eling (eds), *Playing at Peace*, p. 42.
13. For example, Clay Clemens, 'The Antinuclear Movement in West Germany: *Angst* and Isms, Old and New', in James E. Dougherty and Robert L. Pfaltzgraff, Jr. (eds), *Shattering Europe's Defense Consensus:*

The Antinuclear Protest Movement and the Future of NATO (Washington, D.C., 1985), pp. 81–8.

14. Ibid., 88.

15. Jeffrey Herf, 'Neutralism and the Moral Order in West Germany', in Laqueur and Hunter (eds), *European Peace Movements and the Future of the Western Alliance*, p. 370.

16. See Mellon's contribution to Jolyon Howorth and Patricia Chilton (eds), *Defence and Dissent in Contemporary France* (1984), p. 202. See also Wilfried Wiegand, 'Why Is There No "Peace Movement" in France?', *Encounter*, Nov. 1983, pp. 52–4.

17. Cited by Tony Chafer, 'Ecologists and the Bomb', in Howorth and Chilton (eds), *Defence and Dissent in Contemporary France*, p. 218.

18. Roger Chickering, 'Problems of a German Peace Movement 1890–1914', in Solomon Wank (ed.), *Doves and Diplomats: Foreign Offices and Peace Movements in Europe and America in the Twentieth Century* (Westport, Conn., 1978), p. 45. See also ch. 8 of Chickering, *Imperial Germany and a World without War*.

19. See David E. Sumler, 'Opponents of War Preparedness in France, 1913–14', in Wank (ed.), *Doves and Diplomats*, esp. p. 123.

20. Theodore Zeldin, *France 1848–1945*, vol. 2: *Intellect, Taste, and Anxiety* (Oxford, 1977), pp. 879–80.

21. Jolyon Howorth, *France: The Politics of Peace* (1984), pp. 40, 45–7.

22. This view was advanced in 1977 by the Centre des Démocrates Sociaux; see David Hanley, 'The Parties and the Nuclear Consensus', in Howorth and Chilton (eds), *Defence and Dissent in Contemporary France*, p. 81.

23. See his contribution to Howorth and Chilton (eds), *Defence and Dissent in Contemporary France*, p. 248.

24. T. K. Derry, *A History of Scandinavia: Norway, Sweden, Denmark, Finland and Iceland* (1979), pp. 249–50, 395.

25. J. J. C. Voorhoeve, *Peace, Profits and Principles: A Study of Dutch Foreign Policy* (The Hague, 1979), pp. 18, 22, 42.

26. Clay Clemens, 'The Antinuclear Movement in the Netherlands: A Diagnosis of Hollanditis', in Dougherty and Pfaltzgraff (eds), *Shattering Europe's Defense Consensus*, p. 97.

27. Ben Ver Teer, 'The Peace Movement in the Netherlands', *Atlantic Quarterly* 2 (1984), p. 41.

28. Hobhouse, *Democracy and Reaction*, p. 49; J. A. Hobson, *Imperialism: A Study* (1902), p. 382.

29. J. R. Seeley, *The Expansion of England* (1883) pp. 109, 110; XIX HC Deb., col. 1821; Spenser Wilkinson, *War and Policy: Essays* (1900), p. viii.

30. See Martin Ceadel, 'The First British Referendum: The "Peace Ballot", 1934–5', *English Historical Review* xcv (1980), esp. pp. 829, 833–4.

31. Correlli Barnett, *Strategy and Society* (1974), p. 1.

32. Robert H. Ferrell, *Peace In Their Time: The Origins of the Kellogg–Briand Pact* (New Haven, Conn., 1952), p. 263.

33. Robert H. Ferrell, 'The Peace Movement', in Alexander DeConde (ed.), *Isolation and Security* (Durham, N.C., 1957), pp. 87, 90–1.

34. Morgenthau, *In Defense of the National Interest*, p. 78.

35. See, for example, the 1940 survey evidence cited in Gabriel A. Almond, *The American People and Foreign Policy* (New York, 1950), p. 131.

36. Burnham, *The Struggle for the World*, p. 241.

37. Patterson, *Toward a Warless World*, p. viii.

38. Morgenthau, *In Defense of the National Interest*, p. 7. Among many works on this theme see Kenneth W. Thompson, 'The Ethical Dimension in American Thinking about Peace and War', in Booth and Wright (eds), *American Thinking about Peace and War*, pp. 159–86; and R. E. Osgood, *Ideals and Self-Interest in America's Foreign Relations* (1953).

39. Stanley Hoffmann, 'Will the Balance Balance at Home?', *Foreign Policy*, Summer 1972, cited and commented on by Coral Bell, *The Diplomacy of Detente: the Kissinger Period* (1977), p. 35.

40. Cited in Paul Keal, *Unspoken Rules and Superpower Dominance* (1983), p. 224. Emphasis added.

41. H. N. Brailsford, *A League of Nations* (1917), p. 8.

42. Ragner Svanström and Carl Fredrik Palmstierna, *A Short History of Sweden* (Oxford, 1934), p. 333.

43. Amry Vandenbosch, *Dutch Foreign Policy since 1815: A Study in Small Power Politics* (The Hague, 1959), pp. 166, 172.

44. John K. Nelson, *The Peace Prophets: American Pacifist Thought, 1919–1941* (Chapel Hill, N.C., 1967), p. 105.

45. Cited in Charles Chatfield, *For Peace and Justice: Pacifism in America 1914–1941* (Knoxville, Tenn., 1971), p. 311.

46. C. Roland Marchand, *The American Peace Movement and Social Reform, 1898–1918* (Princeton, N.J., 1972), pp. x, xi.

Appendix

1. Hedley Bull, 'Martin Wight and the Theory of International Relations', *British Journal of International Studies* 2 (1976), p. 106.

2. See Shlomo Avineri, 'The Problem of War in Hegel's Thought', *Journal of the History of Ideas* 22 (1961), pp. 463–74; and Andrew

Vincent, 'The Hegelian State and International Politics', *Review of International Studies* 9 (1983), pp. 191–205.

3. Hinsley, *Power and the Pursuit of Peace*, pp. 66–72.

4. Bernard Porter, 'Patterns of Thought and Practice: Martin Wight's "International Theory" ', in Michael Donelan (ed.), *The Reason of States: A Study of International Political Theory* (1978), p. 65.

5. Ibid., 66; and Bull, 'Martin Wight and the Theory of International Relations', p. 105.

6. Bull, 'Martin Wight and the Theory of International Relations', p. 105.

7. Kenneth N. Waltz, *Man, the State and War: A Theoretical Analysis* (New York, 1959).

Index